MW01125104

'Fataar re-constructs brand building for today's complex landscape; packed with insight this is a rich collection of experience, data, observations and recommendations to build brands that cut through and deliver sustained growth.

'In the midst of the revolution of brands, Fataar offers a compelling collection of evidence, case studies and perspectives that lead us to why and how to build brands with cultural resonance. This is the ultimate guide to building brands in culture.'
Julie Bramham, Managing Director, Diageo Luxury Group

'This book holds the key to unlock how to truly use culture to your financial benefit. Fataar captures your attention while simultaneously educating on how culture shifts impact both inside and outside an organization. Her skill in simplifying the labyrinth of culture, of brand strategy, risk management and all the pieces of the intricate brand wheel explained through easy-to-digest diagrams and experiences makes this a must-read book!'
Rachel Muscat, Co-Founder of Humanrace with Pharrell and formerly of adidas

'In an era where culture is the currency of relevance, Leila Fataar's work is a bold manifesto for businesses to act with authenticity, empathy and cultural intelligence.

'It's a vibrant blueprint for NextGen brand-building – one that rejects tokenism and traditional hierarchy in favour of intersectional thinking, collaborative creativity and community-rooted impact.

'Fataar's insights bridge the gap between boardroom and street-level, between strategic planning and real-world resonance. With an unflinching focus on the "cultural front line", Fataar reframes success around values, impact and credibility – proving that culturally attuned businesses don't just survive change, they lead it!'
Martin Raymond, co-founder of The Future Laboratory

Culture-Led Brands

Drive growth, build resilience
and cultivate resonance

Leila Fataar

KoganPage

First published in Great Britain and the United States in 2025 by Kogan Page Limited

Kogan Page
Kogan Page Ltd, 2nd Floor, 45 Gee Street, London EC1V 3RS, United Kingdom
Kogan Page Inc, 8 W 38th Street, Suite 90, New York, NY 10018, USA
www.koganpage.com

EU Representative (GPSR)
Authorised Rep Compliance Ltd, Ground Floor, 71 Baggot Street Lower, Dublin D02 P593, Ireland
www.arccompliance.com

Kogan Page books are printed on paper from sustainable forests.

ISBNs

Hardback	978 1 3986 1901 2
Paperback	978 1 3986 1899 2
Ebook	978 1 3986 1900 5

British Library Cataloguing-in-Publication Data

A CIP record for this book is available from the British Library.

Library of Congress Control Number

2025009750

Typeset by Integra Software Services, Pondicherry
Print production managed by Jellyfish
Printed and bound by CPI Group (UK) Ltd, Croydon CR0 4YY

People call me many things, but my favourite is 'Mama'.

To Jacob,

Doing what I can to clear a path for your generation to thrive.

I love you.

Mum

CONTENTS

LIST OF FIGURES

ABOUT THE AUTHOR

A renowned brand builder and business innovator, Leila Fataar has three decades of senior leadership experience at the intersection of culture, creativity and commerce, underpinned by a commitment to credibility and advocacy for inclusive representation throughout the advertising, marketing and communications industries.

A pioneer of the cultural branding blueprint with her rare ability to speak the languages of culture, corporate and entrepreneurial, Leila has spearheaded an approach from the boardroom to the billboard that positions cultural relevance not only as a marketing nice-to-have but as a key business growth driver.

Working globally brand side, in senior positions at TONI&GUY, adidas and Diageo, and through her own independent companies, Spin and Platform13, across multiple categories, her expertise lies in the ability to read the cultural zeitgeist and signals and translate these into compelling brand strategies that resonate with diverse audiences.

FOREWORD

We live in a world of constant progress, change and upheaval. In this environment, the most successful businesses thrive through deep cultural understanding and insight and working out implications for how their brand (or brands) should show up in the world.

When I first met Leila, I was struck by her deep sense of the world around her, a huge curiosity, and an ability to connect with people across different elements of society. All of this gives Leila the ability to join the cultural dots and use her insight to help brands be attuned to cultural currents and signs.

The natural disruptor in Leila constantly pushes businesses and brands to adapt to flourish, as doing the same will only result in, at best, getting the same and, more likely, in being left behind.

How brands show up 'in culture' can be a fine line, and understanding cultural nuances remains key. Leila understands the importance of a brand being true to itself, its values and its roots, but, at the same time, showing up in a relevant way in an often-chaotic world. Many brands talk about authenticity; knowing how to be authentic is an art, and one that Leila fully understands.

Translating cultural insight into bold creativity is something that I have also always associated with Leila. She knows that brands don't need to just demonstrate that they understand the world, but that they need to do it in a way that cuts through. Big and bold creative ideas help brands to stand out – countless studies on effectiveness show that. Leila is always pushing to be bold, in the relevant way.

Leila's championing of inclusivity has always stood out. She has been a big voice that inclusive businesses are the most successful. Leila has always had that ability to build brand stories that connect across diverse audiences. This will come across in this work.

When we first worked together, Leila came with a remit to ensure that our brands were culturally attuned. She did this, but her legacy was even greater as she impacted the culture of the broader organization. She understood that just writing a culturally savvy brand plan is not enough, but that the leadership overall of the organization needs to embrace a culture-led approach to business. A culturally curious and connected business will lead to winning in the external environment.

So, this book is a must-read for business and brand leaders as they look to shape strategies and plans that fit successfully in the complex modern world. It covers the many critical areas that are all topics that organizations are discussing and grappling with. I am lucky to have benefitted from Leila's cultural wisdom and I am sure that you will get the same from this book.

Edward Pilkington, Chief Marketing & Innovation Officer,
Diageo North America

ACKNOWLEDGEMENTS

I would need a whole other book to list every single person who has been instrumental on my journey…

My family who have always supported, believed in me and encouraged me: Naomi Fataar (my mum), the everyday support system, Luke Davidson (my husband) and Jacob Fataar Davidson (my son) and my three sisters (Farah, Natassia and Sarah) and my friends who are my family too. I could not have done any of this without you. I love you. Thank you.

My Spin and Platform13 teams, both core and curated. What an honour. You share my values completely, you have helped grow my businesses and you have supported me both professionally and personally. Beyond thankful.

My TONI&GUY, adidas and Diageo teams, both in-house, in multiple departments, and all external people I worked with, on all levels. I include my Spin and P13 clients here too. Without your trust and freedom to work on incredible and unique projects, none of my case studies would be possible. I learned a lot. We did a lot. Thank you.

I could never forget my champions in the industry, giving me space and support even when I am vocally challenging the system. And that includes my publisher Kogan Page. Thank you.

And to those who inspire and challenge me every day, even if they don't know me personally, I thank you.

ABBREVIATIONS

API	Application programming interface
AR	Augmented reality
ATL	Above-the-line (marketing)
B2B	Business to business
B2C	Business to consumer
BNPL	Buy now, pay later
CD	Creative director
CDO	Chief data officer
CEO	Chief executive officer
CFO	Chief financial officer
CIO	Chief information officer
CISO	Chief information security officer
CMO	Chief marketing officer
COO	Chief operating officer
CPG	Consumer packaged goods
CRM	Customer relationship management
CSO	Chief strategy officer
CSR	Corporate social responsibility
CTO	Chief technology officer
CX	Customer experience
D&I	Diversity and inclusion
DEI	Diversity, equity and inclusion
DOP	Director of photography
DTC	Direct to consumer
EGC	Employee-generated content
ESG	Environmental, social and governance
FMCG	Fast-moving consumer goods

GDPR	General data-protection regulation
HR	Human resources
IDFA	Identifier for advertisers
IRL	In real life
KBA	Key brand assets
LLM	Large learning model
M&A	Mergers and acquisitions
NFT	Non-fungible token
NGO	Non-governmental organization
OOH	Out-of-home (advertising)
PLA	Product listing ad
POC	Person/people of colour
PR	Public relations
R&D	Research and development
ROI	Return on investment
SEO	Search engine optimization
UGC	User-generated content
UPI	Unified payments interface
VR	Virtual reality

Introduction

Embracing uncertainty in modern brands

Culture is the stuff of life; a reflection of reality and a global connector of communities and intersectional audiences. This rhythm of life has always intertwined heritage, identity, lifestyle, fandom, unspoken codes and so on. It's what we see, what we do, what we wear, what we listen to, how we act, how we communicate, who we connect with. Culture influences us, enables us and lets information spread; it's what affects our lives. Culture affects us all, and that includes a brand's full audience – you, shareholders, employers, investors, employees, consumers, communities and fans. When I say *audience* throughout the book, it means *all* of these audiences.

I have always believed that political decisions, mainstream media narratives (sometimes sympathetic, sometimes weaponized) and technological acceleration and adoption are the biggest drivers of cultural shifts, creating wide-reaching realities for everyone. These shifts drive our behaviours and mindsets and help us decide what we work with and for, and why; what we engage with, advocate for, defend and consume; and why we buy certain brands and goods and services at any given time.

Each era impacts people's behaviours and mindsets, building on each other over time, cascading through generations, directly affecting individuals, their communities and cultures… and, ultimately, their perception of, engagement with and consumption of brands.

For me, culture is about people.

And people, thankfully, don't fit into neat little boxes – our identities are nuanced and fluid. It simply cannot be that one size fits all in traditional age demographics within segmentations like Boomer, Gen X, Millennial, Gen Z, Alpha, Beta and so on – still so widely used in our industry. This, however, has been reflected in industry obsessions with the 'youth' demographic, whether it be in targeting and/or hiring.

It's a mindset, not an age. It always has been.

We need all age groups across everything for true relevance. In this book, for ease of use, I will use broader, more fluid terms like Gen X, millennial, Gen Z and Gen A in the context of era-defining changes instead of the 'age' of particular audiences.

We are in the most exciting, the biggest, the most data-driven, the most radical political, societal and technological transformation since the industrial revolution or the advent of the internet and the smartphone. Meanwhile, we have gone far beyond code red on climate change. There has been a power shift over time, from the traditional establishments created to benefit the few towards more decentralization of power for and by the many. Finding a balance is important now and in the foreseeable future, even changing as this book is written at the close of 2024. For us all, the only certainty is uncertainty. With the threat and promise of an AI-powered future, being human is a competitive advantage, meaning that a new, culture-led approach to brands and business is needed.

Introducing the culture stack

The culture stack, shown in Figure 0.1, shapes our personal identities and how we express ourselves, and how we engage with our communities and the world.

Inherited cultures are unselected; made up of people and communities who have shared and intersectional experiences of place, rituals, norms, language, traditions, religion, values and customs. An example is the New

FIGURE 0.1 The personal culture stack

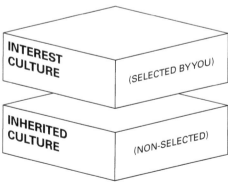

Zealand Haka – a recognizable custom shared by Kiwis no matter their heritage or background. Inherited culture also includes personal characteristics that we are born with, such as gender (whether nonconforming, binary or not). A person is part of a variety of inherited communities (intersectional), whether in their homeland or a wider diaspora and whether these early years have been nurturing or traumatizing. Even if we do not follow these traditions and values later in life, what we learn from these areas form our world-view and shapes why we see things the way we do and impacts the way we make decisions.

I am not a D&I expert or activist, but I do have front-line experience of one of the most extreme forms of racism and oppression: South African apartheid. I have seen that generational impact on my community. Being born and raised of mixed 'race' (Coloured/Malay or whatever labels the apartheid government used to segregate us) in South Africa without the internet has given me valuable skills and tools that I have used throughout my career. I am proud of my heritage and identity and grateful that this way of thinking drives my everyday decision-making and doing, both personally and in business. I left South Africa for London in 1995, the year after apartheid was officially dismantled, so I do not know, nor have I lived in, my birth country after the transition, even though it did start opening up a few years in the run up. This makes 2025, the year of this book being published, my 30-year anniversary in both my career and London. No formal education in business, marketing, communications or advertising has led me to think differently in this world. Instead, bringing new and alternative perspectives enables me to creatively break traditional formulae. My breadth of experience helps me with problem-solving and adaptability. I am proud of my non-traditional career and what seems to be a consistently successful body of work.

I am inclusive. For me, challenging systems that keep down marginalized or historically under-represented people and/or use unfair discrimination in any way, will always underscore who I am and what I do. I also use the word 'diverse' in the most inclusive way and use 'marginalized' for people who have historically been excluded.

I am opportunistic. Growing up in a situation with no Plan B, and not only surviving but thriving in places where I was never supposed to be, is one of my secret powers. When you have no way in and no contacts, you grab any small opportunity, embrace it fully and make it bigger and better. This can help identify the small wins or cracks in brand plans that can grow into bigger opportunities… and the time to pivot.

I can navigate uncertainty. It's in these times that there is a credible opportunity to push things forward, but you need to think creatively and quickly.

I am adaptable and resilient. Being flexible in a variety of situations and environments with the ability to connect with a variety of people on all levels, I 'read the room' and act accordingly.

I am a rapid problem solver. If you are in a dangerous situation, you quickly analyse everything around you to clear a safe path out – rapid troubleshooting is a key skill helping me to make brand work stay relevant and one step ahead.

I am innovative. When you have to make something from nothing, from only what you have in front of you, you find creative and new ways to do that – an entrepreneurial and innovative mindset is the very essence of survival in uncertain times. This also means that I think about any activity through the eyes of the audience, and consumer, and don't speak like a traditional brand person – I don't know the language, but have learned how to navigate my path.

I am curious. My personal heritage, journey and interests are so varied and complex that I have always and will always be interested in why people do what they do. I have always been interested in what influences them, including external factors – both in and out of their control – that impact them. I always dig deeper, and I'm forever curious about everything, with an intangible skill of knowing what resonates. I have been asked many times to codify this, but simply don't know how to.

Our *interest cultures* come into view as our horizons broaden and stack onto (not intersect into) our inherited culture. I was lucky to be surrounded by creativity in my community in South Africa. At home, my independent mum and grandmother were pattern-cutters for fashion and swimwear labels. These women had and have incredible eyes for design and technical expertise. My uncles were musicians who broke racial barriers – their band The Flames is in the Hall of Fame in Durban, South Africa. My school friends and neighbours excelled at sports, sang, danced and more. I have always understood the power of these creative cultures to connect people. For us, access to developing these talents as careers was and is still a challenge for my community in South Africa.

We start to choose the 'things' we are interested in and like to do; the things that add to our inherited identity. These are the things that say something about who we are. This is where brands can play a significant role. (I detail how in Chapter 5.) People's interests can come from overarching and intertwined cultural territories such as technology, sports, fashion, gaming, climate, food, animals, music, art and so on, which can be segmented into the more granular skateboarding, sneakers, cats, Korean food, whisky, Swifties, Star Trek, hip-hop, football and so on. We become fans of these things. Adding to them with our own expressions, we engage with others interested in similar activities, joining communities that are multi- and intergenerational, global and intersectional, connected and unified through this 'identity', this fandom or fan culture.

In my formative years, 90s rave and club culture was my fandom of choice. When I started clubbing in Cape Town in the early 1990s, due to the climate of the country, the scene provided some of the first opportunities to mix 'races'. Connecting with like-minded people in real life or through virtual communities gives us all a sense of belonging; a place to connect and relate to each other on a human level. So, for me, arriving in London at the height of this culture enabled me to find and meet like-minded people from all walks of life, all backgrounds and all parts of the world. For me, creativity and community blended into a joyful connection on a sweaty dance floor – my home from home.

It was the making of me, to be honest.

Back in those pre-internet days, you had to work hard to find your tribe, your community. For us, magazines were our internet and personal word of mouth was how we found out about activities. A community was usually recognized through clothing style, choice of music and shared knowledge of those cultural experiences that you could only know about if you were part of that scene. I landed in London, the home of post-punk in the mid-90s, with a shaved head and a riot grrrl style, a deep love for hip-hop, Prince, science fiction and hardcore, rave and jungle club culture. I had no contacts, very little money and no idea what I wanted to do as a career. I did know that London was a place where people from all walks of life mixed, where you could make something from nothing, where people were celebrated for their differences.

I felt at home immediately.

As individuals, our inherited culture, made up of multiple characteristics, also relates to intersectionality, and forms the foundation on which all our interest cultures (usually more than one) are stacked, adding deep layers of identity and expression. Like inherited culture, interest and fan cultures also show up through storytelling, rituals, languages, myths and artefacts deeply impacted by era-defining communication technologies. This language goes beyond borders, and 21st-century businesses need to understand how to address this. Dig a bit deeper and you will find that the interest cultures that influence us all emotionally, like sports, fashion, music, art and films, always reflect the society of the time. Look at Banksy, for example, for art and activism, and Telfar, a luxury fashion brand with the strapline, 'It's not for you – it's for everyone'. For us all – creators, brands, consumers, fans – our content is archiving the stories of the attitudes and values of our generation, and, in the age of AI, feeding the model for the next generation. Take the 2024 Olympic Games – a clear visible indicator of the connection between wealthy countries and gold medals. Around 50 per cent of these were awarded to athletes from the G7 countries and China, which together account for 60 per cent of global GDP.

This is, of course, expected. So, it makes the incredible feats achieved by people from marginalized countries and groups even more special.[1] These included participating for the first time, like South Sudan in basketball, or, like Algeria's Kaylia Neymour, winning the first African gymnastics gold medal, or countries like Botswana, St Lucia, Albania and Cabo Verde taking home any medal for the first time, and the first medal for the inspirational Refugee Olympic Team, created in response to the 2015 refugee crisis and enabling refugees to compete at Rio in 2016 and every Olympics since then. The Paris Olympics also highlighted deep-rooted gender political issues. Claimed to be the most gender equal Olympics, the host country's ban on its athletes wearing the hijab, and the huge online debate around Algerian boxer Imane Khelif's gender, created an uproar. This made the Netherlands' Sifan Hassan's podium appearance in her hijab for her marathon gold and Imane's gracious gold win (celebrated by the Algerian diaspora – a country colonized by France) in the face of horrendous online bullying, even more powerful.

Our *stacked cultures* profoundly shape not only our personal identities and how we express ourselves, but also how we engage with our communities (both inherited and interest), with the world and with brands. Our personal culture stacks that define who we are and how we see the world can inspire and affect us. A significant element of these cultures are the brands directly associated with or adjacent to those cultures, with an important role in respectfully adding value and fostering that connection, those communities, that fandom.

It's always been about the context

To act in the present and prepare for the future, you have to understand where you came from. This book aims to outline the context and nuances around each topic, but, to be honest, each chapter could be a book on its own. However, this is an attempt at joining the dots of this 'stuff of life' (see Figure 0.2) through a culture-first lens by sharing my 30 years of global observations and experience. For brands, the 20th and early 21st centuries can be divided into distinct phases, with the decisions made by those in leadership responding to the shifts that shape the landscape at the time, their own personal views on the world, and what can or can't be done within a legal framework of operations at the time, while being laser-focused on the pursuit of growth to drive profitability of the business.

The 90s: the most exciting transformation

My first job when I arrived in London at 21 was a testament to that opportunistic mindset honed in my former years in South Africa. In my first week, I headed to the King's Road to see the location of Vivienne Westwood's legendary boutique. Coming out of Sloane Square station, as I walked past a hair salon, I heard its phone ringing out. I went back and forth a few times, and the phone kept ringing. So, I walked in and asked if the salon needed a receptionist. I was asked to work as an assistant receptionist at the soon-to-be-opened hairdressing school the following week. I was so happy, and I could have my head shaved for free (no one wants that grown-out hair) and could meet some creative people in London. I was entirely unaware that this was the hottest international salon group of the 1990s – TONI&GUY. I sometimes wonder whether, if I had known this before I walked in, it would have given me pause. Knowing myself, I think not, but it reminds me of the old cliché, 'If you don't ask, you don't get' – a mantra I still live by today.

This opportunity set me on a career path I didn't even know existed.

I started at the salon's new school in New Oxford Street the following week. I was elated. The dormitory in my hostel was £60 per week, and a huge hole in my very small budget. Now I had a job. I could eat. I could get my hair done. I moved out to stay on friends' floors and sofas, and, after a few months, I had enough for a room in a shared house, then a bedsit and eventually my own flat share. I took on a second job selling tickets at Ticketmaster to supplement my income. I went clubbing every weekend, and always with the best hair. After a year, I asked to be moved to 'that office at

FIGURE 0.2 What impacts culture, the stuff of life

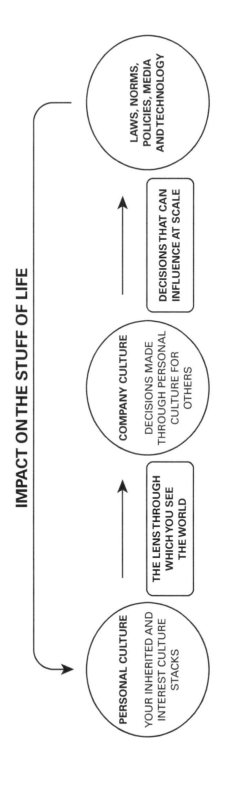

IMPACT ON THE STUFF OF LIFE

PERSONAL CULTURE
YOUR INHERITED AND INTEREST CULTURE STACKS

THE LENS THROUGH WHICH YOU SEE THE WORLD

COMPANY CULTURE
DECISIONS MADE THROUGH PERSONAL CULTURE FOR OTHERS

DECISIONS THAT CAN INFLUENCE AT SCALE

LAWS, NORMS, POLICIES, MEDIA AND TECHNOLOGY

the top of the building'. I had no idea what they did up there; I just knew that I wanted to do more than be on reception, but I didn't want to be a hairdresser.

This job started my pre-internet career in PR and communications. I would, for example, cut up transparencies of products and hairstyles and post them to magazines, fax press releases and assist on anything I could. A key learning from this time was about who really shaped interest cultures – from clubbing and music, fashion and beauty for the wider community and consumers. I knew that there were significant voices behind the scenes – the hairdresser, the make-up artist, the stylist, the photographer and image maker, the journalist, the promoter, the PR and so on – people not necessarily front-facing who were a big part of shaping, representing and moving that culture forward. These friends became the start of my wonderful network of creative and cultural voices – people who shape, influence and represent the culture and community.

Brand leaders, here is a shocker: follower count on social media does not necessarily equal influence.

The 2000s: the most data-driven transformation

I instinctively knew something big was happening in the late 1990s and early 2000s as the internet, or the static Web1, went mainstream. It helped that I was an avid William Gibson reader and had brought his book *Neuromancer* with me from South Africa. The Web2 revolution, e-commerce, dynamic websites, social media and the like, was led by early online pioneers like Jeff Bezos (Amazon) and Larry Page and Sergei Brin (Google), Tom Anderson and Chris DeWolfe (MySpace) and Mark Zuckerberg (Facebook). Like them or not, they changed the game for us all for ever. For the first time, there seemed to be a two-way communication between brands and their consumers, a direct line to sales for early adopters of e-commerce. In the face of this new consumer behaviour, any brands slow to adopt an online channel began to decline as new companies like Amazon understood the potential of global reach. This early online marketplace drove a better understanding of consumers' likes and dislikes about a brand's goods and services, and savvy brands started to segment their audiences. Data was proclaimed as 'the new oil' by mathematician Clive Humby in 2006, with digital and, eventually, performance marketing updating the traditional marketing funnel for the first time in years (and raising valid topics around privacy and ethics, covered in Chapter 11).[2] The rise of social media, and subsequent influencer marketing, took it up a level and transformed how brands interacted with their consumers, enabling consumers to amplify or criticise brands, in public, and allowing a myriad of positive and negative outcomes, which are covered throughout this book. In 2007, Apple introduced the iPhone – a significant milestone in mobile communications, affecting not just the tech industry, but consumer behaviour, mobile computing and the broader cultural landscapes,[3] and, with the launch of its app store in 2008, the rise of new businesses and services. The iPhone played a key role in changing how people consumed media, shopped and interacted online, revolutionized photography, streaming and gaming, powered the rise of social media and enabled on-the-go working models. Accordingly, brands needed to develop plans that went beyond simply showing the benefits of products and services, to also create conversations and build communities in which brands could listen to their consumers to understand their needs and reputations.

Brands that became their own media hubs thrived.

I left TONI&GUY around 2002 to start my first company – generationet.com – an online marketing resource for the fashion industry. It was an exciting time, when anything seemed possible and we could create a new industry. There were no case studies, and it was a time to challenge nontraditional ways of doing things; every opportunity built through innovation and creativity: ideal for someone with my skills. While my first client, *Scene* magazine, failed to actually deploy online, the learnings in trying to move a print magazine onto this new digital medium – the internet – was a huge learning curve and led me to my second client and one of my pivotal career opportunities – the subversive and iconic brand, Acupuncture Footwear. Here, I was encouraged to experiment with traditional and online strategies, given licence to go 'guerrilla' by the wonderful owners Phil de Mesquita and Nikos Nicholaou. After two years, I rebranded to Spin Publicity, finding my niche by offering very early integration of online, social and traditional communications, working in youth culture with a guerrilla-marketing mindset focused on fashion, music and art; literally making up processes and ways of working in this new world.

The 2010s: the biggest transformation

In 2008, the credit crunch took its toll on my independent business, and I was exhausted. I took myself off to Asia on a solo trip, writing articles about hip-hop in mainland China for WGSN and lists of 'Who to Watch' for France's *WAD* magazine. These were amazing experiences and I was inspired, returning to once again rebrand Spin Publicity to Spin Agency – now focused on digital, social and content creation. The early 2010s also saw a transformative shift that has had profound implications on consumer behaviour, the entertainment industry, and beyond. This transition was marked by the rise of streaming platforms like Netflix and Spotify fostering an era of unprecedented access to a global content library, challenging traditional media and entertainment models, and paving the way for a diverse and rich digital culture.

In 2012, I closed Spin and was asked to interview by then global director of brand marketing, Alexander Matt, at sportswear giant, adidas Originals in a newly integrated role as the global PR/social/content director. The remit was incredible: make adidas Originals the sportswear icon of the street. As a corporate newbie, I had no idea how corporate businesses worked, so I adapted processes and ways of working to suit the job I had been brought in to do. (I talk more about that later in the book.) In 2015, after resigning from adidas, I was headhunted by drinks heavyweight Diageo and interviewed with the then European director of marketing and innovation, Ed Pilkington, to be part of his leadership team. We started the first Culture and Entertainment department for Europe with the remit to embed the big brands of Smirnoff, Tanqueray, Guinness, Baileys, Johnnie Walker, Gordon's into this new culture. This sharp education on FMCG big business is still one of my most valuable lessons. It taught me how to make the connection between what I do and business and is why I truly believe that cultural relevance should be one of the essential growth drivers for 21st-century business.

Truth be told, thankfully, I didn't have to apply for these jobs. I didn't have the schooling prerequisites or network to be able to get an 'introduction', which seemed to be the basic entry level of most corporate businesses at the time. At the same time, going in-house was a major culture shock for me. I initially found it really difficult to navigate. But, it is easily one of the best career experiences I've had. Now I speak three languages – entrepreneurial, cultural and corporate – and can easily translate between them all.

A cultural state of mind

While I was brand side, I noticed gaps in the services between the brands and their traditional rostered agencies – gaps that I had learned how to fill in delivering my non-traditional craft. In fact, I was lucky that I was able to flex the processes while I was client side, use my own network and help evolve processes to enable new ways of working. This was also a time that saw traditional business models holding back innovation, and there were industry/agency/company diversity and inclusivity failures stemming from unconscious bias and systemic racism and tone-deaf campaigns, more products than we needed across all categories with waste on all levels, 'purpose' as a buzzword or marketing campaign, brands as culture vultures, repackaged creativity, supply chain issues. The list goes on.

I was convinced the industry needed to move closer to how I had always worked – incorporating real-world insights through the culture stacks, and taking a progressive approach from strategy to implementation rooted in culture and community, underpinned by diversity, inclusion, representation and authenticity. After the consistent successes of the projects I had led while client side, I saw a world where 'cultural relevance' became not only a marketing nice-to-have, but a business growth driver. This would mean brand plans were created with a culture-first approach, built to add value to *all* their audiences… and the world.

In 2017, I founded my second self-funded independent company, Platform13, a new type of big-brand partner ready to answer the challenges faced by big brands in the ever-changing world of consumer behaviour, technology advancements, creative innovation and the swiftly moving cultural landscape. The mission is simple: to create and maintain cultural relevance for big brands, powered by a global and diverse network. Today, the client list includes the biggest and best in the world, crossing categories and industries, with Platform13 strategically set up to flex and shift in line with cultural movements. I had intuitively spearheaded this approach my entire career, and I knew it worked, but, at the beginning, the industry wasn't quite as ready.

In the mid 2010s, two pivotal moments set off a seismic shift in social justice issues, in turn kicking off a major shift of consumer decision-making, and, suddenly, the way I had been working for years started to make more sense. In 2016, quarterback Colin Kaepernick refused to stand for the US national anthem at an NFL game (and took the knee in further games), in protest of police brutality and racial injustice, sparking global conversations about free speech, civil rights and patriotism. Kaepernick had been endorsed by Nike since 2011, and, amid the backlash, the brand took a bold stance of support in 2018. During the 30th-anniversary celebrations of 'Just Do It', Kaepernick featured in a high-profile global campaign with the tagline, 'Believe in something. Even if it means sacrificing everything'.[4] It flew around the world, resulting in increased sales and Nike's stock reaching an all-time high, and resonated with a more diverse and younger demographic, underscoring the brand's values and leveraging the cultural conversation. On the other side, the actions of Harvey Weinstein and others led to the spread of the #MeToo movement, founded by Tarana Burke. It resulted in much-needed conversations around sexual misconduct in the workplace, highlighted a public debate on power dynamics, consent and toxic masculinity,[5] and encouraged industries to advance long-fought-for gender-equality initiatives. The 2010s felt like a time of brand activism, empowered by social media reach and consumers' expectations that the brands they engage with align with their values and demonstrate a genuine commitment to positive change.

The 2020s: the most radical transformation

This first half of this decade has seen the long-trodden path to gender equality widen to include non-binary and trans rights, but these issues continue to be complicated in different cultural norms and global societies. In 2020, the world stopped and kicked us all out of our comfort zones. For brands (and us all), uncertainty became the only certainty. We could never have foreseen the global collapse of industries and services and the cataclysmic effect on the creative and cultural communities, in a few short months, when the Covid-19 pandemic hit. Lockdown enforced a pause in brands' relentless execution schedule, but offered an opportunity for reflection and strategizing, without time constraints, in preparation for the upcoming recovery. We saw innovation like we have never seen before – categories, products/services and communications addressing new consumer and workforce behaviour and needs, usually long-drawn-out digital transformations rapidly kicking in, and what seemed like an overnight rise of online-based services, from grocery deliveries, to video calls for everything, the TikTok craze, all the way to the explosion of Houseparty and gaming apps for those Friday night kitchen raves and get-togethers.

And then...

The social justice movement exploded after the murder of George Floyd in May 2020, sparking much-needed conversations about systemic racism. The injustices behind this massive global uprising were deeply felt, and companies had to dig deep and really think about those 'purpose-led' statements or their stances on DEI.

Meanwhile, Gen Z began to enter the workforce and exhibit significant buying and decision-making power. As digital natives, this segment's comfort with technology had a profound effect on digital marketing and new ways of shopping, forever evolving the consumer funnel. Additionally, Gen Z expect brands and companies to be authentic and transparent, with a clear approach on social and climate issues. This continues to be both a challenge and an opportunity for brands, with an urgent need to address the climate emergency in their core business model to balance people and the planet with profitability. The 2020s have also seen the recognition and valuing of multiple genders, neurodiversity and disability gaining much-needed momentum and influence on workplace policies, legal frameworks, product development and messaging. This shift towards greater inclusivity and accessibility should not be just a matter of social responsibility for brands, but also of changing the narratives in the mainstream at scale. Brands who genuinely embrace these cultural shifts are well positioned to build stronger connections with consumers.

2022 saw the metaverse and Web3 take over our industry but fail to reach the mainstream. Now, in 2024, an AI future feels like both a threat and a promise for our industry and the world at large, accelerating faster than any other technology before it. I will use AI as a catch-all for what the Federal Claims Commission refers to as 'a variety of technological tools and techniques that use computation to perform tasks such as predictions, decisions, or recommendations'.[6] AI, in a variety of forms from large language models (LLM) to generative AI (GenAI), is an intuitive and conversational tool, learning as it goes along to enable more nuanced responses. Because it learns from the data that feeds it, it is imperative that we ensure the best possible data sources are used, and this is also reflected in how we behave online. With AI, the more context it has, the more connections it makes, and the more relevant the responses. A one-off prompt is not enough. Think of it as a dialogue in which a 'speaker' can be challenged and probed for even better outcomes, and maybe one day it will even challenge you back. At this early stage, there also are still many AI 'hallucinations', which Google Cloud defines as incorrect or misleading results that AI models generate.[7]

These errors can be caused by a variety of factors, including insufficient training data, incorrect assumptions made by the model, or biases in the data used to train the model.

If this is the most radically transformational era, 2024, the year this book is written, is the tipping point. We are right in a transitional period in history, so I find myself in multiple and non-binary realities, which may seem contradictory. So, I spoke to a variety of other senior leaders with deep expertise and experience in their areas to find out their realities of where brands and businesses are today and their thoughts on this incoming era, which I have included in the relevant areas of the book. I would like to give a massive thank you to a very senior executive from a global business consultancy, who spoke to me off the record; Sarah Watson, former chair and global CSO of BBH, and now a leadership coach; Ete Davies, EVP at Dentsu Creative EMEA; Keith Cheng, general manager of Umbro, China; Michelle Lavipour, senior head of communications; Ana Andjelic, global brand executive and author; Ayesha Martin, senior director, Purpose, adidas; James Kirkham, brand strategist, business advisor and cultural commentator; Jamie Gill, strategic advisor in the fashion and luxury goods sectors and founder of The Outsiders Perspective; Katie Dreke, founder and CSO, DRKE; Peter Semple, CMO of Depop; Kwame Taylor-Hayford, co-founder of kin and president, D&AD; and Mordecai, chief innovation and strategy officer.

At the moment of writing, it's pretty hard to imagine the world next year, much less in the next 5, 10 or 20 years. 2024 is election year, seeing an unprecedented 49 per cent of the world head out to vote for national leaders in at least 64 countries (plus the European Union), potentially reshaping the geopolitical landscape, and our lives. Governmental changes will lead to sharp policy shifts that directly affect businesses, employees and communities. As much as brands and companies don't want, or even need, to be 'political', your shareholders, employees and consumers either have been or will be affected. This deeply impacts our identity cultural stacks, through which brands are perceived and actions judged. As this new generation expresses their social identities and personal values at and through their work, business leaders need to balance the interests of all their audiences – from shareholders to employees.

Brands need to consider how this personal identity and representation, culture and community, context and nuance, impact on how they are seen, or not, to be culturally relevant. We are at a pivotal moment for humanity and the future of the world, where the choices we all make, the actions we all take and the values we all uphold will define not just our present but the legacy we leave for future generations. This book explores the context of how we got here, the nuances of where we are right now and outlines an opportunity where evolved brand values and cultural relevance can lead to positive growth.

Notes

1 Padovani, Loïc. 'Paris 2024 Olympics: The Nations that Won Their First-Ever Medal at the Games', International Olympic Committee, 13 August 2024, olympics.com/en/news/paris-2024-olympics-nations-won-first-ever-medal-at-the-games (archived at https://perma.cc/7F9P-ERGL)

2 See, for example: Forbes. 'The Digital Gold Rush: How Wall Street Mines Social Media', 1 June 2015, forbes.com/sites/etrade/2015/06/01/the-digital-gold-rush-how-wall-street-mines-social-media (archived at https://perma.cc/R4ZA-BXJQ)

3 MacWorld San Franciso. 'Apple Reinvents the Phone with iPhone', Apple Newsroom, 9 January 2007, apple.com/uk/newsroom/2007/01/09Apple-Reinvents-the-Phone-with-iPhone (archived at https://perma.cc/U2NP-Z2VG)

4 Banet-Weiser, Sarah. 'Nike, Colin Kaepernick, and the History of "Commodity Activism"', *Vox*, 7 September 2018, vox.com/first-person/2018/9/7/17831334/nike-colin-kaepernick-ad (archived at https://perma.cc/XP9X-SMKN)

5 Diaz, Jaclyn. 'Where the #MeToo Movement Stands, 5 Years After Weinstein Allegations Came to Light', NPR, 28 October 2022, npr.org/2022/10/28/1131500833/me-too-harvey-weinstein-anniversary (archived at https://perma.cc/59QH-JQWD)

6 Atleson, Michael. 'Keep Your AI Claims in Check', Federal Trade Commission, 27 February 2023, ftc.gov/business-guidance/blog/2023/02/keep-your-ai-claims-check (archived at https://perma.cc/FG9D-9Y3V)

7 Google Cloud. 'What are AI Hallucinations?', Google, cloud.google.com/discover/what-are-ai-hallucinations (archived at https://perma.cc/C62H-ZXE2)

01

The case for cultural relevance

Evolving the brand playbook

I define a culturally relevant brand as a brand state in which a variety of audiences (marketing target and/or not) consistently connect positively with that brand. Your brand becomes relevant when your audiences share your activities and advocate for your brand, defend it, work for it and buy it at any time – not just in the traditional marketing campaign cycles, product launches, a CSR blitz or last-click attrition. It means being consistently and positively 'in' conversation, ready to be discovered, but not necessarily 'always on' or in the places that can be traditionally measured. That is hard for an industry obsessed with scale, ROI, and measurement and metrics that were set up in the 20th century but are still used as standard.

Culture-led brands can do this because they deeply and respectfully connect with intersectional audiences through their culture stacks, delivering brand activities, products and services relevant in the context of what is happening in their audiences' and the wider world. These brands make audiences feel something, help them solve a problem or support them in navigating the intense cultural shifts that impact us all. This doesn't have to be overtly 'worthy', but it must push things forward with purpose and intention. This means that brands have to make sense in people's culture stacks – their lives, their interests and the world. It's emotional. This is what people buy into, beyond traditional product consumption. Then the right brand activity is fuelled (not bought) by media, driving reach *and* relevance, hype and *depth*; pulling people to your brand, not pushing your brand onto people.

Today's generation is the most brand and marketing savvy. The days of brands having to 'lead the audience' are long gone. Audiences, especially consumers, are not stupid. We see this evidenced in the past few years in TikTok driving new behaviours as Gen Z, Zalpha and Alpha come into view. These are masters at manipulating the algorithms to ensure they see content that they want and discoverability of their passions and connected brands is easy. This cohort will scroll past generic content without a second thought, skip and ignore your ads and jump onto and off what often seem to be random and short-term viral trends. While marketing drives purchase intent, brand drives behaviour, and, all too often in our industry, brand is conflated with marketing.

This results in the frequent misunderstanding that a culturally relevant brand is judged through output *only* – a famous person in an ad, a collaboration, a hit on a trending TikTok topic that your and every other brand jumps onto but which disappears in what feels like hours, a paid influencer campaign, one product virality, and so on. These one-off, fleeting moments of communication don't necessarily benefit the brand because your 'relevance' is only attached to and dependent on the associated element. This is what is frequently and frustratingly referred to as being 'in culture'. For me, this does not make a culture-led brand, because cultural relevance is not an output of a marketing or comms channel. It's a movement, not a moment. Savvy brands should read beyond things that are 'trending' to uncover *why* this 'conversation' is happening in the first place and then decide if it is relevant to them.

Building a brand through cultural relevance is in the *input*, and, for me, that's always been connected to its unique role for people, internally, externally and in wider society, incorporating its values and, importantly today, its impact on the planet and people. To do this, cultural relevance as the objective and the outcome is the key to 21st-century business success (see Figure 1.1). Done right, a culture-led approach creates meaningful audience resonance and adaptable brand resilience in today's most uncertain of times.

Your cultural positioning leads to brand and business strategy

Today, transparency and authenticity are not buzzwords. They are what audiences judge your brand and business on through the lenses of their culture stacks. Audiences are monitoring your responses to monumental global events and major impactful cultural shifts, and they are digging deeper

FIGURE 1.1 The cultural relevance table: objective plus outcome

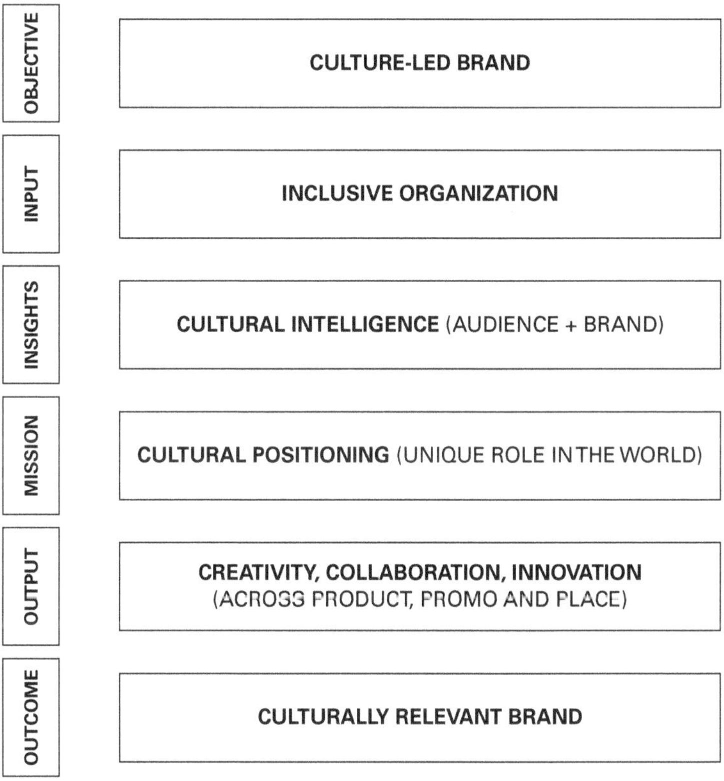

to understand *why* your response is what it is and *how* your brand, product or service is relevant to them. It starts with a deeper understanding of why, how and where the ever-shifting cultural landscape affects and influences their behaviours and attitudes – real-world insights through ongoing cultural intelligence.

To be relevant, it's no longer about what the brand says about itself; it's about how the brand impacts people positively and what they say about it to others. This is how I have always tried to work. The ideal outcome of a positive 'Did you see what (the brand) did?' is what you want people to think, feel and care enough to share – in fan cultures, on their channels and word of mouth with friends, work colleagues and families – driving that all-important attention for discoverability, and then keeping them engaged, interested and invested for loyalty. You will only get that crucial loyalty if your brand is relevant to that person.

That's why all my work starts with what I call a *cultural positioning*.

This unique methodology, created and honed over my 30 years' experience, analyses your specific business and brand challenges at any time by exploring *why* your brand/product/service makes sense for your audiences through their culture stacks. This work incorporates your brand DNA, your brand positioning, your values and your expertise, and carefully and surgically intersects your brand and product or service with real-world insights as they happen, translating this into unique cultural positionings to drive relevant brand and business plans for today (and tomorrow). These insights are always created through cultural intelligence by and from a diverse, global network of cultural voices and experts (both lived and professional experiences) who shape, represent and influence the relevant culture.

Your cultural positioning unlocks your differentiator – your role beyond your product or service – to positively impact all your audiences, internal and external, to encourage them to choose you, credibly embedding your brand in their culture. This system finds a role that only that brand can do for *all* its audiences. It comes to life creatively in the way only that brand can do to enable informed decision-making and to stand out and pull away from the competition, guiding both strategy and implementation. A recurring theme throughout this work is identifying existing consumers and communities that the organization does not engage with because it's not part of its business strategy. These are not necessarily niche communities. I call them

FIGURE 1.2 Cultural positioning framework

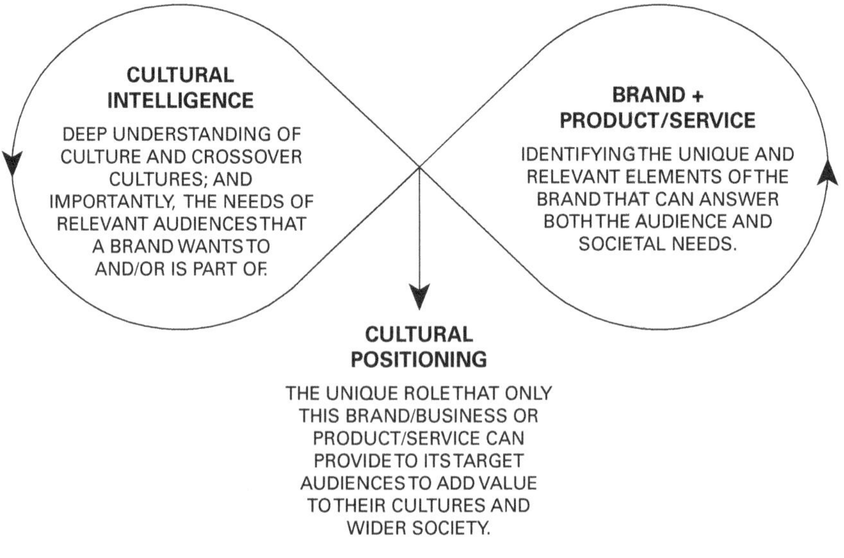

CULTURAL INTELLIGENCE

DEEP UNDERSTANDING OF CULTURE AND CROSSOVER CULTURES; AND IMPORTANTLY, THE NEEDS OF RELEVANT AUDIENCES THAT A BRAND WANTS TO AND/OR IS PART OF.

BRAND + PRODUCT/SERVICE

IDENTIFYING THE UNIQUE AND RELEVANT ELEMENTS OF THE BRAND THAT CAN ANSWER BOTH THE AUDIENCE AND SOCIETAL NEEDS.

CULTURAL POSITIONING

THE UNIQUE ROLE THAT ONLY THIS BRAND/BUSINESS OR PRODUCT/SERVICE CAN PROVIDE TO ITS TARGET AUDIENCES TO ADD VALUE TO THEIR CULTURES AND WIDER SOCIETY.

latent audiences. Once I understand *why* your brand is or could be credible for your audiences, and what their needs are for your brand and product at any point in time, the *how* is easier, enabling you to make the right decisions to be and stay culturally relevant.

The framework in Figure 1.2 looks simple, but it's not easy because culture is living and breathing, always evolving; your inbox choked with mountains of data, trends and insights to connect your brand and business to, both externally and internally. One of my intangible skills is to identify and marry all the right inputs for a brand, an uncodifiable ability to understand what will resonate, unlocking new and latent audiences (and how to engage credibly with them) and foreseeing incoming challenges and credible opportunities for brands who want to be part of that audience's life.

The benefits are clear.

Your cultural positioning can help to address your most pressing business-critical challenges and keep you up to speed as audiences impacted by culture reshape how they can and want to be reached. This means a deeper understanding of how global shifts and local nuances impact all your audiences' (internal and external) culture stacks, behaviours and demands, and determines what you need to do about it. This clarity of the role of your brand in culture will help with critical decision-making, meaning these expected and unexpected shifts and ever-changing debates and policies that impact your audiences – from technology to politics, music to film, DEI to ESG, AI to privacy issues and more – are efficiently and credibly identified and effectively addressed in the right way before they become a crisis or a missed growth opportunity. This clarity drives culture-led creativity beyond simply the craft of beautiful advertising, supporting Ipsos 2023 findings that campaigns with fresh creative ideas combined with 'empathy and fitting in' are more likely to be effective and perform 20 per cent better on short-term sales lift potential.[1]

KWAME TAYLOR-HAYFORD

If you are a great company, you make a great product because you have to. It's essential to success. When you connect that great product to an issue of our time in an authentic way and you move the needle forward on that issue, it becomes a force multiplier for your brand and business. Gen Z, young millennials, Gen Alpha, will disproportionately choose your company, your products, over others. They will come and defend your company in times of crisis because they connect with what you're about, and you connect with the issues that they think are important in the world.

Your cultural positioning can help you to identify new and latent audiences and, importantly, why and how to engage with them, driving new opportunities for growth. It can define how your product or service should show up for your audiences where they are, and credibly – whether through mindsets and values, physically, digitally, virtually and behaviourally. The interconnectedness should ensure that resonant work through the business and, importantly, brand reputation and resilience become increasingly important, which can reduce the risk of call-out culture and deliver brands' positive impact for their audiences and wider society. It mitigates risk, helping you decide what is (or is not) credible for your brand or business to engage with, which 'trends' are relevant and whether that 'shiny new thing' should even be invested in.

This exercise is not static or a one-off.

My version of ongoing cultural intelligence continues to read and analyse relevant shifts specific to the brand's cultural positioning. This empowers brands to flex their plans creatively as culture shifts, create audience-resonant content and experiences, innovate products and services, explore new media and platforms, experiment with emerging commerce and evolve business models accordingly.

Brands go global

In the past, branding livestock denoted ownership to deter theft. From ancient civilizations, there are many examples of symbols and engravings by artisans who created products made of pottery and leather goods to differentiate between each other. Industrialization and globalization from the late 19th century saw mass production, with competition exploding for every type of goods and service.[2] Early branding on the products helped with identification, mainly consisting of logos of the companies that manufactured that product. While at Diageo, I learned from the Johnnie Walker archive that the bottle was made with corners so it could be distributed globally without rolling around on the ships – a particular type of bottle production operation that directly reflected the time.

At the beginning of the 20th century, with scale now the name of the game, brand owners developed marketing plans to connect products to 'associations' such as luxury or love, finding ways to reach and sell to as many people as possible. In this world before the internet, mass media controlled the narrative around monumental movements and day-to-day political messaging. Their leadership steered the type of coverage, according to their personal culture stack – this mass reach able to spread messages, raise awareness and shape public opinion, mindsets and behaviours at scale. For brands, this meant that push marketing, one-way messaging and traditional advertising reigned. The more budget you had, the louder you shouted through limited communications channels such as radio, TV and print publications, and the bigger you became. That business model expanded with the introduction of brand-owned retail stores. This was done using hero advertising campaigns in the mass media with a clear role for the brand: help people make purchasing decisions. This meant the bigger and more complex your company became, the more organized and efficient you had to be to create processes to reduce costs to make the most profit.

In the 1970s, with computers entering the workplace, the division of labour between humans and digital technology made processes even faster. Such processes are the reason why big business is big business, helped by corporate structures that are hierarchical, fixed and departmentalized. Things become difficult when these siloed processes, created to optimize different departments vertically, are not always co-created, used, integrated or shared across the organization horizontally. In these set-ups, employees are directed by their managers, who are directed by their managers, and so it goes up the corporate ladder. This system is still widespread today.

Brands go cultural

The late 20th century saw my generation, Gen X, come of age; a resourceful cohort with access to personal computers, early video games and MTV, raised amid divorce going mainstream, the AIDS epidemic driving safer sex practices, the end of the Cold War, the fall of the Berlin Wall, the dismantling of apartheid in South Africa, the first successful space shuttle voyages and other dramatic developments.

Cultures like hip-hop, clubbing, skateboarding and many other scenes were born in this era, as this cohort strove to create a new future through 'interest' communities. As these scenes grew, the interconnectedness of these diverse cultures and communities became apparent. Take basketball and hip-hop connected by sneakers: savvy brands like Nike, adidas and Converse started to associate themselves with the cultural voices representing both communities (and fans).

During the pandemic, when *The Tiger King* and *The Last Dance* gripped Netflix viewers, I wrote a piece for *Campaign* magazine outlining some learnings that brands could take from the phenomenon of one of the most culturally relevant brands, Jordan.[3] I talked about the impact of representation and Black American culture of the 1990s in apartheid South Africa and how the crossover of cultures spread across the world even before social media. I highlighted how diversity breeds success, with coach Phil Jackson understanding how to create a winning team dynamic. I highlighted how timely storytelling can engage people outside 'categories' and introduce them to a brand, how breaking the formula can transcend category leadership, why brands should guard relevancy and, importantly, how this brand drove outsized and sustained growth.

Such cultural nuances seeped into other advertising with the forever-iconic Budweiser 'Whassup' ad from 1999 that went viral before social media as we know it today.[4] It felt fresh and authentic, relatable, funny and infectious; impacting me very early in my career. Unpacking it now, it was one of the first times a cultural nugget of gold – a representative cast including the director of the ad (and the short film the idea was inspired by), Charles Stone III – was used to connect to the brand and engage audiences outside the core Budweiser target audience.

These brands delivered growth through acquisition of new audiences by optimizing their current products or creating new products to market in new and exciting ways in line with the growth of this new era. From my own experience, during my five-year tenure at TONI&GUY, I launched Mascolo In-house, an internal bookings agency for the global artistic team (and for the teachers at the TONI&GUY academy) to style hair for credits in fashion magazines or music videos to further enhance the brand and extend it beyond the category of beauty for the mainstream. It was so successful that, at one point, there was a shortage of teachers.

Brands go online

The late 1990s saw the internet and email – the Web1 era – drive the next profound shift for the role of brands. Consumers shopped differently, they shared their views on products publicly and with each other, and business analysts could track data on how consumers were interacting with products. Previous mass one-way messaging between brand and consumer started to feel ineffective to this new generation, as consumers who adopted these technologies became less reliant on brands to help them make purchasing decisions. In the early 21st century, smartphones became mainstream, social media took off and, with it, the rise of the creative industry.

This time saw a slew of new world lifestyle brands providing new products connected to this new world, and innovative creator tools and platforms built to support a new channel of communications: influencers – bloggers, vloggers and social media – had arrived. I revisited that time when I worked on a Platform13 project exploring the rise of the distinctive and transformational Dr. Martens Jadon boot from 2013 to 2023. We created a mini-doc that explored an interplay of global perspectives, uncovering communities past and present, and how the early explosion of online blogging and social media shattered traditional ways for the world to see and hear new people, cultures and style – catapulting the boot to the status of cult icon, adopted by both fashion and music industries still today.

Back then, with new demands on how to engage with them, brands had to shift to showing up where their consumers were, in ways relevant to them, to start creating 'experiences' across multiple channels and using these new influencers. The era of brand storytelling had arrived, yet established brands continued to operate with a 20th century structure.

My guerrilla era

This was also the time of innovative and experimental brand marketing and the golden years of boutique agencies, one of which I opened in 2002 and closed 10 years later. I had no investors, partners or formal education in this area, but I was personally a very early adopter of online and social technology.

Ours was one of the first hybrid companies in fashion and youth that mixed digital and traditional comms from day 1. Not because it was in a trend report or a media plan, but because that's how we communicated in real life. We didn't realize how different that was. Spin clients were an incredible mix of music-, art- and fashion-oriented and adjacent brands, including a young *VICE* magazine and Carhartt WIP, among many others. These brands were open to trying new things that blended well with my forever non-traditional, guerrilla mindset. We made early collaborations with our friends (other brands, upcoming creatives and even new media like Hypebeast) to build our audiences; 24-hour stores because we couldn't afford retail rents; flyposting (also known as wildposting) because we couldn't afford OOH, and many many many events. Importantly, we connected all those channels together. At this time, I hadn't even heard of the words 'channels' or 'silos'. We experimented with a new online world opening up, from online forums to social media.

It was an incredible time.

Eight years in, as traditional PR became more difficult, and after a solo trip to Asia to find inspiration, I rebranded to Spin Agency – this time focused on digital marketing, content creation and social media. Any disciplines I have worked in since then will always be underscored by the storytelling and messaging skills honed by this background – it is still prevalent in how I work today.

I'm so thankful it was my 'training'.

After 10 years, I was ready for my next challenge – bringing my culture-led approach in-house.

My brand-side era

By the 2010s, youth, sneaker and streetwear culture had taken over the world. After closing Spin, being headhunted in a 'pinch me' moment to head up the global PR for adidas Originals was amazing. In 2012, my first corporate adventure at the German HQ began. As the storyteller of the brand, I immediately requested integrating social into my team, which had previously sat as part of the digital function, ensuring that this input was integrated upstream in planning. I was adamant that this new PR/social area needed to be the voice and face of the brand to drive those all-important two-way conversations with the sneaker community, its fans and the end consumers. This also meant global responsibility for all the content and activation across the PR and social functions.

The time spent tweaking traditional processes and bringing in new systems was worth it. But it wasn't easy.

I built a brand-new team that included people who were deep in sneaker and youth culture and curators with experience in social and in publishing. The blending of all our skills in collaboration with a diverse and talented network of freelance creatives and cultural voices feels like an early version of today's in-housing. Upon reflection, my entrepreneurial mindset, honed through creating and running a 10-year company, enabled me to both challenge using rostered agencies and update existing processes, such as finding new ways to reduce payment times to my global network – the people I worked with to deliver the projects. This was one of the fundamental shifts in how the organization worked, to do the work I had been sourced to do, changing how we did marketing from new reporting lines to new integrated processes, budgets and objectives.

For me, brand is product and product is brand, so, connecting the two and cohesively bringing them to life in the most credible way, in the places and spaces where the audience is – whether through online content, collaborations, partnerships and/or IRL events – still gets me excited today. I was the executive creative director and executive producer on all the activations and content under my watch, whether commissioned through my incredible network from years at Spin and/or live on set or at the event. The comms were meticulously and cohesively planned in-house, and we delivered compelling cross-channel storytelling that resonated with all audiences internally and externally. We executed hand in hand with our network of creatives who were using exciting visualization techniques in these new spaces, building long-term relationships with the cultural voices of our community, connecting online and in real life in an on-going series of brand activities – the annual calendar was packed.

There have been so many career-defining highlights from my time at adidas. One of the proudest was the rerelease of the iconic Stan Smith line through a multichannel cultural platform – Stan's Back – and a multidiscipline creative platform – the Green & White Takeover – integrating PR, brand activations, influence, social and online. The ultimate praise came years later on the main stage at Cannes Lions when Stan Smith himself said: 'When Stan Smith relaunched in 2014, it felt like a new brand.' *Business of Fashion* analysed the relaunch in 2017:[5]

> Thanks to a well-orchestrated promotional blitz, this unlikely hero has made one of the greatest comebacks in marketing history, from a declining brand popular with suburban dads into a must-have for the 'fashion-savvy'... a campaign designed to look grassroots, but which was in fact choreographed from start to finish with a goal of making the shoes de rigueur for people whose parents may be too young to recall the last time Smith played at Centre Court.

But it wasn't only brand relevance; it drove serious business too.

This was the beginning of my understanding that this way of working could also drive serious sales. As *Business of Fashion* continued:

> Sales of the shoe jumped dramatically, to 8 million pairs, in 2015, bringing total sales over the past four decades to more than 50 million. While the company hasn't released figures, researcher NPD Group Inc. estimates US sales rose fivefold last year. adidas says sales of its Originals collection, which includes the Stan Smith, and another top-selling retro model called the Superstar,

popularized by rappers Run-DMC, increased by 80 percent in the US last year, more than three times faster than footwear for team sports such as basketball and American football.

Another highlight was the launch of a completely new silhouette, ZX Flux, where I had no real product samples to work with, only a render on a page. From narrative and message-creation in October to delivering generated creative assets over the end-of-year holidays to an IRL launch in January, and with record-breaking sales of the shoe by the end of the year, we continued to prove that culture-led work could drive growth and the brand – and in only a few years if done right. The next two years continued to be fruitful for me and the brand. I delivered several incredible career-defining projects by continuing to iterate internal processes until I left. This included, in 2014, getting coverage of the first adidas x Farm (from Brazil) womenswear collab in male-oriented Highsnobiety. I was especially proud of the work on the womenswear apparel business – from injection packs to seasonal products and collabs. I was told that, at that time, that business was growing faster than the men's apparel.

In 2015, I stepped into my next corporate role on the leadership team at Diageo, Europe, with a new level of seniority, a new industry and the new Culture & Entertainment department I had set up to work across the brand portfolio. My remit: embedding the portfolio of big brands into culture, with a licence to disrupt, incorporate some new ways of thinking and adapt some processes to enable me to do the work. A good example was a hugely successful campaign for Captain Morgan in 2016. 'Only One Captain Morgan' – in tribute to Leicester City's captain Wes Morgan – was a fully integrated cohesive campaign ideated and delivered in less than a month, and included partnerships, content, product and media (earned, owned and shared). We led from in-house at a time when the power of social was so new for the business, fandom wasn't even a word in the industry and corporate agility was a dream. It was tough, but we did it and the results spoke for themselves – from both the industry and the community we were targeting. It's comments like the following from chief client officer of the Ingenuity Group, Richard Robinson, that really do make it all worth it.

RICHARD ROBINSON

I judged this in the final round of the Marketing Agencies Association Awards that year. The whole room was bouncing at the authenticity and sheer audacity of the idea. The thing that really stood out, beyond the outstanding cojones of everyone involved in creating, approving and believing in the idea, was the craft and operational discipline needed to make this happen. A true case study in celebration of the people who make stuff up and the people who make stuff happen. And all this after you have to consider Leicester City had to win the Premier League, a feat believed impossible by almost everyone, to make the idea reality. I have a clear memory of one of the people quoted as a testimonial being a convenience store owner in Leicester who was quoted alongside the usual suspects of Kantar, Ipsos, Neilson and the like sharing the impact the bottle design had on his customer base. It was the most beautiful of anecdotes, cutting through the sea of data every other entry included, and telling the very real story of a job done well. I loved it.

Both my tenures brand side required me to spearhead a number of organizational transformation initiatives in order to do the work I had been chosen to do. These worked because my teams created briefs that incorporated a variety of wide business insights and I had the autonomy to deliver the response in the way I thought best. Importantly, these activities were integrated across internal functions, all embedded in the brand vision. I do need to acknowledge Alex Matt (adidas Originals) and Ed Pilkington (Diageo), who saw something in me and supported my way of doing things, even when they weren't sure about it. Without them giving me the opportunities and the cover to try new things and challenge the status quo internally, my career could have been very very different.

Brands go 'purpose'

This was also the time that millennials started to become serious consumers and enter the workforce en masse, in a world that was starting to be negatively impacted by the overproduction of the 20th century. Awareness and understanding about issues around sustainability and diversity meant this new generation demanded that brands become more than the product they sell: to have purpose, to be true to their principles, to have a point of view and a voice that could influence, to do better – and they would let you know if you didn't.

For brands, the era of 'purpose marketing' had begun. But, for me, purpose marketing simply doesn't work. I prefer to embed brand values in culture work because that is what impacts the culture stacks. One of my favourite projects at Diageo was for Smirnoff. The 2017 Equalising Music project was set-up to add real value to one of the brand's key cultures and occasions: festivals.[6] We developed a three-year plan to double the amount of female, non-binary and trans headliners across Europe after the global team shared that only 17 per cent of headline DJs were female. Through an ongoing programme to support aspiring DJs gain the technical skills and confidence, to champion the cause at industry events like the Ibiza International Music Conference, and by leaning on our partners like Live Nation and Spotify to support them authentically too, we could drive resonance in the community like never before.

JAMES KIRKHAM

If you want to exist in a successful way as a brand or product right now, you need to connect with your audience by participating in conversations that they're having or the communities that they're building. That is cultural relevance to me. If you are not part of the fabric of this cultural conversation, consumers and audiences will ruthlessly filter you out. Period. I've said for years, we have a line that's: instead of interrupting what your audiences are interested in, you need to become what they are interested in.

But a client-side targeting would be: I'm James, I'm a 40-something in Richmond; I quite like music. We are so multifaceted, multidimensional, and, thank God, one of the good bits of social, or rather the evolution of digital in this, was that. That understanding that the more you respond to these crossovers... this crossover is absolute and everywhere right now, and it's not down to TikTok. TikTok is a catalysing factor. That means it's happening quicker and it's more arresting, and young people especially expect that sheer juxtaposition, like cultural roulette. It's like barbecue, football, news, lifestyle, art, style. We expect it. So, crossovers happen all the time. Therefore, everyone needs to treat their audiences like that, too, their consumers.

Era of culture-led brands

Now, in 2024 and probably for a few years yet, the pace of AI innovation is accelerating faster than the regulations, with deep fakes and virtual influencers already in the public domain. There are justified concerns around the worrying impacts on climate, ethical issues, compliance, data privacy, potential biases, and the overall transparency and effectiveness of AI systems. In its world-ahead outlook, *The Economist* suggests that 2025 is crunch time on 'the biggest gamble in business history'.[7] Blending new AI models with modern, human-oriented working systems is an exciting move, shifting brand evolution and business transformation even faster and in more ways than we thought possible. *The Economist* notes a significant difference between the companies that are driving the pace and commitment of AI and data-driven transformation versus those who aren't. For those pushing hard, it's very much about accelerating the commercial side of the business and applying the analytics to consumer engagement, making smart choices about how to invest in growth, and lining that up with the supply team so that products get delivered to the right places at the right time. AI also presents a new way of supporting and helping front-line decision-makers across the business. We have an opportunity to develop operations and productivity with redesigned workflows and processes that can, and must, address the key challenge of the siloed way of working in big companies, many of which were set up in the 20th century as organizations built for category leadership and maximum profit.

These fundamental issues need to be prioritized and resolved by evolving rigid old-world processes to adaptable new-world ecosystems because cross-business challenges and opportunities are linked, and this way of working is not fit for purpose today. Ideally, new forms of synchronized efficiency can free us up and enhance the best of what only humans can do – seeing the bigger picture, empathetic creativity, emotional intelligence and ethical connection through critical thinking. We must focus on building softer skills like communication and collaboration to improve work and inspire team-work, all the while learning, experimenting and evolving with new technologies. Without these sharp and smart human interactions, questions and inquiries, the output will be generic and the outcome non-transformative. Additionally, we should ensure ethical, human and cultural insight is at the forefront, with a continuous skill–upskill–reskill infrastructure for talent built in. If we don't include those inherited culture-led human viewpoints, and if we don't invite and empower people on all levels of the organization to be part of the transformation, we risk losing the trust, inspiration, empathy and energy needed for commitment to long-term and ongoing change. At this stage with AI, there may be resistance or inertia to change, with the prospect of potential job losses and scepticism on a personal level. In my experience, how everyone in the organization responds to change determines the success of it, so, finding elements that truly resonate with people is essential.

I've said it for years and will say it again: making cultural relevance a growth driver is just good business. Done right, cultural relevance fosters an internal mindset of curiosity and possibility. This can help break the traditional formulae, push innovation through the business and encourage creativity in the places and spaces where the audiences are. That means that, externally, a culture-led brand retains existing audiences, attracts latent and new ones – from employees to advocates, fans to consumers – and can drive relevance beyond its category to culture.

This means culture must be brought upstream in brand and business strategy, with a new way of thinking about all brand audiences and their behaviours as critical.

Notes

1 Ipsos and Effie UK. *Dynamic Effectiveness: Ipsos & Effie UK, Volume 2: The Empathy Gap and How to Bridge It: Giving Creativity's Other Half the Airtime It Deserves*, 2023, ipsos.com/sites/default/files/ct/publication/documents/2023-12/Ipsos_Effie_The%20Empathy%20Gap_December2023.pdf (archived at https://perma.cc/ZU6L-9HVU)

2 O'Neill, Erin. 'A history of branding', London College of Contemporary Arts, 27 December 2015, lcca.org.uk/blog/education/history-of-branding (archived at https://perma.cc/ZSK4-HXNK)

3 Fataar, Leila. '6 Brand Lessons from Michael Jordan's The Last Dance', *Campaign*, 27 May 2020, campaignlive.co.uk/article/6-brand-lessons-michael-jordans-last-dance/1684290] (archived at https://perma.cc/X4KL-74ER)

4 Barker, Matt. 'How Budweiser's "Whassup?" Ushered in the Era of Viral Ads', *MarketingWeek*, 24 January 2020, marketingweek.com/inside-story-budweiser-whassup (archived at https://perma.cc/G3GP-83DF)

5 Bloomberg. 'Can Adidas Repeat Its Stan Smith Success Story?', The Business of Fashion, 3 May 2017, businessoffashion.com/news/news-analysis/adidas-hits-marketing-gold-with-stan-smith-shoes (archived at https://perma.cc/9F6H-PGF5)

6 Gumble, Daniel. 'Smirnoff Kicks off Equalising Music Campaign to Mark International Women's Day', *Music Week*, 8 March 2017, musicweek.com/brands/read/smirnoff-kicks-off-equalising-music-campaign-to-mark-international-women-s-day/067740 (archived at https://perma.cc/6LGZ-DA8Q)

7 Shanbhogue, Rachana. 'Will the Bubble Burst for AI in 2025, or Will It Start to Deliver?', *The Economist*, 18 November 2024, economist.com/the-world-ahead/2024/11/18/will-the-bubble-burst-for-ai-in-2025-or-will-it-start-to-deliver (archived at https://perma.cc/88PP-LG7N)

02

Redefining organizational structure for cultural agility

The Covid pandemic fast-tracked and supercharged digital transformation in the most collectively disruptive way, building online connections and communities faster than ever. The lockdowns meant that everyone in the world, including brand and business audiences – from shareholders to employees to customers to consumers – all had to adapt simultaneously. The changes were significant, heralding a new era of connected globalization and related behaviours. Now, business is global by nature and being able to bridge cultural gaps across the business, borders and backgrounds is essential for success.

Importantly, this expanded cross-border working at scale, customers, consumers and employees is always diverse and intersectional. This deep interconnectedness through trade, technology, social media and travel blurring the lines between what it means to be global and local, and the rapid exchange of goods, services, information and cultural practices have immediate impacts that ripple across regions and into the workplace.

ETE DAVIES

The things that you say that you want to be as an organization – which is what attracts talent to come and work with you – you have to be almost uncompromising about those values and that kind of integrity. Otherwise, you don't build loyalty or trust within the teams. People talk about values, and, to a certain extent, the concept of organizational values can be perceived cynically, but that's going back to culture. It's so central to who we are as people and as companies. And the reason people leave is because so many organizations have compromised them. Values are what you are and what you live by. And if you're not going to live by them, then they're not your values. That's the truth.

FIGURE 2.1 The company culture stack

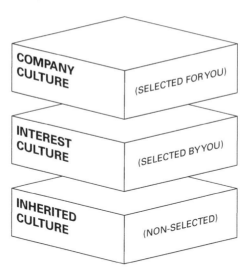

This is where company culture, as part of the culture stacks (Figure 2.1) – beyond traditional bonuses and financial incentives, free beer or a ping pong table – comes sharply into play. *Forbes* describes company culture as 'the secret sauce of an organization, the living, breathing persona of your company, capturing the norms, values and behaviors of the business'.[1] It's important to note that company culture is determined by business leaders' personal culture stacks; their business decisions are rooted in societal communication styles and personal lived experiences and are impacted by unconscious bias (which we all have), personal ambition and corporate politics, which in turn cascade down into how a business is run and the type of people within it. So, in this time of radical transformation, if your leadership is monoculture, set in its way, inflexible in thinking and impossible to convince to adapt rapidly, it begs the question about where that may leave a globalized brand or business today and in the future.

Cultural agility transcends borders

Cultural agility is the ability to understand multiple cultural and local contexts and work within them to make business decisions that obtain positive business results. For me, cultural agility goes beyond borders and must incorporate the culture stacks too.

Let's start with the obvious. I'm sure we can all remember times when frustration occurs because of a language barrier, and which could be a major challenge when it comes to inter-, cross- or multicultural communication and behaviours. Step forward Microsoft, who, at its Ignite 2024 conference revealed Interpreter in Microsoft Teams, a tool that delivers 'real-time, speech-to-speech' in up to nine languages.[2] Translation is not simply the exchange of words into another language; it needs to be understood with nuance and in the context of that culture for accuracy and effectiveness – this is important both internally and externally. Take the word 'freedom' – it means different things to different people depending on where they are from or how it is seen or experienced through their inherited culture stack.

Workplaces need to positively impact, motivate and engage an ever-more borderless cultural and global workforce and multiple generations with different work attitudes and ethics all working together. Hiring people from diverse backgrounds is not enough. Businesses need to establish inclusive organizations that enable people from different backgrounds to thrive and for innovation to truly break through. It's about fostering respectful relationships by helping people from different cultures (within their stacks) and backgrounds (including someone who has never worked in a corporate environment) understand each other.

Personally, I did not know anyone from a corporate setting when I was growing up, so, understanding this language and way of working was a culture shock when I went in-house – from the vocabulary, to the systems, the ways of working and more. As an 'outsider', there are two examples of my needing support in the corporate environment that spring to mind. Very early on in my first corporate role at adidas, I struggled with both my department and cross-functional communication. I asked Rachel Muscat, who also worked there at the time, for advice. She simply said, 'They speak in the language of decks and PowerPoint.' It was a real 'a-ha' moment and I quickly taught myself how to use PowerPoint and to share my ideas and work in this format. Being able to package my non-traditional ideas in an understandable way meant success all round. Another example was at Diageo, where I struggled with having no experience in the FMCG industry. Ed, my boss at the time, organized an incredible coach, Jane Upton, to support me in navigating the business and relationships in the business. These supports have been career-changing for me, and are just two examples of what may seem to be standard to people who have had access to these environments but could easily be overlooked. Offering ways for diverse employees to learn how to navigate your business can make the difference in their work success and career progression, and finding ways to help them deliver *their diverse perspective*s can make the difference to your business.

This is where company culture and cultural agility play an essential role.

A generational shift

What's always interesting to me is how cultural shifts will create new values and norms, driving innovation across working practices, products and communication. Your workforce keeps your brand and business in business, so it's in your interest to ensure your employees' experience is positive and engaging to maintain loyalty and reduce employee turnover. One place to start is with an understanding that there is a distinct generational shift and widening gap between traditional and contemporary work culture, which is compounded by 'Boomers' and early Gen X retiring, millennials entering leadership and Gen Z flooding the workforce.

This younger workforce grew up or adopted internet culture and early side hustles, and is increasingly taking responsibility around climate and social issues. In 2018, I delivered a global culture-led strategy for Johnnie Walker, aimed at rebooting the brand for new audiences. I knew side hustles were on the rise due to the internet. Having dug deep into the history of the brand, I discovered that the founder, John Walker was a humble grocer with a side hustle – a passion for whisky and a genius for blending. His son, Alexander Walker was an innovator and disrupter. Using ships' captains as sales agents, he created the square bottle to be able to export globally (without the bottles rolling around on deck) and the slanted label to stand out from the crowd. For my part, 2018 was a time when consumers started to want their brands to be more human, to be more than their product, to add value to their lives. For me, it was clear. Johnnie Walker had an authentic opportunity to become relevant to this new audience and to continue to drive its brand values of progress and its decades-old 'Keep Walking' strapline in a new, culturally relevant way. It felt like a unique opportunity to develop a credible and relevant brand to champion and support the culture with resources that that community needed, and show contemporary occasions and new ways to consume Johnnie Walker that matched with this new audience's lifestyle.

The Covid pandemic saw many of us gain a new respect for each other and the front-line workers who held us all together, creating what I hope is a more empathetic mindset and appreciation for the power of community. This attitude burgeoned as the public developed a deeper understanding of systemic racial injustices; and, with heightened knowledge of the climate emergency doubling down on both planet and people, employees started challenging their businesses and industries. Covid also shifted how we all saw the nine-to-five. We saw that working hours could be staggered and flexible, allowing better and much-needed connections with friends and family. Today, that work–life balance is expected to be built into company culture. Wellness and wellbeing have become much more important, with not only physical but mental health finally and firmly on the work–life agenda. This employee shift has driven some big brands to offer paid self-care time to their employees. While it shows a corporate shift forward, it could be unsustainable if the traditional workplace systems that drive stress and burnout in the first place – such as unreasonable workload, toxic environment, new types of leadership or a feeling of not belonging – are not addressed. Failing to truly nurture wellbeing as part of company culture is a business risk as younger generations unashamedly prioritize work–life balance in the face of millennial-era 'bossing' and 'hustle harder' cultures that label Gen Z as lazy, uncommitted or unwilling to work hard.

These new-generation mindsets and behaviours underpin healthy work attitudes, so, creating a company culture that adapts accordingly is directly reflected in the success of the business and the brand in the long term. To succeed, brands need to ensure that the work 'place' is positively productive of outputs that are credible and authentic for the brand. Always remember that your employees are also part of cultures and communities. We know that the new generation of incoming intersectional talent wants to work for brands and companies who have a point of view on the world and stand up for what they believe in. As they prepare to transform, it's critical that businesses today have the mindsets and behaviours of their people and their consumers at the forefront.

Applying my cultural positioning framework can help with understanding the unique role that only your brand or business can have for employees or society. The output directly impacts and may evolve current hiring, HR and people management and procurement practices, making them fit for purpose for your brand and/or business today.

Skills-based hiring

Opening the gates to non-traditional candidates is a key pillar to build a diverse organization today and in the future, and will help to level the playing field. This is especially important for talents who, for no reason of their own, come from situations where gaining a degree was wishful thinking, or people like me, who, even with a degree have had to self-teach in their chosen career. This also extends to those who have not had experience in or access to these environments.

JAMIE GILL

Look at all the leaders in our industry and observe how power is distributed. Today, ethnically diverse communities represent the majority of the global population, and here in London and in other major cities across the world, we're seeing that play out in the Gen Z population. It's time we focused on bringing ethnically diverse populations' skills into our business in a way that will drive innovation and customer understanding. Industries such as the finance sector are way ahead of us while we should be leading on this given our market growth strategy and marketing outputs.

In November 2024, the Sutton Trust shared new research that found what we all instinctively know:[3] that in the UK, education and class background have huge impacts on people's ability to reach the top of a creative profession; that access to creative degrees, in subjects such as music and art, is skewed towards the privileged elite. The Trust found that at four of the most prestigious universities – Oxford, Cambridge, King's College London and Bath – more than half of students on creative courses come from upper-middle-class backgrounds. So, it was a proud moment when Platform13 ran the strategic comms reboot of the prestigious D&AD charitable organization and its Shift programme. Our insight was clear: the traditional pathways into the global design and advertising industry are inaccessible to people from under-represented communities and there are nuanced reasons specific to each city. Access should not be one-dimensional and neither should the talent, so, we wrapped all the comms from the Shift programme to D&AD together, beginning a new, tangible movement under a new and cohesive platform, Shift Creativity. This was a call to action to shake up the old industry paradigms to benefit self-taught creative talent and enable them to access and flourish in the commercial creative industry. The programme aimed to address certain key areas. First was shifting raw skills, in a direct response to challenges faced by self-taught creatives from under-represented backgrounds through free, industry-led night schools in Sydney, London, New York, Berlin, Hamburg and Sao Paulo. Second was shifting the industry through D&AD's strong and deep links in the industry to help bridge the gap between under-represented talent and careers.

The business of people

From the Great Resignation of 2023,[4] attitudes to the traditional workplace set-up, corporate life, stress and burnout continued to significantly impact work culture across 2024, along with the huge number of lay-offs debunking the myth of corporate job security, and a reassessment of what success means today – it's not always financial wealth or a career at the top of the corporate ladder.

Even as early as 2019, it was reported by Earth.org that 90 per cent of its assessed net-zero plans of 35 major emitters, including the European Union, which together accounted for about 82 per cent of global greenhouse gas emissions, were unlikely to be achieved.[5] Today, the labour market remains unsettled in distrust of corporations, especially after the widespread deprioritization of DEI and the reduction in climate net-zero targets. This means that these entrepreneurial generations, concerned about both of these issues, are more likely to start their own businesses to disrupt and challenge the traditional brand and business landscape, follow non-linear career paths and/or be unafraid to leave a job if it isn't working for them. But, 20th-century businesses need these innovative and entrepreneurial mindsets and skills to transform into 21st-century organizations. Savvy business leaders should create environments that can attract, recruit and retain this diverse, multicultural and ever-more-global workforce. Previously, you had to be where the global HQ was to do a global role. Anyone who has worked for a brand knows all too well the struggle between global and local, inside the business and ultimately, externally to consumers. The requirement to stay at home in 2020 catalysed a huge change in work life for many of us. The acceleration of virtual working was an immediate adjustment for people and companies, with the logistics of remote working achieved at super speed. This was not simply working from home on back-to-back video meetings; it was a change of mindset and working methods for both employers and employees. New workplace systems, technologies and processes, including those video calls and meetings, but also digital collaboration tools and remote productions, changed how we worked and how we thought about work forever. The Covid pandemic made workers and businesses see remote, flexible and hybrid working as viable options, offering an unexpected opportunity for companies to not only re-evaluate *where* they work, but *how* they work and *who* they hire.

This also means a Global South workforce historically marginalized and also deeply affected by both their own traditions and politics and those of the Global North, are finding some new opportunities in a digital world that has normalized remote work. While it's true that technology usage and adoption is increasing around the world, there are still inequalities in infra-structure and access to it, including the internet, which means that there are still major discrepancies in opportunities for people across the world. Therefore, hiring for experience, skills and attitude over just a traditional degree is essential, marking a huge change for recruitment, and I was happy to see this happening in Gartner's *Future of Work Trends for 2024*.[6]

Human power over human resources

Cultural agility establishes credible relationships and builds trust, so, 21st-century businesses must develop cultural competence and communica-tion skills to connect with diverse colleagues and colleagues in new markets. With remote or virtual teams, there are additional challenges of missing non-verbal communication such as body language or reading between the lines.

JAMIE GILL

That's why we emphasize the importance of bringing in talent with deep insights from those markets. They understand how things are done and can provide the invaluable intel that's needed to succeed in those areas. But I think the fear is that bringing in new perspectives might dilute the brand. There's a concern that these new voices won't fully understand or respect the brand's heritage and values. What we're saying is, of course there's an onboarding process, of course there's a marriage of these ideas, of understanding where the constraints of the brand values that we've now established and know are concrete. With the proper support in the transition into industry, no one is going to go rogue. And I think that's the belief – that people from 'outside' will go rogue.

It means lifting barriers, opening the gates and embracing a wide variety of cultures, perspectives and knowledge to ensure that everyone can engage, participate and feel seen in our collective future. That means the rise and need for adaptable and coach-like leadership skills to foster trust and teamwork to leverage the power of humans by treating people as humans instead of business resources. This in turn promotes productivity, efficiency and effectiveness across both the business and borders. These are skills that go beyond only technical expertise and are directly related to personality and ethics. They include open communication and collaboration, active listening and critical thinking and a considered approach to empathetic cross-cultural relationship building. They incorporate cultural sensitivity around traditions, and strategies and processes to positively resolve employee conflict or misunderstanding because of beliefs or political affects related to people's culture stacks.

Successful teams trust each other. For multicultural teams, building that trust can be hard. A good first step is examining how your inherited culture impacts your own behaviour and then recognizing your own biases to people from different cultures. Working successfully and building trust with partners and colleagues in that market needs deep and sensitive respect for their cultures. They will also have a perception of your culture. Taking the time to appreciate and understand foundational business norms, such as working practices, negotiation methods and communication styles, will go a long way. Additionally, understanding societal norms, such as eating arrangements and engagement with elders and children, can make all the difference in connecting credibly with people. This is also true for people from different cultures in the workplace and why inclusivity practices are crucial. One thing that is clear for us all is that inclusivity is no longer just a nice-to-have. Ignore this at your business risk.

Markets vs culture

In the 20th century, especially in the Global North – ironically where these polarizing movements have seen the most support – there has been an influx of immigrants from the colonies for a number of reasons. The UN's *World Migration Report 2024* estimates 281 million international migrants worldwide, with the number of displaced individuals due to conflict, violence, disaster and other reasons surging to 117 million, the highest levels in modern-day records, underscoring the urgency of addressing displacement crises.[7] This stems back to the slave trade's forced migration of an estimated 12–15 million Africans to the Caribbean, the Americas and Europe. Then, during the two world wars, large numbers of non-European troops worked for the Allies and settled in the areas where they were deployed. Since then, decolonization has led people to move to Europe because their states ceased to exist. Another historical reason was a huge demand to fill post-war labour shortages and rebuild the economy, for example the Windrush Generation of thousands of people encouraged to leave the Caribbean for the UK from 1948 to 1971, changing the face of the UK for ever. Migration has increased over the past five decades, whether through those trying to find a better life, for educational opportunities, cultural opportunities or as refugees fleeing a terrible home-country situation. In 2015, 65 million people had been displaced from their homes by conflict or natural disaster. That year, more than a million refugees entered Europe after fleeing wars in the Middle East, Africa and Central Asia.

As an immigrant and a person who was segregated by colour inside both my country and city, I have always been fascinated by the movement of people in the world, how borders are created and, importantly, by whom. My motivation to leave South Africa and move to London was absolutely based on my culture stacks. First, I wanted to live in a society that had 'laws' around security, racism and discrimination. And I also wanted to live in a city that was mixed, where you would be accepted for just being you, no matter your colour, ethnicity and background. For me, there is still no better city in the world for that than London. This was further reinforced after the worrying far-right riots in the UK in 2024, sparked and spread by misinformation. An act aimed to divide, it resulted in pulling communities and cultures together, themselves taking to the streets in peaceful solidarity and unity against racism. Second was access to my interests. At 21, club culture, music and fashion were important to me from a self-expression and identity perspective. I wanted to be at the epicentre of the type of music and fashion that I have always gravitated towards but had no access to in South Africa. Third, and still to this day, connected to both, was a perception of a London attitude that felt reflective of me – as punk and rave, defiance and acceptance. 2025 marks exactly 30 years since I landed at Heathrow, and I still love that energy.

The inherited culture stack is soon to become extremely relevant for brands and businesses. Global population dynamics are shifting significantly, seen in the interest by 159 countries in de-dollarization, around systems like Brics Pay from the Brics bloc.[8] These countries include major world powers, such as China and Russia, and countries that are influential on their continent, such as South Africa and Brazil, and can profoundly affect the global financial landscape and economic growth. With President

Trump warning this collective that they would face 100 per cent tariffs if they created a new currency to compete with the US dollar, much is riding on the responses during Trump's second presidential term.[9] As mentioned in Chapter 1, creativity and innovation breed in places where there are no other options.

On the other hand, from now until 2050, half of the global population increase is expected to originate from just nine countries: India, Nigeria, Pakistan, the Democratic Republic of the Congo, Ethiopia, Tanzania, Indonesia, Egypt and the US, with sub-Saharan Africa likely to see its population double in contrast to Europe's projected decline.[10]

JAMIE GILL

Regarding the rising markets and India's emergence as a superpower, along with overconsumption and the need to gear up the production for growth, my gut feeling is that, as some markets strengthen, others are softening, so, what we're really seeing is a counterbalance, not huge growth. This means the supply chain is in place already; it's just currently geared for other markets. The planning needs to be in whether the supply chain can translate as is, or if adjustment is needed for the emerging markets. My feeling is it's going to be a smaller growth trajectory over time that's just counterbalancing where we're losing markets such as China. If we are speaking specifically about markets such as India, a market I know well, it's exciting because I've observed a distinct brand journey. Historically, the Indian market wanted heavily embellished looks that Western brands weren't offering, so they would go to a tailor and have their clothing made but buy into leather goods, shoes, jewellery etc. Now, I've watched markets where consumers are starting to enjoy the cut, the fit and the craft that goes into luxury ready-to-wear. This evolution is happening in India, just as it is in Africa, particularly in Nigeria, which offers hope in the emerging markets where larger markets aren't showing the stability in growth they once had.

New market, their culture

Penetrating a new physical market and/or culture is tough. In the face of the momentous shift in global population dynamics, industry and businesses need to be ready to invest and strategically partner in new territories.

Traditionally, global brand and/or marketing teams create expensive advertising campaigns that local markets need to support and optimize through media spend. Local markets, however, with their own regional differences, may feel like those global campaigns don't resonate with their audiences and value systems, so prefer to adapt the global assets or even use their marketing and/or media spend differently.

ETE DAVIES

No one has a model that works perfectly, because there's always the battle of brand consistency, commercial and operational efficiency. If you're trying to be culturally relevant, then autonomy and primacy has to be given to local markets to deliver creatively, for work to really resonate and be something people actually feel connected to. Key brand elements need to be consistent so that there is a consistency of the brand experience; for example, out of 100 per cent of the control of the brand, there's 20 per cent that should be the global foundation, and then the other 80 per cent is locally customized.

From colours and symbols having significance to local laws, regulations and customs, and tailoring messaging and providing better customer service, cultural awareness is essential for successful international trade. In a commentary for *Campaign* magazine in 2023, I reflected on how the luxury fashion sector is transitioning from status-driven motivations towards a focus on cultural credibility.[11] I observed a significant shift as luxury brands move beyond traditional retail settings in established fashion capitals, venturing into innovative strategies and brand experiences in unexpected locales. If done well, we create not just engaged audiences, but committed brand advocates.

JAMIE GILL

Firstly, there are significant growth markets out there that are ready to be tapped into. It's already understood from marketing; we need to start representing these markets with our ambassadors and influencers who are going to resonate with these consumers. While it's great to see more diverse campaigns that speak to global audiences, it's also key to have the talent in-house, at the global HQ level.

All big decisions are held at HQ level so that's where you need representation for your global business. In local markets, it's obvious that you need a local workforce, but to not have that voice represented where the decisions are made is detrimental to business growth and success. The point is business needs highly skilled professionals, and part of the analysis of skill in our industry is to understand the customer. To not then develop a representative workforce means you'll be missing key skills. It's why diverse teams have been proven time and again, to be better performing in terms of profitability, innovation and adaptability.

These are professional, skilled people who truly understand these communities of consumers, how to communicate with them to tap into their spending behaviours. Nuances such as knowing traditions around dress at Indian weddings is key to tapping into this growth. For example, the mother of the bride might want as many outfit changes as the bride, so do the sister, the cousins and the aunts. The market is underserved from an international luxury brand perspective where there's a huge opportunity to build out the brand proposition to this audience. I see an immense opportunity for established luxury houses to really start tapping into that at a couture level. But we have to ask how a brand can truly understand how to engage with that market without representation of that market in decision-making roles in-house. This is what The Outsiders Perspective is addressing – enabling skilled talent from ethnic minority backgrounds to transition into luxury, fashion and beauty.

Take China, for example – a key target for many global brands. Major cultural shifts include *guochao*, a return to young people celebrating Chinese culture and trends. We see this across Asia, as young people reject hard-sell Western influence. These shifts are drastically changing the 'face' of current and future consumers and their needs in this region. On the other hand, global brands introducing their product or service to new markets provides incredible opportunities for cultural exchange from their home country.

This opportunity is also true for product creation and innovation. When working with Dr. Martens to unpack challenges facing those who are under-represented in the music industry worldwide, assumption, trend reports and desk research would never be enough. To deliver a recommendation for how this fashion brand could make a positive impact credibly in music, our first port of call was curating the right team of literal Dr. Martens boots on the ground, in Japan, Germany, the UK and the US. Our work unlocked country-specific nuances and an approach that incorporated these with a credible and actionable role for the brand. Similarly, we brought this outside in through another Dr. Martens project to truly get to know the personalities and faces behind their quantitative data – and to build a rich qualitative global portrait of who represents the brand UK, US, Japan, China and Germany. Our report was delivered to global teams in an extensive, multimedia way through a dedicated password-protected microsite, including a six-part content series bringing to life each consumer segment. We further engaged the global internal teams by hosting four global virtual panel discussions with each segment, so they could ask the participants any specific questions they wanted, hopefully resulting in actionable insights from product creation, sales and marketing, and potentially even opening up new and previously unexplored areas for the brand.

For modern brands, relevance involves crafting adaptable and flexible brand and business strategies responsive to locally nuanced cultural insights.

ETE DAVIES

You have to look outside the Global North, Western society and economically developed countries to see how innovations are really shaping culture. If you look at Asia, Africa, South America, you can see how, globally, technology innovation shapes culture – because everyone's getting the technology at the same time, but everybody's circumstances are very different.

KEITH CHENG

The fast-growing awareness of health and sports in China led to a rapid change in the way people dress. When Umbro officially re-entered the China market in 2023, we launched a campaign called 'Anytime Anywhere'. The campaign focused on a collection of blokecore style products with functional fabric. We invited key opinion leaders in design, styling and music to generate their own content to tell the story of how they can dress in blokecore style in different scenarios – be it at the gym or a social gathering. Social media gained the first wave of online awareness, leading to a big offline event in Guangzhou. The event drew a big crowd of football fans, Umbro fans, and cool kids, to celebrate the love of football culture, and generated buzz in the market, paving the way for Umbro to regain the position of sport lifestyle brand in China. Establishing a clear connection to the brand's culture of football lifestyle helps to drive a long-term relationship with the core consumer group. As for the Umbro brand, we aim at creating a football and football-lifestyle culture in China, which, in business terms, enhances traffic, conversion and margin to build up a sustainable growth model.

Like it or not, in every part of the industrialized world, communities are mixing and blending across cultural stacks – both inherited and interest – catalysing substantial social transformations, with identity and self-expression increasingly transcending traditional ethnicities. This results in the dismantling of and/or building upon historical context and heritage nuances, reshaping the cultural landscape for us all. An inclusive, culturally agile organization is the key to entering and succeeding in these spaces and attracting, engaging and retaining audiences through the full culture stack. To do this credibly, insider knowledge of the people, rituals, language and semiotics of that country and culture – both in real life and in the online space, both inherited and interest – is essential.

The ability to successfully navigate and adapt to diverse and global cultural practices and backgrounds is becoming more important than ever for global organizations to succeed. It means both being aware of cultural differences and respecting cultural diversity, whether in or between coun-tries, and is, in fact, a competitive advantage. By positively leveraging the differences for business success, cultural agility goes beyond borders and country-specific norms and languages. That means driving company culture evolution like we have never seen. All well and good in theory, but impos-sible in reality if your current business or organizational processes are not fit for purpose.

For your outcome to be different, your business must update internal systems, foster new ways of working across the business and borders and build new capabilities in this new era of work.

Notes

1 Wong, Belle. 'What Is Company Culture? Definition & Development Strategies', *Forbes*, 30 May 2024, forbes.com/advisor/business/company-culture (archived at https://perma.cc/8EPM-6JQ4).

2 Microsoft. *Microsoft Ignite 2024 Book of News*, 19–21 November 2024, news.microsoft.com/ignite-2024-book-of-news (archived at https://perma.cc/N5X9-CJVS).

3 Tibbs, Lewis. 'Research Reveals Stark Class Inequalities in Access to the Creative Industries', The Sutton Trust, 13 November 2024, suttontrust.com/news-opinion/all-news-opinion/research-reveals-stark-class-inequalities-in-access-to-the-creative-industries (archived at https://perma.cc/HRM4-LG9A).

4 Savage, Siobhan. 'From the Great Resignation to the Great Reskilling: The Next Era of Work', *Forbes*, 28 July 2023, forbes.com/councils/forbeshumanresourcescouncil/2023/07/28/from-the-great-resignation-to-the-great-reskilling-the-next-era-of-work (archived at https://perma.cc/8V5N-9E8Y).

5 Igini, Martina. 'About 90% of Top-Polluting Countries' Net-Zero Targets Unlikely to Be Achieved: Report', Earth.org, 12 June 2023, earth.org/net-zero-study (archived at https://perma.cc/R726-HD3D).

6 Gartner. *HR Toolkit: 9 Future of Work Trends for 2024 Key Insights and Actionable Strategies for HR Leaders Crafting Organizational Resilience*, Gartner, 2024.

7 IOM. 'World Migration Report 2024 Reveals Latest Global Trends and Challenges in Human Mobility.' IOM UN Migration, *World Migration Report 2024*, 7 May 2024, worldmigrationreport.iom.int/news/world-migration-report-2024-reveals-latest-global-trends-and-challenges-human-mobility#:~:text=With%20an%20estimated%20281%20million,urgency%20of%20addressing%20displacement%20crises (archived at https://perma.cc/MC7W-Z9T9).

8 BBC News 'Brics: What Is the Group and Which Countries have Joined?', BBC, 1 February 2024, bbc.co.uk/news/world-66525474 (archived at https://perma.cc/A24H-F3RR).

9 Muzaffar, Marosha. 'Trump repeats 100% tariffs threat to Brics nations if they attempt to replace dollar', *The Independent*, 31 January; 2025, independent.co.uk/news/world/americas/us-politics/trump-brics-nations-tariffs-us-dollar-b2689644.html (archived at https://perma.cc/9VXG-SVRB).

10 United Nations. 'World population projected to reach 9.8 billion in 2050, and 11.2 billion in 2100', UN Department of Economic and Social Affairs, 2017, un.org/en/desa/world-population-projected-reach-98-billion-2050-and-112-billion-2100 (archived at https://perma.cc/ZG95-JC99).

11 Arrigo, Yasmin. 'Redefinign the Runway: How Luxury Brands Embraced the LFW Experience', Campaign, 6 March 2023, campaignlive.co.uk/article/redefining-runway-luxury-brands-embraced-lfw-experience/1814890 (archived at https://perma.cc/5BPK-SU4U).

03

Culturally informed leadership

The new expectation for CEOs and CMOs

In this era of an ever-changing, globalized, polarized world impacting you and your audiences' culture stacks, a change of approach to 21st-century brand and business has been much needed. The PwC's *27th Annual Global CEO Survey* should be a wake-up call for brand and business leaders.[1] A shocking 45 per cent of 4,702 global CEO respondents doubted their company's current trajectory would keep them viable beyond the next decade – up from 39 per cent just 12 months earlier.

SARAH WATSON

How do you lead things that wouldn't have meant anything a few years ago and now can paralyse a workplace? I will tell you what I'm really learning about leadership – it's to physically hold a space where everyone can hold their position. The role of leader is not to hold the position yourself. It's to create an environment for everyone else to hold their position safely.

A business consultant I interviewed goes further, stating that he doesn't think that the future of leadership can rest on the shoulders of just one individual with a singular vision. He feels that the complexity of what lies ahead requires a dynamic interplay of perspectives and expertise. On one hand, we need leaders capable of taking people on bold, often uncomfortable, journeys of transformation – navigating uncertainty and embracing change. On the other, we need those who can steadfastly uphold the frameworks that keep it all grounded – observing structure, rules, ethics, responsibilities and the broader metadata that ensure accountability. He is convinced that both mindsets are critical, and both need an equal voice in shaping the way forward – it's about mastering a balancing act. So, companies must navigate competing priorities – short-term needs versus long-term strategy, growth and profit versus employee wellbeing, and sustainable value versus immediate returns. It's not an either–or scenario; it's about finding equilibrium in a way that drives progress while staying anchored to purpose and responsibility.

Something has to change.

We have seen big business structures evolve from product-led to customer-led to consumer-led to service-led. All these business strategies competitively play to win in category, with short-term profit the ultimate measure of success. Pivoting and reshaping business strategy to focus on positive impact on and for all audiences – including employees, customers, consumers, fans and wider society – and help to create a better future for us all must start with a redefinition of success; in other words, how that brand can add value to the world, while still making a comfortable profit.

For this, we need resilient leadership with an entrepreneurial mindset and skills focused on the role of the brand or business in addressing climate change and its impending tipping point for the planet and people, upcoming and ongoing technological disruptions, acceleration of AI and Industry 5.0, demographic shifts both globally and nationally, a fractured and polarized world of geopolitical destabilization and social instability and the much-needed fight to dismantle deep systemic social injustices directly connected to generational health and wealth inequality. These are serious and life-affecting challenges for everyone.

Identifying your brand's unique role in the world through my cultural positioning framework could be a start. This culturally informed and led North Star would enable the cohesion and integration of people, technology and new working systems to build a new business foundation fit for today and tomorrow. Cascading this into your brand values and business strategy will enable both survival and the capacity to thrive in this new era of radical transformation. It means that those with company-wide decision-making powers, the C-suite, need to challenge the status quo of 20th-century leadership, and collaborate and evolve their roles and their relationships with each other, the workforce, their industry and governments, and focus on connecting the dots between their audiences (beyond only the shareholders) with responsible positive business outcomes.

ETE DAVIES

There are two camps of leaders: those who are living it – either through passion or community – and then the 'scientists' – those who are objectively studying it. The latter get their cultural insight or understanding primarily from research, whether that is surveys, social listening or lifestyle publications and editorial. They tend to take a very educated view on what is the trend and on brand frameworks, strategy and what's happening in the macro society and environment. The other type of leaders are those who live it. They live the culture because they're from a community where the culture is being generated. Particularly in the UK, a lot of the diaspora from the Global South and other places are the generators or modern popular culture. That intimate tie means there's that connection which gives a first-hand experience and perspective that the scientific leaders sometimes struggle to truly understand beyond theory, to understand actually what's really happening in culture, and the inexplicable trends. These leaders usually have a few deep-lying areas of passion and interest, whether that is fashion, photography, music or even sport. And, because they are so deeply immersed in what is ultimately a passion for them, they're right into the subcultures and the communities and what's emanating out of that – because culture is massive, multifaceted, it's all the things that we experience. And so, people with lots of those passions and those deep touchpoints and connections tend to be more plugged in to what's happening in various cultural sectors, which then gives them a more informed view because of all the adjacencies between fashion, music, sport, art, technology and so on.

Culturally informed leadership is increasingly essential for CEOs and CMOs. It involves cultural agility, understanding and appreciating diverse cultures, values and beliefs, which helps leaders make well-informed decisions that consider the impact on global stakeholders. This approach fosters inclusivity and builds trust within organizations and their audiences and communities. Today, agile, adaptable, entrepreneurial, innovative, culturally informed leadership needs to come to the forefront, not to 'fix' the problems of the 20th century, but rather to dismantle the old and create new systems for today and the future, driving that all-important emotional connection to audiences, wherever they are, consistently.

New leadership fosters an inclusive culture where employees feel valued and that they belong. This type of leadership encourages collaboration through employee empowerment and results in employee motivation, engagement, effectiveness and loyalty. This type of leadership considers the impact of that business on people and the planet, and acts accordingly from the implementation of wellbeing strategies, digital and AI literacy, product and service innovation to a business's ESG strategy. This type of leadership understands the concept of responsible growth based on brand values and the power of community and creativity, while planning for multiple future scenarios.

And it flows from C-suite.

For this approach to succeed in the face of uncertainty and multiple potential future scenarios, a solid but adaptable business agenda with adjustable goals and priorities will need to be set. A leadership team with both the capabilities and mindsets to push that agenda forward positively will need to be built or developed. Leading with softer skills that include self-awareness, empathy and open communication results in much-needed innovation and better employee performance, necessary for brand and business survival and growth.

JAMIE GILL

I think people believe it's going to hurt the brand. And, let's be honest, while that surface conversation might be happening, there's often an underlying belief. As we highlighted in our UK Fashion DEI Report, leadership is crucial in driving these initiatives – true change needs to be led from the top. What we are not saying by 'lead from the top' is wipe the entire C-suite clean and start again. We're not attacking the current regime, but we are asking them to think differently. Leaders need to lean into the conversation, be allies, and truly understand the importance of what we're advocating for. No one is saying that anyone must give up their job. There's a fear that by embracing diversity, people think they'll lose their positions. If leaders are feeling insecure, they're less likely to let go, fearing that bringing in others might take their place, rather than seeing how it could enhance the business.

Leading with emotional intelligence (EQ) – rather than education or technical knowledge – recognizes and understands both your and others' emotions, enabling better and more compassionate decisions for everyone. This type of leadership would understand the importance of a culturally relevant brand

and making cultural relevance a growth driver. It starts with diversifying the C-suite to rewrite the rules and change the face of leadership today.

Diversifying the C-suite

Historically, white men have been most able to climb up the corporate ladder and become CEOs. Usually taking the top job with their education and technical or financial expertise, leading with a hierarchical control-and-command style. As society norms changed, so shifted the styles and expectations of leadership, evolving to more democratic ways of working. The turn of the century saw the rise of visionary leaders such as Steve Jobs with product and/or engineering backgrounds reflecting the explosion of the tech industry.

Who knows, the next cohort of leaders could very well be gamers.

A 2024 article from SHRM looked at the profiles behind the top 10 roles at Fortune 100 companies since 1980, and reported that the face of the C-suite is changing, even if it is at a glacial pace.[2] Some interesting findings include that the average age of C-suite leaders is 57, about the same as in the 1950s and reversing, in around 2001, a brief trend for younger leaders. Major movements have come from 'foreign born leaders'. The study found that, since 2011, this group grew more quickly and now accounts for 15 per cent of the top executives, with the UK and India the two biggest sources. It is no surprise that 36 per cent of top executives have MBA degrees and Ivy League alumni continue to dominate, making up 23 per cent of all top executives. The share of C-suite leaders with finance backgrounds jumped from 19 per cent to 32 per cent. Since 2001, as technology and the internet became normalized, there has been a huge shift in needed leadership skills, with a doubling of external talent and an increase in cross-industry talent brought in since then, reducing the traditional in-company promotions. Regarding gender, it was found that, in 1980, there were no women CEOs, but, today they make up 27 per cent, still far under the 47 per cent of women in the workforce.

Male and white CEOs still top the stats, even though there are countless studies and reports from multiple verified sources that link diversity across the business (and on the board) with positive business outcomes. Add the missed benefits of intersectionality and the picture is even more frustrating. A 2023 article in *Raconteur* notes that there are also few leaders who are known to be LGBTQia+ (even though Apple's Tim Cook came out as gay nearly a decade ago) and that leaders with known disabilities are similarly under-represented.[3] Importantly, the article highlights that, in the UK, there has never been a woman of colour at the helm of a FTSE 100 firm. I had a play with the *Raconteur* calculator to find out how I compare with the average FTSE 100 CEO. Education and experience ticked the boxes, but the results were not surprising, with a clear 'fail' around gender and ethnicity.

JAMIE GILL

I think the reality is that there are two parts to it. When you are part of any diverse group, you've often experienced being in the minority. However, if you combine the diverse groups, we actually form a majority. So, when we conducted the Fashion DEI Census, we found that the majority of people identified as part of a protected or diverse group, with the true minority being able-bodied individuals and non-protective classes. This means, fortunately, you are a custodian of this diverse group you are a part of, shaped by the struggles you've faced.

So, if you've had to fight your way up, especially if you're intersectional – whether from a lower socioeconomic background, an ethnic minority, LGBTQ+, or any combination of these – you've faced significant challenges. To reach a position of influence or leadership, you've had to work harder. You could argue that you've worked twice as hard to get to where you are compared to those in non-protected, more privileged positions. From my perspective, those who have reached a position where they can open doors for others have not only learned but also demonstrated capability. They've understood that what they've achieved is everything they were looking for, and it's not so much driven by insecurity. The doors are going to open now because of everything I've been through. That fight is deeply ingrained in me. What I'm saying is, you've worked hard to reach a position of leadership and influence, and now the opportunity is right there. I see many leadership roles that have been attained through connections rather than merit. It's been the 'business on the golf course' thing, where the advantage comes from who you know, rather than the quality of your skills. That's where I see insecurity resulting in people not helping those coming after them. It's bred from insecurity.

A 2024 *Women in the Workplace* report from McKinsey, in partnership with LeanIn.Org, collected information from 276 participating organizations employing more than 10 million people from corporate America and

Canada, providing an intersectional look at the specific biases and barriers faced by women of colour.[4] It found that, since 2015, the number of women in the C-suite has increased from 17 to 28 per cent, and the representation of women at the vice president and senior vice president levels has also improved significantly. All good, right? Not when that progress for women of colour is lagging behind, with the report finding that, although women represent roughly one in four C-suite leaders, women of colour represent just one in 16. It also found that, in 2023, for every 100 men promoted from entry level to manager, 87 women were promoted, and trending the wrong way for women of colour: 73 women of colour were promoted to manager for every 100 men, *down* from 82 women of colour last year. The authors call this the 'broken rung', where women, especially women of colour, fall behind and can't catch up. Another finding calls out microaggressions (I talk more about this later in the book), making women – and especially women of colour – who experience it three times more likely to think about quitting their jobs and four times more likely to be burned out. In addition, they are likely to still carry out a disproportionate amount of childcare and household work. These are some of the reasons why hybrid and remote working and a focus on work–life balance might be more attractive to them, but should not be accompanied an assumption that they don't have the same ambition or dedication as men.

A 2021 *Harvard Business Review* article based on an analysis of more than 150 companies found that, after women join the top management team, firms become more open to change and less open to risk, and that they tend to shift from an M&A-focused strategy to more investment into internal R&D.[5] The article highlights that, when women join the C-suite, they go beyond new perspectives to shift how the C-suite thinks about innovation, ultimately enabling businesses to consider a wider variety of strategies for solving problems, creating value, and championing progressive ways of working.

So, it's a shame that so few of us get there.

A 2024 article in *The Economist* unpacks the impact of motherhood on a women's career through a study across 134 countries.[6] It presents shocking statistics of what is dubbed 'the Motherhood Penalty' – 95 per cent of men aged between 25 and 54 are in the workforce, while, for women in the same age group, it drops to 52 per cent. This means that company culture must incorporate work–life balance, especially at leadership levels, where traditional societal norms mean women are more likely to take the carer role at home, disproportionately affecting career prospects.

The article also mentions career gaps, when having a baby means delaying or missing out on promotions. Even when women are up there, an interesting perspective from the World Economic Forum on gender parity in leadership is the concept of 'the male blueprint', referring to a set of characteristics, behaviours and expectations attributed to traditional masculinity.[7] These gender stereotypes include assertiveness, decisiveness, competitiveness and confidence, which have been valued and emphasized in leadership roles and reflected in the media narrative across multiple cultures. It appears that women not only have to match that style, they have to constantly prove that they can do even more than their male counterparts. Additionally for many, menopause matches this hugely important leadership career stage. According to the World Health Organization, in 2025, over a billion people will be in menopause.[8] Thankfully, it looks like millennials are openly starting to address these previously hidden life-stage effects of perimenopause, and they are expecting their businesses to not only listen but provide supportive workplaces.

There is still much to do, however, to move the dial in diversifying the C-suite, especially beyond simply gender.

It's not rocket science to understand why diversifying makes sense. Different perspectives challenge the status quo, instigate personal growth and drive innovation and transformation. Not only that, attracting and retaining diverse talent and consumers becomes frictionless, when they can see themselves reflected across the business, especially in leadership. Additionally, diversity at the top table plays a hugely important role diversifying the all-important leadership pipeline. It doesn't stop there. In a world of corporate missteps impacting brand reputation, legal teams can further err on the side of the cautious, while much-needed relevance drives creative and bold ideas. A diverse cohort checking and challenging assumptions can ensure positive business decisions in a world where reputation and sensitivity across cultures is essential. For the C-suite, that means learning from their direct reports and through the organization and external agencies and partners to help fill the gaps to drive a new growth mindset.

The CEO: growth driver or blocker

CEOs are under pressure from all sides, from shareholders to regulators. After all, big brands need short-term, profit-driven goals to stay *big* business. This can cause decisions based purely on these goals, with success calculated on short-term results.

ETE DAVIES

The old and traditional school of thought around CEOs and leaders was that they've built long and storied careers and they're clearly accomplished people to get to where they want to get to, which unquestionably makes them experts in many things. The new mindset of CEOs is to constantly take themselves out of their comfort zone into areas where they're going to experiment and to hire people that keep them on their toes in terms of knowledge, so they are continually learning and are more connected to teams who are plugged into 'what's new'. This new leadership mindset is essential now because of the pace at which culture and communities are evolving.

One brand that has faltered in recent years has been Nike, for a few reasons. A *Business of Fashion* article noted that, in December 2023, Nike slashed the outlook for its fiscal year ending in May, predicting sales would grow 1 per cent.[9] That would mark the company's worst performance since the late 1990s, other than the pandemic year of 2020 and the 2009 recession. The effects of decisions made in 2020 by a new CEO with a consulting background, John Donahoe, are clear. These included waves of lay-offs during a restructuring that reorganized the sports business units or categories around gender. This move lost decades of knowledge and expertise, possibly costing Nike its unique ability to create game-changing innovative products. Another strategy to place all growth bets on a DTC business model meant walking away from deep, long wholesale relationships – from 'mom and pop' stores to independents and key retailers. These are not only the distribution points, but also community hubs – the lifeblood of this brand. I can only imagine there was immense focus, effort and budget on data-driven performance marketing to feed that business model that had to be moved from brand building. This may have felt transformative for investors at the time, but Nike was built on innovative, cultural and creative nous, deeply connected to multiple communities that love the brand. It's also one of those brands with all it needs for a turnaround at its disposal. It needs to just do it. The wonderful stories from the 2024 Paris Olympics offer a moment for the brand to leverage its incredible athlete roster, including Simone Biles, Noah Lyles, Yuto Horigome, Sha'Carri Richardson and more.

Not only lifestyle brands like Nike, but also CPG brands are feeling the burn. A July 2024 Reuters article highlighted P&G, Unilever and Nestlé all reporting below expected sales growth.[10] P&G saw shares falling 4.8 per cent due to price increases, weak spending in its second-largest market, China, and continuing boycotts of Western brands in the Middle East, among other issues. Price increases also saw McDonald's sales fall 1 per cent over the April to June 2024 period compared with a year earlier – its first decrease since the Covid pandemic. Starbucks sales dropped 3 per cent globally at stores open for at least a year, including a 2 per cent fall in its home North America market, as reported by CNN.[11] When the founder of Starbucks (Howard Schultz) makes a comment on LinkedIn about the state of a business he is no longer with, you know something is in the air.[12] For Schultz, even more than the China slow-down, he believes Starbucks' US operations are the primary reason for its problems. For him, the answer does not lie in data, but in the stores, and the need for an obsessive focus on the customer experience, through the eyes of a merchant, someone with real on-the-ground insights. Meanwhile, luxury brands are also struggling. Another 2024 *Business of Fashion* article highlighted a synchronized global slowdown and low consumer confidence as a hangover from the Covid pandemic, while, looking forward, it predicts a continued period of slow growth in advanced economies, although it expects an eventual bounce-back.[13] A factor is the deprioritization of expensive fashion in the face of a post-Covid reality. Even the 1 per cent (of wealthiest individuals), in the face of formulaic luxury products and the decrease in true luxury experiences are expecting even higher levels of personalized and curated services, bespoke products and a sense of real connection to the brands they spend on.

For any CEO, whether new in the role or having dealt with the last few pivotal years, assessing the need and level of business transformation or remodelling for an unpredictable future is crucial. In a world where external issues are so momentous, CEOs may focus on the internal things that they can control. We all know that a two-to-three-year restructure wrapped as transformation generally means cost management. We also understand the need for the quick wins of departmental transformation with traditional measurements and metrics and generally as a top-down vertical directive and bottom-up execution. This time, however, we must start with a specific definition of what responsible positive growth means for the brand, its category and the world and how that growth will be achieved by and within that business; in other words, how that brand can add meaning and value to the world, while still making a profit. A cultural positioning identifies the unique way that the brand or business can do that. Building this into your brand values and business strategy will enable you to thrive in this new era of radical transformation. As Industry 5.0 becomes a reality, CEOs need to be well read and prepared for cyber-attacks and the corresponding security, especially as data, privacy and global payment systems drive new behaviours and business models.

KWAME TAYLOR-HAYFORD

I think there needs to be an alignment of incentives across some of the leadership teams. Because everyone is chasing a slightly different objective, it's a challenge because they're working in silos – CMO has their thing, the chief product officer has their thing, everyone's got their thing.

This means fostering new collaborations between roles like the CFO and CISO in a positive way, mitigating business risk and keeping the organization safe and compliant. An interesting trend is the CFO to CEO journey. In 2024, the *Financial Times* reported that, of 674 companies featured in the Fortune 500 and S&P 500, 8.4 per cent of vacant CEO positions were filled by CFOs in 2023 – the highest percentage dating back to 2013, when the level was 5.8 per cent.[14] The article warns that, while these skills may be needed in a financial crisis, as there has been in the immediate post-Covid world, it may not translate to driving the demand and transformation needed for the future. Even worse, *Raconteur* noted that women still remain largely under-represented in the role, reporting that, of 163 CFOs appointed worldwide in the first six months of 2024, just 44 were women.[15]

The CMO: growth driver or cost centre

The CMO role – the title here again, gone again, back again, often also incorporating chief growth officer, chief brand officer, chief creative officer and so on – is deeply cross-functional, ever changing and ever expanding, needing an on-the-pulse hand that can cohesively add and join multiple disciplines to move the brand and business and, ideally, the category and culture forward.

PETER SEMPLE

I'm a believer that you're likely to do the best work if you're deeply engaged with the thing you're working on. Not everyone has that luxury, and sometimes you need to take the job that's in front of you. But I've been lucky enough to find my way into roles where I can marry all the things that I'm deeply passionate about. Even if you're really smart, you really don't necessarily understand all of the cultures you're trying to interact with. And so, surround yourself with people who do, or have a revolving cast of collaborators. We do the thing here of having a relatively small skeleton crew and then a revolving cast of creative talent, strategic talent, inspirational talent, so that we're able to have the right conversations with the right people.

KWAME TAYLOR-HAYFORD

CMO tenures are getting shorter and shorter. There's so much pressure on CMOs to drive business results today. And that's important, but when you have a great CMO, their job is to help you think much more long term and focus on your brand and focus on how your brand and its values manifest in the world. They stay busy keeping up with changing consumer perceptions and changing consumer habits. CMOs are struggling right now because it's all about immediate growth and performance, and results. Very few brands are leaning into experimentation, imagination and investing long term. Real value is keeping an eye on long-term growth and doing brand work that espouses the values of your brand and organization, aligns with what consumers are looking for, ultimately even allows you to understand consumers so well that you can start to feed those insights into product innovation.

ANA ANDJELIC

Corporations started separating those who make creative stuff from those who make commercial stuff, those who make things and those who sell them. And, unfortunately, marketing fell under this latter part of those who sell things, narrowed down to that media planning role. Marketing almost comes in at the end, and today the question is how we are going to target consumers to buy this?

No matter the ever-changing job or team title, one thing is certain: in a world where audiences are brand and marketing savvy, this department – as the brand-building department in direct contact with these audiences across a proliferation of channels on behalf of and as the voice of that brand's audiences inside the brand – is a key growth driver for culture-led brands. When it comes to the work, the role to be done hasn't changed: attract and retain consumers and drive growth.

How this is done has changed.

Traditionally, the job was to implement a marketing strategy clearly focused on product-oriented mass marketing and big media spend. Today, demands include smaller budgets, a fragmented media landscape and the need for consistent messaging in the languages of multiple and growing channels and platforms; consumer expectations; the creation of compelling content that resonates and gets over the difficulty of earning audience attention to engage core and acquire new audiences; among other expectations and behaviours. All this means that the required skillsets may be lacking. So, a culture-led entrepreneurial CMO mindset is required to deliver dynamic communications and seamless customer experience. These should be based on real-world insights, aligned with strategic growth priorities, mixed with real-time market and consumer activity, and take account of constant feedback from everyone and anyone in the comments sections and/or through UCG on social media. This requires adaptable planning and rapid responses as standard. These are less common in the mindset, behaviour or organizational set up of traditional big brands, but are imperative for success.

For marketing transformation, that relationship and partnership with the CIO and CTO and their team is essential to ensure the marketing tech stack is relevant and optimized. This will help to drive good growth through both brand and performance marketing, cohesively and not in competition with each other. While there has been much digital transformation since 2020, AI and first-party data, with related privacy issues and the proliferation of channels to reach, optimize and measure, means that brand transformation has its backbone in data and technology. Today's CMO needs this understanding and those soft skills outlined earlier. It's a tough job, no doubt about it. It does not mean the end of traditional marketing skills, but it does signal the need for upskilling and progressive marketing transformation from an organizational perspective.

PETER SEMPLE

The marketing world that CMOs face these days is – unsurprisingly – ever more complicated. There are myriad new media channels and kinds of advertising properties that you interact with and engage with across the platforms where people spend time, so you need to keep up with what is technically possible. And then, all of the things that we know to be true of culture, the things that people are experiencing, the things that are influencing their decisions, are moving at a faster pace than they ever have done before because of the barrage of things that people consume every single day. There's more and more that you have to try to get to grips with and try to have at least a rudimentary understanding of, to understand the tools within the toolkit.

But I feel that, as a marketing leader, and I suppose the same is true of being a CEO, you need to have a really firm idea of what your business is capable of today and tomorrow, and where the ambition for that lies.

In a culture-led brand, CMOs must be included in strategic business information-sharing and critical decision-making at the highest level, evolving traditional CMO relationships with the CEO and other members of the C-suite, especially the CFO and legal teams. CFOs prefer predictability and measurability, while legal teams can be overly cautious especially with provocative ideas, which can sometimes lead to risk-averse efficiency at the expense of broader and longer-term effectiveness. This can cause under-investment in brand marketing, especially in tough economic conditions and where reputation is important, which is, of course, counteractive in a world where everything is changeable and there is an urgent need for new growth opportunities and demand-generation. In 2024, *The Drum* reported that only 22 per cent of CFOs believed that their CMOs demonstrated 'excellent' value to the business' bottom line (the majority stating 'good' or 'average').[16] For them, the input is as important as the output, so, finding a common language would be a helpful unlocker of budget and understanding.

Ultimately, CMOs must understand how their decisions affect the growth drivers of the business and what levers they can and need to pull to drive growth. Success will only happen if CMOs can demonstrate and communicate both the value of and method for creativity and communications – beyond traditional advertising ROI metrics – which focus on marketing inputs that directly impact business outcomes. Perhaps this needs to be reoriented around how CMOs can drive pricing power through brand-building instead.

KATIE DREKE

Based on what I've observed with clients, and through conversations with former colleagues, I can sense that the past few years have been especially tough for CMOs because the world is in the midst of a turbulent age, and the majority of CEOs do not come from a creative background. When the business fundamentals start to rumble and shift, it's quite natural for people to instinctively retreat to their wheelhouse. Not as many CEOs have a wheelhouse of communications and brand development, and therefore don't immediately lean into the power of creativity to drive business decisions and outcomes. But imagine if they did. Business could become more highly differentiated, enhanced and leveraged under experienced creative leadership. Like the former CMO of Nike, Davide Grasso, moving into the CEO role at Converse, and then again at Maserati. As well as the former CMO of Jordan, Sean Tresvant, recently taking on the role of CEO at Taco Bell. I think we will begin to see more of these such moves in the coming years.

To be fair, CMOs also must hold up their end of the bargain, and raise their business game in order to spar successfully with commercial leaders and CFOs. But, at the end of the day, I don't think the classic rules of marketing are necessarily useful for where we're going next. The landscape is being rewritten at the moment. To hold traditional tenets of marketing too tightly in your hands is a dangerous move. This is not a moment to be looking in the rear-view mirror.

I found myself disappointed to see the CEO as a creative blocker highlighted in Lions' 2024 *State of Creativity* – a report that analyses inputs from close to 3,000 global marketers and creatives.[17] The report found that, while there is growing optimism in brands and business, a key challenge is CEOs' lack of trust in creativity for growth. While there is much talk of creativity, the reality for this cohort was that CEOs reverted to tried and tested strategies favouring short-term tactics that impact the bottom line, rather than engaging with new ideas. Statistics in the report support creativity as an accelerator for growth. Brands that predict higher growth (for 2024) are six times more likely to promote creativity, and 4.6 per cent more likely to have a higher marketing spend (than in 2023). I can concur with this to a point. (Chapter 4 includes more about culture-led creativity, where a brand goes beyond the craft of creativity, creating a win for everyone.) The Lions report includes excellent suggestions to make creativity work for the 21st-century business – idea sharing, success celebration (made even more impactful with a shout-out by the CEO), better feedback loops, especially with agency partners, and, an important one, reframing failure. This last aspect could be a game-changer for brands today. It would mean taking risks when, in the past few years of survival mode and the need to protect the bottom line, and keeping stability in uncertain times, this is not likely the first thing on a CEO's mind. But being overly cautious and conservative in today's world means that more innovative agile businesses can easily challenge your top spot. My experience in the leadership team at Diageo was a real insight into big business operations, giving me a unique perspective and focus on the work I do.

In 2023, McKinsey found that CEOs who place marketing at the core of their growth strategy are twice as likely to have greater than 5 per cent annual growth compared with their peers.[18] Today, as we move to a new era, it may be time for that CMO to jump to CEO.

Test, learn, iterate

Mintel's 2024 report on the role of innovation finds that, while every region has seen a decline in CPG innovation, the trend is most pronounced in North and Latin America.[19] The highlight is that, even in the US, home to the innovative Silicon Valley, only 29 per cent of CPG launches are new products for the first five months of 2024, well below the global average. Interestingly, and in contrast, the Middle East, Africa and Asia-Pacific are the regions innovating the most in the CPG industry. This is a reflection of their faster rate of economic growth than more mature markets, and fuelled by a more innovative 'growth' mindset. It's clear that future-proofing your business can only be achieved by exploring multiple future states and scenarios for the brand, its product or service offers and new ways of reaching consumers.

In this new world order, at this transformational time, I believe a good and reasonable budget and effort to experiment with cutting-edge ideas must be allocated to ensure that big brands stay relevant, survive and grow. For legacy brands, with new products and companies biting at their lead and answering the unmet needs of their audience, they can no longer only compete through traditional strategies. A dedicated test and learn department, headed by an imaginative, experimental, creative C-level leader and with a diverse team would enable the business to explore fast-moving societal and cultural changes and diversify a brand's products and services in a proactive, not reactive, manner. There may not be a sale or tangible impact directly linked to this straight away; there would need to be freedom to challenge and disrupt the status quo, and there would have to be an acceptance that projects and pilots out of this department may fail or take a bit longer to work. But that's ok.

ETE DAVIES

There's a number of ways we cascade innovation, but an approach that seems to work particularly well is to build excitement and inspiration by making or finding out cool stuff that other people will look at and just be amazed by. It's stuff that will really ignite people's curiosity, might shock them, might force them to rethink, so that then they start to lean in and re-evaluate and reappraise their perspective. And then the other way is small incremental success and momentum.

For clarity, this is different from, and beyond, traditional innovation departments. While these R&D areas have a crucial role in developing core products and services relevant to the category of the brand, growth today can come from many places, whether in category, in your cultural territory – known by the brand or not – or from a completely different place. Take Guinness, for example, and its long-awaited Guinness 0.0, created for those who love the taste, but don't want the alcohol,[20] or our Platform13 project for the Guinness rugby heartland, 'Never Settle', or our project for Guinness in Caribbean culture. They all make perfect sense. (More of this will be covered in Chapters 4 and 8.) But, I have always wondered if Guinness, an iconic brand, could be a live, experiential brand? What would that look like? Compare it with, for instance, the *Michelin Guide*: who would have thought the origins were in a clever strategy from 1900 by the Michelin tyre company to encourage driving (and therefore the demand for automobiles and ultimately tyres)? Today, the brand is (also) a global signifier of the fine-dining scene.

Making cultural relevance a business growth driver, an innovation catalyst and a marketing output can transform your brand and reimagine your business. But, culture-led brands need to be driven by culturally informed leaders, hand in hand with new-world agencies and partners. They need to be flexible business ecosystems with diverse teams to build legacy projects, ensuring true resonance with their audiences and, ultimately, sustainable business growth.

Notes

1 PwC. *PwC's 27th Annual Global CEO Survey: Thriving in an Age of Continuous Reinvention*, 2024, pwc.com/gx/en/ceo-survey/2024/download/27th-ceo-survey.pdf (archived at https://perma.cc/6W29-KFQ4).

2 Cappelli, Peter. 'The Changing Face of the C-Suite: Older, More Diverse and More Experienced', SHRM, 16 Febuary 2024, shrm.org/executive-network/insights/changing-face-csuite-older-diverse-experienced (archived at https://perma.cc/X8W4-JRPZ).

3 Murray, Clara. 'Is the Face of FTSE 100 Leadership Changing?', *Raconteur*, 2 May 2023, raconteur.net/c-suite/the-changing-face-of-ftse-100-ceos (archived at https://perma.cc/449Y-XAUW).

4 Mckinsey & Company, LeanIn.Org. *Women in the Workplace 2024: The 10th-Anniversary Report*, 2024, mckinsey.com/featured-insights/diversity-and-inclusion/women-in-the-workplace (archived at https://perma.cc/B7TV-BA8K).

5 Post, Corinne, et al. 'Research: Adding Women to the C-Suite Changes How Companies Think', *Harvard Business Review*, 6 April 2021, hbr.org/2021/04/research-adding-women-to-the-c-suite-changes-how-companies-think (archived at https://perma.cc/LF7V-QKTP).

6 Economist, 'How Motherhood Hurts Careers.' *The Economist*, 30 January 2024, economist.com/interactive/graphic-detail/2024/01/30/how-motherhood-hurts-careers (archived at https://perma.cc/2RQ6-3XWJ).

7 Wiesner, Silvia. 'The Male Blueprint – What It Is and How It Stops Women from Reaching the C-Suite', World Economic Forum, 8 March 2024, weforum.org/stories/2024/03/the-male-blueprint-what-is-it-and-how-does-it-stop-women-from-reaching-the-c-suite (archived at https://perma.cc/4BB4-ZSSY).

8 World Health Organization. 'Menopause', 16 October 2024, who.int/news-room/fact-sheets/detail/menopause (archived at https://perma.cc/ZDF5-UUYM).

9 Miller, Daniel-Yaw. 'How Nike Ran Off Course', *The Business of Fashion*, 5 February 2024, businessoffashion.com/articles/retail/nike-sportswear-market-challenges-john-donahoe (archived at https://perma.cc/88Q3-VY9M).

10 Rajesh, Ananya Mariam, and Jessica DiNapoli. 'P&G Posts Surprise Sales Drop as Demand Slows Despite Price Restraint', Reuters, 30 July 2024, reuters.com/business/healthcare-pharmaceuticals/procter-gamble-misses-quarterly-sales-expectations-2024-07-30 (archived at https://perma.cc/33A3-KRNT).

11 Meyersohn, Nathaniel. 'Starbucks Sales Tumble as Customers Reject High-Priced Coffee', CNN Business, 30 July 2024, edition.cnn.com/2024/07/30/investing/starbucks-coffee-sales/index.html (archived at https://perma.cc/U5W8-PTKR).

12   Schultz, Howard. 'Howard Schultz on LinkedIn: Starbucks Announced Earnings Last Week…', LinkedIn, 2024, linkedin.com/posts/howardschultz_starbucks-announced-earnings-last-week-and-activity-7193044402255110144-y4mN?utm_source=share&utm_medium=member_ios (archived at https://perma.cc/4PJ3-ASGE).

13   Amed, Imran. 'Is this an Inflection Point for Luxury Fashion?', *The Business of Fashion*, 3 August 2024, businessoffashion.com/opinions/luxury/is-this-an-inflection-point-for-luxury-fashion/?utm_source=linkedin&utm_medium=newsletter&utm_campaign=LINewsletter030824 (archived at https://perma.cc/U2KB-ZDBP).

14   Raval, Anjli. 'Why More CFOs are Becoming CEOs.' *Financial Times*, 13 March 2024, ft.com/content/fb4a8289-f8df-44d3-b6f0-48d476e775c2 (archived at https://perma.cc/38U7-VUJW).

15   Birchall, Sam. 'Diversity in the CFO Role: What is Going Wrong?', *Raconteur*, 7 October 2024, raconteur.net/finance/diversity-in-the-cfo-role-what-is-going-wrong (archived at https://perma.cc/8HL8-VDJV).

16   'How Can CMOs Find Common Ground with CFOs for B2B Brand Building in 2024?', *The Drum*, 8 January 2024, www.thedrum.com/news/2024/01/08/how-can-cmos-find-common-ground-with-cfos-b2b-brand-building-2024 (archived at https://perma.cc/K2FY-XYM4). Accessed 12 Dec. 2024.

17   Lions Advisory. *State of Creativity 2024*, Lions, lionscreativity.com/advisory/state-of-creativity?utm_medium=pr&utm_source=lions&utm_campaign=pr-em-lions&utm_content=2024.03.20&utm_term=noterm (archived at https://perma.cc/3RPK-E4G5).

18   Brodherson, Marc, et al. 'The Power of Partnership: How the CEO–CMO Relationship Can Drive Outsize Growth', McKinsey & Company, 26 October 2023, mckinsey.com/capabilities/growth-marketing-and-sales/our-insights/the-power-of-partnership-how-the-ceo-cmo-relationship-can-drive-outsize-growth (archived at https://perma.cc/A5CL-8AVE).

19   'The Role of Innovation in the Future of the CPG Industry', Mintel, 3 October 2024, mintel.com/insights/consumer-research/role-of-innovation-future-cpg-industry (archived at https://perma.cc/36CU-3S2W).

20   Guinness. 'Guinness 0.0: Non-Alcoholic Beer with Our Iconic Taste', guinness.com/en-gb/beers/guinness-zero (archived at https://perma.cc/B6J2-C2PH).

04

Mapping the cultural landscape

What it means for brands today

From new social media platforms to monumental world events, it can sometimes feel difficult for marketers to keep up. The need to read and analyse cultural shifts, signals and conversations that impact the world, communities and fans, and flex accordingly, is more important than ever. Take the expected TikTok (and TikTok Shop) ban in the US. If it happens, the ripple effect would be massive on the 170 million US users and impacting brands as they seek and invest to engage with this generation of consumers and creators.

There is no doubt that, today, brands are built through fan communities and cultures, accelerated and amplified on social media via UGC and memes, and discussed in online communities like Reddit. YouTube's 2024 *Fandom* report found that 85 per cent of people online (aged between 14 and 44) describe themselves as 'fans', meaning that they turn to their object of fandom for connecting socially and for self-care, which will ultimately feed into their identity.[1] For brand leaders who used to think of fan culture as niche (usually and wrongly translated as small) and connected only to 'youth culture', these diverse and multigenerational tribes are both highly influential advocates and economic powers, if engaged in the right way. 'Awareness' and 'eyeballs' are no longer enough, meaning you can no longer just shout louder than everyone else and deploy a huge media budget focused on traditional reach channels and that 1990s 'hero', the ad. This would hold the brand back because brand activity would be dependent on and relentlessly executed against the schedule of the media buy, the retail space windows' calendar, industry awards or traditional drawn-out production schedules.

KATIE DREKE

Cultural relevance happens when you're lucky enough to establish a toehold in people's hearts and minds, and manage to live there rent free for a bit of time. Sometimes it's because your brand is naturally and genuinely showing up where a resonant audience is also naturally and genuinely showing up. It shouldn't ever feel forced, allowing connections to be familial or friendly and expected. And, perhaps most importantly, if you're absent and missing, they would notice and likely miss your presence.

To be discovered, brands have to gain audience attention credibly by reaching them where they are, engaging them in the way that they want. This chapter focuses on the marketing, media and comms landscape and how to create and maintain relevance through attention and discoverability, and loyalty through communities and fandom.

The culture stack underpins fan culture

The culture stacks have always impacted fan culture, and technology has always driven innovation and communication around and within fan culture. So, even though interest cultures are connected globally, when and where (inherited stack) these fan cultures come to life can differ. For example, skate culture in California is different from that in Palestine or Ethiopia or China or Brazil, and different today from in the 1980s. Successful brands need to be able to credibly tap into these cultural nuances to become and stay relevant and adapt for growth or even survival. This resonance happens if the brand positively impacts their audiences' lives in the ways that matter to them, in the spaces and places they inhabit and with a deep understanding of their nuances, rituals and language (and no, I don't mean their generational slang).

As with cultural agility in new markets discussed in Chapter 3, in fandom, a brand needs to make the same effort by immersing itself in the fans' world. Fans connect deeply with brands, products and services that authentically add value to their communities and cultures, reflecting or adding to their identity, saying something about them and sharing their codes and values. In 2018, after signing another 10-year sponsorship of the O_2 arena and 19 Academy venues across the UK, O_2 tasked Platform13 to create a cultural approach and positioning to drive meaningfulness around its iconic live music category. Through filmed interviews with established cultural voices, organizations and companies in live music and the UK music economy, a deep-dive focus group with 20 O_2 customers with an interest in music, and a full-day workshop with relevant senior stakeholders, which included a panel of music industry heavyweights, we delivered a cultural opportunity and clear roadmap for relevancy and impact for the next 10 years. Similarly, in 2024, Platform13 developed and ran an internal workshop for the adidas North American Purpose team as part of its UK immersion trip to help reimagine and reframe the approach to driving purpose marketing strategy and community action, by taking a culture-first approach to sport, with a special focus on football. We explored how football culture in the UK has evolved over time, its wide-reaching impact and how it connects communities. From that, we developed an interactive workshop that featured insights, discussions and in-person interviews with grassroots and community leaders in the categories of football media, impact and grassroots football clubs.

This sort of project doesn't have to be 'worthy' – it just needs to be relevant and unique for your brand. In advertising, this manifests in, for example, Budweiser's 'Whassup' (mentioned in Chapter 1), 'Raise your Arches' from McDonald's and Nike's industry benchmark 'Nothing Beats a Londoner'. What makes these campaigns successful are the cultural nuggets of gold that come from understanding the unspoken signs that only fans or specific communities would know about.

This is where brand love is born and thrives.

JAMES KIRKHAM

Entertainment strategy is always about seeking out and discovering, rather than just interrupting and so on. I think those strategies have always been vital. Within something like Copa90 and sports, there was an inherent belief that the fans themselves were important. That was predicated on necessity, because Copa90 did not have rights to show football matches. So we went, 'Oh, well, it would it be really interesting if we spent time with fans.' Historically, a beer brand would go, 'You've got an armchair fan, you've got a super engaged fan... maybe there's one more.' That's rubbish. There are actually about 20 different facets of fans. There's the fandom of legacy, of a dad going with his son or his daughter. You've got cathartic fandom, which is about that moment. If you've got the escapism, which 90 minutes gives you from the drudgery of normal life, you've got loyalty, you've got the identity of the badge. And all of these are true areas of fandom that any brand can play in. But some people just think, 'Oh, you're an armchair fan.'

Culture-led brands go further. During the Covid pandemic, while it was good to see established brands and companies support their staff and teams, the cultural and creative sectors – the sectors that brands spent much time and money aligning themselves with, those coveted interest territories of music, art and design, food and drink, sports and the associated creative industries – went into crisis mode. And with them the independents, the self-employed, the freelancers, the newbies, the ones that make their industries exciting and dynamic, the cultural voices who push and drive culture and conversation forward. So, in this era of culture-led brands and the need for diverse perspectives and cultural agility, there is a clear opportunity to bring in people (cultural voices and fans) or work with those who know how to.

The cultural pipeline drives brand resonance and relevance

To succeed in fan culture, respect of the culture stacks and knowledge of how information spreads through the fan stages and across different fan cultures is key. This is also a type of cultural agility, along what I call the cultural pipeline – from subculture to emerging (sometimes called niche), to popular/mainstream culture. This pipeline arrangement is a dynamic relationship where ideas and feedback flow all ways, inspired by and contributing to the ever-changing landscape. Leaning into fandom can only be achieved by knowing and understanding how information spreads and is shared along the pipeline, enabling the evolution from sub to emerging to mainstream. Here, it is not just an option but a necessity for a successful brand to be remembered – and celebrated – for the right reasons. Securing that invaluable engagement and priceless word of mouth, delivering special cultural artefacts and/or activity that drives advocacy and activism along the pipeline means that the brand is credibly part of and primed for long-lasting growth. Maybe those surprise-and-delight guerrilla-style tactics could be useful again today.

Subculture tends to be related to inherited culture and is where alternative perspectives to the mainstream can be found. A good example is Gen Z's response to millennial culture on social media: from the popular and mainstream, highly produced, styled aesthetic of product and content to new on-the-fly lo-fi expectations of true reality; and Gen Zalpha moving to new community channels like gaming while social media becomes even more mainstream; and so on.

It's never been about the channel.

Audiences will move to the next space, so brands need to present themselves credibly where their community is. This is not necessarily where your traditional high-reach media plan says it is. For brands, subcultures are rich early insights into understanding new ideas that could impact popular culture later. By keeping an eye on subculture and tapping into emerging culture through cultural intelligence, relevant signals can help a brand see potential incoming changes that will affect all their audiences and potentially help them find new ones. While brands should not necessarily play a role in early subculture, the right cultural intelligence, filtered through your cultural positioning, reads, analyses and identifies relevant nuggets to help you understand if, where and how along that pipeline your brand (and its products) can or should show up (Figure 4.1).

Ideas from subculture that find roots emerge to bridge subculture and popular culture, bridging inherited and interest culture is where brands can really start building brand equity in and for the culture. It's at this emerging culture stage when engaging credibly means that brands need to ensure that they are truly supporting and not appropriating or simply monetizing it, but adding value.

FIGURE 4.1 The cultural pipeline: communities, brands and cultural intelligence

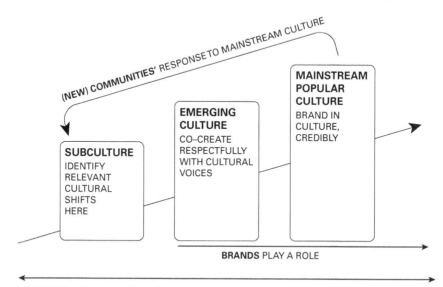

One of my favourite Platform13 projects unlocked a new audience for a brand that is rooted in subculture, Dr. Martens. In the past few years, their 'alternative' has gone mainstream; the iconic Dr. Martens boot moving from a badge of rebellion to a desirable, but still alternative, look. So, we dug deeper into today's music culture, a credible space for the brand, and identified a new 'alternative' movement that went beyond gender norms, a community proudly intersectional, an inclusive generation who stand up for what they believe in when it comes to politics, art, music, style and more, and who are borrowing from multiple influences to create something new, undoubtedly bold and alternative. These audiences should have been wearing the brand that we all associate with this subculture, but they weren't. We delivered a new identity, with detailed creative and comprehensive through-the-line global comms guidelines and plans to reach and engage this new consumer with the brand and AW23 innovation product. This included creating a direct link to Dr. Martens long-standing music culture through a dedicated TikTok activation to find new gen talent to showcase at a special gig and to start building an ongoing relationship with. The activation was even shortlisted for the 2023 TikTok Awards.

The most credible way for a brand to engage in any culture is by building strong, transparent and open relationships with the voices of that culture or community. This was a key pillar when I launched Platform13 in 2017 and how I worked on the brand side too. Project teams are assembled according to category, culture and community, and blended with the right partners, creatives and creators able to bring that activity to life in new and exciting ways. These may or may not be the same people, but for me, both lived and professional experience are essential. Supporting and co-creating and collaborating with these cultural voices across financial, research, marketing, product and business resources can almost always ensure credibility, authenticity and relevance for the brand.

ETE DAVIES

What we found is that, when we encourage partnership, the organization is initially reluctant because the belief was always that if you start partnering with external parties it adds extra management. But, in reality, we have seen that, because we're partnering with people who already have advanced knowledge, we're getting through things quicker and there's a lot less rework. So, actually, it's more profitable for the business in those areas, rather than trying to do everything ourselves, which has been a real eye-opener for our finance teams, who are often among the main voices for us not to partner with anyone else – for fear of trading revenue – but that turns out to be a false economy if you're in a service area where you don't really have the expertise or the credibility, and then it's just wasted effort for poor-performing work when actually you can work with a specialist to get to better work faster and more effectively, and this in turn leads to more briefs from the clients.

For brands, these cultural voices can include people, but also calendar moments, other brands, products, events, platforms and even TV shows. Take Red Bull Music Academy – a workshop and lecture series that travelled the world for 21 years, investing in aspiring and emerging music talent. It successfully played in that space because its product made sense and was used organically in the scene. And instead of simply trying to sell more, it added value to that culture. It is still seen as a benchmark brand activity by those in music culture who were there and benefitted, with its alumni recognizable names in music today.

Also at this emerging stage, an exciting phenomenon happens. Interest cultures start to cross over and intersect, enabling multiple points of entry for adjacent brands and categories, if done respectfully. Take football culture. While LeBron James and Drake invest in AC Milan,[2] and Ryan Reynolds and Rob McElhenney have taken charge of Wrexham AFC,[3] branded jerseys are now worn by everyone from a variety of communities – from the terrace to the catwalk to the street, by actors, DJs, music artists and festival goers and, as personalized UGC in Roblox by brands, gamers and fans of other cultures.[4] Images of people from all these communities shared across multiple platforms drive wide interest and engagement, discoverability and loyalty. For the brands (and adjacent brands), the opportunity is massive, if it's done right.

Another example is the typically elite tennis. The US Open was a moment for the United States Tennis Association to introduce the tournament, and sport, to a younger demographic.[5] It updated its 'Champions of the Court' in the US Open experience on Roblox, in partnership with Ralph Lauren Polo and Emirates, enabling gameplay and rewards for these audiences. Expect to see the merch soon. Luxury brands have been at it too. With tennis superstars like Serena Williams and Roger Federer as red-carpet regulars, Gucci wanted a piece of the action. Locking into their shared inherited Italian culture, the brand selected tennis talent Jannik Sinner as a brand ambassador in 2022. His understated personal style perfectly reflects the new CD Sabato De Sarno's almost minimalist aesthetic. It was Sinner's 2023 appearance at the most traditional, historic and prestigious tournament in tennis, Wimbledon, sporting his all-whites and a custom Gucci duffle bag with its distinctive iconic GG monogram, highlighted further by the recognizable green and red straps, that caused a stir online and a frenzy on our feeds.[6]

There is also a very special space in between sub- and emerging cultures, where communities and fans from completely different spaces and backgrounds appropriate and adapt your brand, with no connection to your brand strategy. These latent audiences, or audiences unknown or unengaged by the brand, have great potential for positive growth. Think of the rise of Formula 1 fandom today,[7] or the association of Timberland with hip-hop culture in the 1990s, or brands and music artists in gaming culture today.[8] Being able to credibly leverage opportunities can be a clever way to connect with fans. Strategically incorporating this into brand plans can be tricky and the right hands are needed to do this well. It can be risky too if it feels like your brand is simply jumping on the bandwagon and attempting to appropriate that culture without credit to that culture or it attempts to represent that culture without knowledge of the nuances. At BOF Voices,[9] on stage with the legendary Dapper Dan, I explained that cultural appropriation occurs when brands just drop in and out of different cultures when they want to. We talked about how this isn't just borrowing – that it's indicative of a deeper power imbalance where the powerful feel entitled to the expressions of the less powerful without accountability. When brands engage in genuine exchanges and initiate real conversations with the cultures they are drawing from, it changes the dynamic entirely. This is the difference between the types of brands holding onto the past and those looking to the future – the former are about protection of their power through ownership and control, the latter are where resources are shifted to move things forward together.

KWAME TAYLOR-HAYFORD

To me, it's about understanding that it's not about you. If you come into that moment and you make it all about your brand versus the consumer or the community and what they need or what they stand to gain, that's when you get it all wrong. It's about platforming the people.

Culture goes mainstream when the media and/or people who influence at scale – these could include celebrities or those within or adjacent or connected to that culture – advocate for and/or are paid to endorse and amplify it. This type of reach can drive mass brand discovery and attract new segments of people who only engage or buy into that culture around specific global moments like Formula 1 races, the Super Bowl, the World Cup and the Olympics. Choosing the right, but often unexpected, partners and collaborators really works here to cut through – after all, most global events are experienced through the content they generate. Take Snoop Dogg as the unofficial US correspondent at the 2024 Olympics as a case in point,[10] delivering meme gold, especially when he brought out his BFF, Martha Stewart, delivering iconic, sharable, relatable and sharp content,[11] setting him (and brands) up and ready for when the Olympics hits his home town of LA in 2028.[12] For me, it was his hot takes with Kevin Hart that made this make sense.[13] It's definitely worth googling.

Once a brand hits popular culture, this is where it becomes tricky to maintain relevance. Particularly interesting going forward is the acceleration of AI – its ability to identify and reflect patterns of behaviours and trends, and usability by all audiences, will enable it to spread these to an even wider audience, scaling mainstream culture (and associated brands, and potentially your competition) faster than ever.

This is where brand loyalty needs to kick in, and leveraging fandom respectfully is key.

A hallmark of fandom is the depth of knowledge and expertise its members often have about their particular interest. This can include details and nuances about the subject's history and theories about unsolved questions or future developments. For established or big brands, fandoms can contribute to the evolution or growth of the brand by engaging with it, offering feedback and creating derivative works. For example, the Oasis reunion announcement of 2024 led to an instant sell-out of gig tickets across generations of people, 30 years after the band's heyday. The attention-grabbing roll-out was a masterclass, and not dissimilar to how I planned sneaker drops back in the day. It started with the rumours, driving fan curiosity and noise. This was then followed by the tease of the date, while the multi-generational fandom went into overdrive with memes, memories and what I can only imagine as a flurry of relevant brand partnership activity in the making. This gives even more opportunity for driving hype through leaks and limited editions, driving on all the way to sell-out in 2025.

Such events also occur because of the proliferation of internet culture – so much so that new definitions and uses of words like 'brat', 'demure' and 'manifest' were 2024-made words of the year by Collins English Dictionary,[14] Dictionary.com,[15] and the Cambridge Dictionary,[16] respectively – which says a lot about how things are shared online. This shows that today's and tomorrow's fans are no longer passive; they are platform-agnostic creators, active participants and collaborators, using ever-evolving digital tools and platforms to personalize their content and forge deeper connections with their fandom, communities and each other. They understand how to create content that resonates with their community, how to capture attention and ultimately shift consumer behaviour. They help in keeping the brand legacy alive, often introducing it to following generations and ensuring its cultural significance endures – but brands need to let them lead that. This is where brands have to join in a two-way dialogue with fans, delivering exclusive experiences that stimulate participation and foster interaction among members. Importantly, giving special access to that brand can strengthen a sense of belonging and identity with it.

ANA ANDJELIC

With AI, brands are going to become filters on the world. So, we're going to say, 'Chat GPT, give me the vacation from Prada's perspective', or 'give me a vacation from Chanel'. I think it's more like rethinking what the role of brands play, and we are not really there yet. It's in that world when creativity is very much automated, when you can have these very elaborate brand universes that are actually filters on the world.

Community-first drives credibility

In recent years, brand 'collaborations and partnerships' with 'communities' have become the go to tactic for 'cultural marketing' or anything that has the word 'culture' in it. I use these terms in quote marks here because they seem to be used in many different formats and contexts and sometimes, disappointingly, can feel that a logo lock-up and a short-term hype activation for your 'community' is as far as it goes. Unexpected but credible cross-over brand partnerships through the culture stack are the key to true community projects. If they are deep in the culture or the cultural conversation, but at the same time make perfect sense for your brand, they are good vehicles for that. It's a win for the brand and the culture and community it's a part of.

> KATIE DREKE
>
> The consumer, the audience, the citizen is savvy and smart. They have a friend who works at your company and knows what it's like on the inside. They don't buy your marketing just because you spent 50 million on it. It's all about tangible observable behaviour. Show me. Don't talk to me about it. Show me.

For me, a proud career highlight while at Diageo in 2015 and at Platform13 in 2021 was for Guinness and Caribbean culture. For those who don't know, Guinness has been exported to the West Indies and Africa since the 1800s, so Guinness is as much part of Caribbean and African culture as Irish culture.[17] In the UK, the annual Notting Hill Carnival, celebrating Caribbean culture, is also important for the coming together of communities that makes London the place we can all belong to, even if we weren't born here. I have been going since I arrived in London. In 2016, at Carnival's 50th birthday, myself and Boiler Room wanted to show the positive side to an event that has stood for diversity and love for 50 years, but that is usually marred by a few disorderly idiots. With Guinness and its then tag of #madeofmore, we created a career highlight for me and legacy for the brand. Through a series of interviews and live broadcasting from eight of the original sound systems across that weekend, merch that went viral and our own sound system hand in hand with Deviation, we told the stories of the people who made and make the 50-year-old Carnival what it is – those people who are #madeofmore and those standing up for one of London's most loved, culturally important and relevant street events. In 2021, Platform13 created a new cultural platform for Guinness – to partner with people from communities where Guinness is deeply embedded as part of their culture, to tell their story, their way. For Carnival 2021, which did not go ahead due to Covid, Platform13 wanted to celebrate that with none other than Caribbean food sensations Original Flava and their amazing Nanny (RIP), who used Guinness in her cooking and drinks for years. Key for us was Nanny front and centre as the inspiration for her grandsons, the wonderful Craig and Shaun. A city-wide poster campaign and Nan's BBQ and recipes for Guinness jerk chicken and Guinness punch generated goosebump-inducing comments as the community felt seen and shared accordingly.

It's about moving from appropriation to appreciation, from exploitation to collaboration, from reach to depth.

Flex the codes to break the formula

In 2020, live experiences, retail and socializing were completely reinvented, and online shopping and digital services exploded. For everyone, the blurring of work, life and play drove new entertainment channels such as gaming, and online connections drove fan culture at scale across a multitude of platforms from YouTube to TikTok to Pinterest, Roblox and Discord. Creating an online Roblox birthday party for my then 10-year-old son, in lockdown, was a sharp learning experience, for sure.

For me, Travis Scott and *Fortnite*'s 'Astronomical' event during lockdown was a turning point for innovative forms of creativity, entertainment and brand narratives for today's generation and how they discover and engage with music and artists.[18] For brands in survival mode in an immediate post-pandemic world, the objective was simple: keep audiences' attention. This has driven the massive uptick in the last few years in performance marketing, with content following us around the internet while automated creativity runs the risk of not delivering distinctivion or differentiation. For too long we have had to deal with the same ideas repackaged, the same formats repurposed with the same type of mindsets saying the same thing in the same places. Brand narratives and messaging must now be delivered in all the spaces the audiences inhabit, through the creative language of the cultural zeitgeist. Who knew that Gen Z would feel so much about Y2K and 90s culture, nostalgic for a time they didn't even experience? Perhaps it's a response to the perfectly produced and similar-looking aesthetic of algorithmic millennial visual culture, harking back to a time when the internet was wild and life felt more unfiltered, more 'real'?

Traditionally, global brand guidelines outline the brand positioning, messaging and tone of voice, a comprehensive brand identity incorporating a toolkit of logos, palettes, typefaces and the like, and how they show up in the same way across different media. This was all in service of showing brand familiarity at all consumer touchpoints, a way to win category leadership. And it does work for traditional marketing touchpoints. It worked well back in the day, when the touchpoints were limited to print advertising, billboards, direct mail and brochures. For brands today, however, they need to break the traditional formula of long-drawn-out content creation and layers of approvals, deeply attached to rigid brand worlds.

Unlike legacy and big brands, while you might have brand recognition, your name or reputation may not be enough to gain that all important attention; whereas the decades-long building of iconic brand assets are now perfectly poised to play, whether online or in real life, and can be integrated across the whole media landscape. In a world where the digital and virtual became more seamless, adaptable brand universes can bring brand experiences to life in ways we can only imagine, breaking the formula currently limited by our traditional status quos, and freeing up the power of instantly recognizable key brand assets (KBAs) and core products. This mechanism has always been one of my personal favourite creative techniques – used while both at adidas to personalize the Stan Smith tongue graphic and generate social profile photos, and changing the figure on the Captain Morgan label to Leicester City's Captain Wes Morgan to celebrate his team's unlikely win – it really roots the creativity in the brand authentically. And do I even need to mention Barbie?

These new ecosystems also include evolving traditional OOH and outdoor formats in new ways through CGI, AR and 3D. This was brought to life when the Jacquemus Bambino bags trundling around the streets of Paris hit our feeds in 2023. Using CGI techniques felt like a taste of things to come and, for me, welcome excitement in a sea of generic product storytelling. Beyond the mere attention-driving moments, such brands coherently tell their product stories across every single touchpoint at each moment, whether through product, online or IRL, and build the brand narrative further every time, immersing us all, fans and others, in their world, connected through visuals and messaging.

KATIE DREKE

One of the biggest 'unlocks' of the last 10 years is that brands no longer have the luxury of creating a completely static brand. I'm talking about a locked identity system that is singularly consistent everywhere around the world with the same tone of voice, same rigid rules, same look and feel. That model has been broken. Brands who try to hold something like that together in our modern context will burn their gears out in the attempt, because what consumers expect is a more fluid, dynamic, resonant brand that can read the room, adjust and participate with culture as it happens.

JAMES KIRKHAM

Different entertainment strategies suit those different behavioural needs at different times, and definitely borrowing unashamedly from each industry, too. And I think it's such an important thing for young people, but across the board, the moment you're siloed and sat there in your brand, it will slowly wither, because it's just not the way we live our lives.

Today, with serious competitor FOMO – the fear of missing out on what your competitor is achieving – there has been an increase in what is known as blanding, where everything looks the same, be it simplified brand logos, colour palettes, shot style and so on. Clearly, this has meant a decrease in interest and attention as the same old same old is rolled out. At this stage of development, if GenAI is only used as a creative output, it can easily go down this generic path. It reflects what's already online, which means the output (as it is now) can look exactly like your competitor's. This formulaic homogenization of a brand world is the exact opposite to what we should actually do – that is differentiation, personality, possibility and expression.

Transmedia content fuels fan culture

Brands, if part of the pipeline in a credible way, are amplified via fan cultures that cross over and/or are adjacent to others along the cultural pipeline through vast online communities across a fragmented media – YouTube, Instagram, TikTok, Snapchat, Pinterest and so on – across multiple disciplines and channels, and multiple formats within those channels.

A transmedia strategy – enabling content, activity and experiences delivered across multiple platforms in the right format for the same fan and introducing and engaging new audiences and consumers at a multitude of entry points – is where culture-led creativity shines, reaching more people faster than before. Keeping up to speed with online platform styles is key to creating the right content – activating correctly and engaging platform specific audiences, so the days of your single community manager are long gone. A lesson for brands here: always remember that you don't own your social pages. They are owned by the social platforms and the platforms own their algorithm. On Instagram, for example, followers mean everything, especially when organic and paid is coordinated, so, as the algorithms change, so does access to your followers, and that can happen at any time. Meanwhile, on TikTok, followers are not the focus at all, so, if you depend on traditional paid social ads on this platform, it simply won't work. Here, users demand entertaining creator-led content, and the platform algorithm prioritizes the niches, which connect directly to sub- and emerging culture. Even YouTube, the closest to TV for this generation, needs relevant adjacent and cohesively planned content on other platforms, with the right blend of traditional broadcast mechanics and creator-led activity. On immersive channels like Roblox, participation is the name of the game (covered in more detail in the next section).

All of this makes that fight for attention almost impossible to react to or even measure within the confines of the traditional marketing or tentpole moments. It breaks the traditional agency model, unless it is truly collaborative and integrated. Transmedia content drives commerce, which means creativity and product innovation go hand in hand. So, brands have to rewrite their own rules to find exciting, interesting and relevant ways to, first, be discovered and then close that gap to conversion; showing up, credibly and authentically in the places and spaces where their audiences are, in the formats they want, but still in the language of the brand. This takes a brand that can flex and change but still be recognizable. An adaptable brand ecosystem responds to, foresees and matches the cultural shifts impacting both current, target, latent and potential consumers. It blends product, brand and business strategy meaningfully and activates the brand in the language and spaces of those audiences, consistently and without losing brand recognition. This is done by incorporating a cultural positioning, responding to cultural intelligence, opening traditional brand worlds up to play with contemporary semiotics, to surprise and delight audiences and to enhance KBAs. It can also work well reactively – take the hilarious Coors Light foul fan can,[19] created almost overnight to commemorate LA Angels' Shohei Ohtani's long ball that damaged the LED board displaying an ad for the beer. Worth an internet search, for sure.

Shareability drives brand discoverability

Gen Z, Zalpha and Alpha are already on platforms like YouTube, TikTok, Minecraft, Discord and Roblox as these start to transcend entertainment and gaming to become places of discovery, learning, community and shopping for new and multigenerational audiences. With intuitive Web3 behaviours of decentralization, co-creation and co-owning, users are conscious of their personal data too. This cohort is teaching themselves how to build their own games, finding their communities and fan groups.

They are active, doing the jobs of curators, creators and players. So, for brand activity that involves interaction over passive consumption and that all-important 'discovery' of the brand through fan and creator connections, across the cultural pipeline, here their behaviour is shifting from creating and consuming content to include ownership and participation at scale, and amplifying these activities on the more traditional social platforms. Brands are already flocking to these spaces, but they need to consider how they show up.

Platforms such as Roblox have become key areas for brand engagement, and with incoming Gen A audiences pretty tough to impress, brand strategy in these spaces needs a different approach to success. These platforms are now an essential part of the media mix and the new revenue streams, so, simply inundating platforms like Roblox with the same old mechanics of a traditional brand-out activity goes right against this brand-savvy generation's dislike of being interrupted. I like IKEA's 'Co-Worker' game on Roblox,[20] amassing over 178,000 applications over the two-week application window, for one of 10 paid roles in the virtual store. The activation was the first part of its new Careers Done Different campaign, which aims to give players a taste of future careers at IKEA, imprinting it as a desirable place to work, not just to shop.

On platform, users who actively choose to engage initiate Roblox's new ads, and are embedded within Roblox experiences by the creators themselves, making sure they resonate authentically with the creator's vision.[21] This approach ensures that, when users interact with your brand's message, it's meaningful and engaging, rather than being intrusive or easily ignored. As Roblox potentially becomes inundated with brands, this savvy cohort may move to the next new 'niche space' or subculture. Soon, 3D social spaces like Zepeto could be the next social, and wearables might even be our smartphones. The 2023 launch of the early adopter Apple Vision Pro generated a variety of funny memes across our feeds, and gave us a taste of an incoming immersive future, where real life meets augmented reality meets virtual reality, and where commerce is no longer binary.[22] In these new social and immersive platforms, where personalization and customization is expected, the participatory aspect is the key unlocker. As these behaviours start to become even more widespread and normalized, this could diversify revenue streams and uncover new ways to elevate fandom and content. Further, the rise of digital fashion might be a medium for self-expression and could support underconsumption through reduction in production, while also being a revenue driver for new commerce. I believe that this generation could ignite new and exciting subcultures where people appreciate the value of originality and creativity even more.

A word of warning, however, as marketers vie for that attention to monetize the new world-builders, remember that their motivations to engage with and expectations of your brand are different from those of previous generations. Positive growth will only happen if they feel that the brand is respectful of their culture stacks and positive for the world they are going to inherit. Going forward, this directly feeds back to how brands are perceived by future generations through their culture stacks. These skills and mindsets are the blueprint for a new future for us all, and so the cultural pipeline flows freely and widely.

Where this type of cultural agility fails is when brands do not involve people from the communities or cultures in both strategy and decision-making across commerce, product development or marketing initiatives. Wrong assumptions could cause lack of audience resonance and can risk brand reputation. In the hands of the right people, in-house and/or with new partners that are adaptable, flexible and experienced in coordinating special-izations, cultural relevance can be ignited, breaking traditional formulae to push the creativity of your brand and show up credibly in the places and spaces where the audiences are.

That means the traditional procurement, pitch and briefing processes also need to change. Culture-led brand partners cannot be valued across time sheets. The priceless value is in our cultural knowledge, our wide and deep network and our trusted community relationships. These simply cannot be shown in a 30-minute pitch process or benchmarked cost-wise against tradi-tional agencies. Instead, it's about matching energy and values, and a collaborative way of working to credibly answer your brand challenge can be much more fruitful.

Notes

1   YouTube. *Culture & Trends Report: Fandom*, 2024, services.google.com/fh/files/misc/youtube-trends-fandom-report-2024.pdf (archived at https://perma.cc/F8UM-EZ8X).

2   Davey, Jacob. 'Drake and LeBron James are Joining Forces to Invest in AC Milan', *Versus*, 31 August 2022, versus.uk.com/articles/drake-and-lebron-james-are-joining-forces-to-invest-in-ac-milan (archived at https://perma.cc/7GJK-BBXZ).

3   PA Media. 'Ryan Reynolds and Rob McElhenney Complete Takeover of Wrexham', *The Guardian*, 9 February 2021, theguardian.com/football/2021/feb/09/ryan-reynolds-and-rob-mcelhenney-complete-takeover-of-wrexham (archived at https://perma.cc/BT8T-QZGJ).

4   Shutler, Ali. 'Manchester City Uses "Roblox" to Unveil New Football Kit', *NME*, 5 August 2022, nme.com/news/gaming-news/manchester-city-uses-roblox-to-unveil-new-football-kit-3284154 (archived at https://perma.cc/3BKF-JZFE).

5   US Open. 'New US Open Gaming Zone Features Fortnite, Roblox, TopSpin 2K25 and More', USopen.org/USTA, 16 August 2024, usopen.org/en_US/news/articles/2024-08-16/new_us_open_gaming_zone_features_fortnite_roblox_topspin_2k5_and_more.html (archived at https://perma.cc/RSR9-C6VF).

6   Gucci. 'Global Brand Ambassador Jannik Sinner Embodies the House's Heritage Ties to the World of Tennis in a New Campaign', gucci.com/uk/en_gb/st/stories/article/gucci-is-a-feeling?utm_medium=geolocation&utm_source=gucci-nl&utm_campaign=overlay (archived at https://perma.cc/93SH-5WYA).

7   Faulkner, Noelle. 'The Fast and the Curious: Inside the Rise of Formula 1 Fandom', *Esquire Australia*, 23 May 2024, esquire.com.au/inside-the-fandom-of-formula-1/#:~:text=The%20go%2Dto%20narrative%20for,70.5%20million%20social%2Dmedia%20followers (archived at https://perma.cc/MXN9-5Y7Q).

8   Webb, Alysha. 'How Hip Hop's Love of the Iconic Yellow Workboot Helped Make Timberland a Billion-Dollar Company,' CNBC, 20 December 2020, cnbc.com/2020/12/20/how-timberland-became-billion-dollar-company.html#:~:text=Throughout%20the%20'90s%2C%20New%20York,by%204%25%20in%20clothing%20purchases (archived at https://perma.cc/ZB7A-SG91).

9   Fernandez, Chantal. 'Dapper Dan Discusses Power, Respect and Cultural Appropriation', *The Business of Fashion*, 30 November 2017, businessoffashion.com/videos/news-analysis/dapper-dan-on-the-line-between-cultural-appropriation-and-cultural-exchange (archived at https://perma.cc/8878-XXDU).

10 Pratt, James. 'Snoop Dogg "Likely" to Reprise Olympic Role at Milano Cortina 2026 for the Love of Sport, His Country, and Fashion', Olympics.com, 18 October 2024, olympics.com/en/news/snoop-dogg-milano-cortina-olympic-role (archived at https://perma.cc/82MP-8MHJ).

11 Pengelly, Martin. 'Snoop Dogg Steals Show at Olympic Dressage – Despite Fear of Horses.' *The Guardian*, 3 August 2024, theguardian.com/sport/article/2024/aug/03/snoop-dogg-olympic-dressage-fear-horses-martha-stewart (archived at https://perma.cc/NF8E-QZCF).

12 NBC. 'Snoop Dogg Excited for "Super-Sized" LA 2028 Games.' NBC Olympics, 2024, nbcolympics.com/videos/snoop-dogg-excited-super-sized-la-2028-games (archived at https://perma.cc/WMA9-3TRX).

13 Ferme, Antonio. 'Kevin Hart and Snoop Dogg are Going to be Recapping the Olympics', *Variety*, 23 June 2021, variety.com/2021/tv/news/kevin-hart-snoop-dogg-olympic-highlights-peacock-1235003590 (archived at https://perma.cc/T67E-4J8E).

14 Collins. 'The Collins Word of the Year 2024 is...', collinsdictionary.com/woty (archived at https://perma.cc/RY48-Y3S9).

15 Dictionary.com. 'Dictionary.com's 2024 Word of the Year is...' 25 November 2024, dictionary.com/e/word-of-the-year-2024 (archived at https://perma.cc/R2ZN-4YEL).

16 Cambridge Dictionary. 'The Cambridge Dictionary Word of the Year 2024 is...' Cambridge University Press, dictionary.cambridge.org/editorial/word-of-the-year (archived at https://perma.cc/74DY-UVM5).

17 Guinness. 'The Story of Guinness', Guinness Storehouse, guinness-storehouse.com/en/discover/story-of-guinness (archived at https://perma.cc/5HB9-AXMU).

18 Frank, Allegra. 'This Weekend's Coolest Concert is Happening in Fortnite', *Vox*, 25 April 2020, vox.com/culture/2020/4/24/21235196/travis-scott-fortnite-concert-livestream-the-scotts-music-video (archived at https://perma.cc/W797-FPNX).

19 Foley, Joseph. 'Coors Light Hits a Home Run with Hilarious Commemorative Can Design', Yahoo!Life, 10 September 2023, yahoo.com/lifestyle/coors-light-hits-home-run-050018822.html (archived at https://perma.cc/BP4H-A2BY).

20 IKEA. 'IKEA is Now Live on Roblox – Get Your First Look Today', IKEA press release, 24 June 2024, ikea.com/gb/en/newsroom/corporate-news/ikea-is-now-live-on-roblox-get-your-first-look-today-pub3a269100 (archived at https://perma.cc/DU5K-LTT8).

21 Roblox. 'Roblox Solution: Advertising', Roblox for Brands, 2025, brands.roblox.com/solutions/advertising (archived at https://perma.cc/LU5V-GAQZ).

22 Apple. 'Apple Vision Pro Arrives in New Countries and Regions Beginning June 28', Apple Newsroom press release, 10 June 2024, apple.com/uk/newsroom/2024/06/apple-vision-pro-arrives-in-new-countries-and-regions-beginning-june-28 (archived at https://perma.cc/RBG9-3WDD).

05

Decoding consumer shifts

Insights teams at the forefront

Today, consumer decisions are complex. It's no longer as simple as price differentiation. They are made through the culture stacks, impacted by social issues, economic uncertainty, politics, the media narrative and technology updates beyond audiences' control and changing almost overnight. But, this chapter is not a 2024/25 consumer trends report. Rather, I will focus my perspective on how I identify behavioural shifts through a culture-first lens, to view current and future opportunities for a brand, company or business through analysing shifts, trends and signals to unlock meaningful and relevant insights. Cultural shifts, as defined in Chapter 1, result in a shift in behaviours in people – and these are additive. Understanding this and filtering through a cultural positioning, enables a brand or business to gain insights to help project what could be interesting to audiences in terms of product and communications.

Insights are defined in many ways and mean different things to different people. Some methods of research to get to insights – polls, surveys and so on – can be flawed because responses are based on things that have already happened, and these are ultimately seen through respondents' culture stacks. This means there is unconscious bias from the outset. We all have it. Additionally, self-reported responses can be rational and filtered, and, in group settings, challenger voices might struggle to be heard. However, this type of research may be a way for people to earn some regular income. And who can blame anyone in the cost-of-living crisis we are all in?

Even social media monitoring can support your brand tactics and communications effectiveness, but, for me, this is still short term, about being 'competitive' in your category. Additionally, the consumer data we receive from our websites, third-party cookies and mobiles show purely factual transactional behaviour.

All of these absolutely have a role, because these data inputs, based on logic, show us what consumers are doing or have done, enabling brands to create better customer experience to deliver purchase intent. Using only these methods, brands can struggle to uncover why consumers choose a brand and its product or service and what emotion drove that purchasing behaviour, which I outlined in Chapter 1. Being culturally relevant means understanding how global shifts impact your audience behaviours and how your product or service makes sense for them, where they are, both in mind-sets and behaviourally, encouraging innovation where and when necessary. That means brands need to respond to the noise that hasn't yet reached big data points or big brand research agency levels – the timelines and places where products are usually created and adapted dependent only on the 'now'.

It's impossible to do this purely with consumer data. The right insights are needed. I call it cultural intelligence.

No matter what you call it, the right cultural intelligence, filtered through your unique cultural positioning can identify signals *relevant* for your brand, industry and the world, ensuring you have an awareness of what's coming in next or what's rising both from a macro level (for example through politics and climate) and through the cultural pipeline specific to your brand, and can act accordingly. Doing this right is what makes your product or service relevant in your audiences' lives and gives you knowledge of unmet needs that only your brand can solve. This means you don't have to focus so much on the competition when it comes to innovation. As always, for culture-led work, it's important to have the right input, which means the right people working on it. 21st-century brands need to go beyond the traditional demographics to understand both audience behaviour and their needs to make your product or service relevant to them.

ETE DAVIES

If you're not relevant to somebody beyond just utility, if you don't again align with their values, understand their world view, or hold a position in their mind that they value – which will come from cultural relevance – then your brand or business isn't going to grow. Why would someone pick your products or your service, or choose your brand, or recommend it? For anything that's a consumer-facing product or service, culture is a central pillar to how it performs because, very, very simply, it's about its relevance to people. Ultimately, anything that has some level of interaction with a human being has to have some cultural relevance – even if you're making a hammer. The brand behind it has to understand who the hammer is for and how it could be used, because it could be everything from artists to plumbers. That's where culture is super important. If brands and agencies don't take heed, they will become irrelevant and obsolete, which is what I think will happen with some of these big global companies.

At Platform13, our research and insights project teams are always made up of people with lived experience and deep knowledge of the culture and category. They are part of the team from the start, not only in the 'testing' phase – it's too late by then. They have deep connections to and in their specific communities and cultures; they bring diverse perspectives; they are able to source the right experts, ask the right in-depth questions and find the right answers on the right platforms, with the right people. This always unlocks what I call cultural nuggets of gold, whether worthy or not, ritualistic or not, symbolic or not, but always through the lenses of the brand's audiences. Most of the time, these link to universal truths, important for brands today.

Real-world and real-time insights drive cultural intelligence

With higher consumer demands of transparency and authenticity, matched with speed, personalization and data privacy expectations from brands and what seems like the definite deceleration of mass branding, things are changing at pace. Now we need to consider people's new relationships with brands and tech at the same time intuitive technologies seamlessly integrate into our lives, how consumers see price value and how brands credibly tap into fandom advocacy as it grows through new types of marketing-savvy communities. I believe that businesses need to treat the right audience behavioural signals like a crisis to stay relevant. Those signals, filtered through your cultural positioning, fall into three intertwined and intersecting types of cultural intelligence – real world, real time and ongoing – helping brands to act in the present and plan for the future. Addressed in the right way, this can drive brand and business relevance, resonance and resilience.

Real world cultural intelligence analyses the impacts of cultural shifts on audiences' culture stacks. Worryingly, *Politico* magazine found a huge upsurge in very active far-right parties across Europe, highly anti-immigration, both cultural and economic, with young people buying into it.[1] Since 2015, when more than a million people arrived in the European Union, most of them fleeing from wars in Syria and other Global South countries, migration has become politicized, framed as a crisis by the media and leveraged by an ever normalized and mainstreaming of right-wing opinions. There also seems to be a gender divide in some European countries, with young women often reporting support for the Greens and other left-leaning parties, while anti-migration parties did particularly well among young men. This seems to coincide with an article by the *Financial Times* that caught my attention.[2] It found that, in countries on every continent, younger women are often hyper-progressive, while young men are becoming more conservative. It seems, on every continent, an ideological gap has opened between young men and women. The article suggests that the #MeToo movement was the key trigger that empowered young women with fiercely feminist values to rise up against long-running injustices. In addition are the pressures of being a young man today, as the codes of traditional masculinity, while changing, are still enforced by some parts of the generation before them and 'ordinary' men have to contend with what were previously hidden areas, now available in the internet, around incel culture and violent misogyny. Today, smartphones and social media mean that young men and women now increasingly inhabit separate spaces and experience separate cultures, but converge through the relentless scrutiny of their lives and identities on social media and dangers such as cyberbullying and online predators. This is a binary view, of course. As we, hopefully, move towards a new golden age of inclusivity, with the continued breaking down of gender stereotypes, addressing the widest spectrum of gender is and will be a political, corporate and brand focus.

MICHELLE LAVIPOUR

In a world of global business and brands, teams are becoming much more versed in responding to scenarios that have multiple geographical implications or require multiple markets and geographies to be at the table. This can mean navigating diverse contexts, pressures, cultural settings and political environments. While it can be challenging to land on one global position – in a truly digital world it's essential that your brand shows up consistently across geographies.

Real-time cultural intelligence enables you to proactively ask consumers what they need from a brand or industry like yours, identifying problems *only* your brand can solve. Cultural positioning, anyone? This type of research can be done via social polls and interactive features, and/or reactively, through unfiltered UGC on social media and platforms like Reddit by 'listening' about your brand, product or service (both good and bad) and acting accordingly, by responding on the platform and delivering offline.

KEITH CHENG

The way to map cultural landscapes is so different now compared to 25 years ago. With the heavy reliance on mobile, social media and online sales platforms, we are able to discover new trends very easily. What it informs about brand strategies is, firstly, we need to build robust, quick reaction programmes in the whole system, including design, development, marketing and supply chains. Secondly, brands need to be laser sharp on priority and strategy, so as to make the best decision to go after certain trends, and, more importantly, to not go after certain trends.

Forums like Reddit are where real humans can gather and share actual opinion and conversation on any number of topics, including your brand or category. It's where you can find out what people are really thinking, where people learn about brands and products and services, helping inform purchasing decisions outside algorithmic social media. There are no incentives to be fake, as the community has organized the conversations themselves. Savvy brands can also use these channels in innovative marketing ways. Take the award-winning Super Bowl campaign for CeraVe.[3] It started on a Reddit thread with mass speculation around the claim that *Superbad* actor Michael Cera was the founder of the skin care brand CeraVe. And the rest is history.

Ongoing cultural intelligence, incorporating both the real world and real time, as part of all the phases of the cultural pipeline (outlined in Chapter 4) enables you to identify the right and/or new opportunities for your brand.

ETE DAVIES

We've had a few campaigns where brands have tried to do things in culture, and sometimes it's worked, sometimes it hasn't; sometimes it's been really bad and no one's ever been able to work out why. I always ask, 'Has anyone ever tried to do small things like looking in subcultures and community groups on social channels, for real world insights?' Where people are talking about the brand, you'll suddenly see that discussions happened which meant that, whatever you were shouting about, in the upper funnel of mass media, it was not resonating with the audience because they're mentally and emotionally in a different place. You soon realize that 'point of contact' research, often the end of planning, should be the start.

Niche does not equal small

In today's online world, subculture or niche scenes do not equate to small or under the radar – you just may not be aware of them, yet. On platforms like TikTok, you can find any type of community interest or passion area with complete cultural aesthetics and languages. Similarly, Roblox is a space where a brand could test digital products and experiment with marketing in new and exciting ways, hand in hand with a new generation of consumers, who think really differently from the generations before.

These platforms are valuable tools to sense-check any bubbling trends, sub- and emerging cultures and new communications channels. An example is that of the climate emergency's impact on seasonality in a category like fashion. I talk more about extreme weather and general shifts in temperatures around the world in Chapter 9, but, from a business perspective, fashion brands could explore the impact on product innovation, merchandising and supply chain, and the shifts that need to be implemented in that industry model. Imagine if the right intelligence had seen the K-culture signals coming through a while ago. From 2024, according to the *Japan Times*, global spending on Korean cultural products is forecast to nearly double to $143 billion by 2030 (from new research released by TikTok and analytics company Kantar).[4]

It can mean that culture is being flattened by the algorithm driving a world of conformity, making individuality stand out. If you find your community of like-minded people, new sub-/niche cultures become interesting for brands to keep an eye on. Add the right AI models and you are going to be able to deliver more and, more precisely, on what's important for an individual.

Technology rebalance

In April 2024, an article in the *Atlantic* outlined an opinion I have been sharing for a while, especially as a mother of a teenager.[5] Across multiple countries, a pattern has been forming since 2010. Rates of depression and anxiety in the US – fairly stable in the 2000s – rose by more than 50 per cent in many studies from 2010 to 2019. The suicide rate rose 48 per cent for teens of 10 to 19. For girls aged 10 to 14, it rose 131 per cent. While I am a firm believer in the good that can come from social media, and I agree that this generation is not a monolith, these are stats we all need to consider as we vie for the attention of younger and younger people.

On a positive note, there is a definite awareness around how these factors can cause anxiety, depression and mental health problems, and help is widespread, although there is still a way to go. A *Business of Fashion* article in October 2024 outlined the type of regulations being planned in the US to regulate phone and social usage for teens, with Instagram and TikTok already tweaking their policies to align (I cover this more in Chapter 10).[6] As these types of policy spread, it will have far reaching consequences on reaching these consumers.

Communities and consumers are also showing signs of screen, feed and algorithm exhaustion and passive consumption fatigue, indicating that they are seeking privacy, tangible connection and intimacy in a social-tech-algorithmic-heavy world. With 'brain rot' – defined as 'the supposed deterioration of a person's mental or intellectual state, especially viewed as the result of overconsumption of material (now particularly online content) considered to be trivial or unchallenging' – becoming the Oxford University Press word of 2024, and explained by Casper Grathwohl, President of Oxford Languages, as one of the perceived dangers of virtual life, this speaks volumes about how we are using our free time.[7] At the time of writing, there was already an 88,000-strong Reddit community around 'r/dumbphones',[8] and an article in the *Business of Fashion* in October 2024 highlighting the return of the printed magazine.[9]

We can see communities rebalance their online lives into real-world gatherings like the incredible rise of DJ AG online in London in 2024,[10] giving access to music artists to perform on the streets, the content shared far and wide and on smaller specialist apps and brands like the Offline Club.[11] We see this in running culture in 2024 with brands like Hoka, ON and Satisfy, apps like Strava and stores like Distance in Paris. Such scenes may have started back in the early 2000s, but have resulted in the ongoing rise of the community collective over the hyperconnected individual, and the need for trusted curation – a bit like the 1990s cultural pipeline, to be honest.

There is a need for physical spaces where communities and fans can gather and meet in real life, places where we in culture have always built our communities through connection. These might be storefronts or pop-up style spaces that combine retail activations, brand experiences and media to deliver enhanced and augmented brand storytelling that captures the right attention and interest. Examples were launching and activating a network of key city stores when I was at adidas, exploring third-space activity as we called it at Diageo and programming the Vans store basement at Platform13. We see in China that Gen Z and Alpha's ACG (animation, comics and games) culture is already on its way to shaping the future of retail, with malls and unoccupied office spaces transformed to fan spaces and in-person shopping experiences that online can't offer. For the right brand, this could be an opportunity to enter that market credibly.

Customization (different from personalization) is an interesting behaviour for brands to explore in that it's how a person decides their preferences for themselves. During this technology rebalance, an overwhelming amount of algorithmic and AI in life is driving the need for human connection. Perhaps one's own free will and choice, to go deeper than the 6-second piece of content, to sit with discomfort could become the next era's backlash to the always on, faster, faster, faster mainstream.

Cost vs value

In 2024, the luxury slowdown dominated the consumer headlines. My thoughts on this are that traditional luxury has never been a product-based category, so, once it started 'competing' and a branded T-shirt by a luxury house seemed to be both simple merch and a rip-off, for me, that's where the wheels started to come off. For me, luxury is about impeccable service and skilled craft, it's about one-off things, the scarcity is the value – all the things mass market isn't. I don't want to overpay, but I will pay a bit more if I feel something has a value for what I am looking for at the time.

A Bain report in November 2024 warned that the personal luxury goods market was seeing its first slowdown since the Great Recession, excluding Covid, as consumers cut back.[12] It found that the luxury customer base had shrunk by about 50 million over the previous two years due to continuing economic uncertainty, price elevation and declining customer advocacy, particularly among younger generations – your Gen Z target audience. Interestingly, the report found that there were pockets of luxury growth around experiences, including hospitality and dining, and experiential goods geared towards high-net-worth individuals. *Jing Daily* in 2024 doubled down on its prediction around the shift from quantity to quality – and from material goods to experiences.[13] It foresees this as likely to intensify, presenting an opportunity for luxury brands to offer even more personalized and exclusive experiences. This is a reflection of this generation's belief that expensive does not necessarily equal 'good'. The *Jing Daily* article suggests that pricing power among luxury brands may no longer be as robust as it once was. It highlights that brands will need to justify price increases by demonstrating added value, quality or exclusivity.

We see this in the normalization of dupe culture – legal copying of a product – and the rise of cheaper alternatives of similar quality – a clear signal that being transparent around pricing and costs will become the norm. A deep dive by the *Guardian* in 2024 confirms my belief that this is a long-term shopping behavioural shift, and brands need to take heed.[14] The outcome of this behaviour is that brands need to lean into transparency of their impact on the planet, on people and ultimately the cost of what people are paying (price) for their products. This also leads into the next topic.

Conscious consumerism

Don't get me wrong, I like nice things, but I think we can all agree, the climate emergency is one of the most pressing, real and urgent issues to address (more on this in Chapter 9). By addressing this proactively, a brand can drive that much-needed and real 'emotional connection', real cultural relevance.

In the early 2020s, flexing your TikTok hauls became a way to satisfy that dopamine hit and a mechanic for brands to use as a sales tool. Hauls, a rapid trend that spread across TikTok, encourage users to flaunt their hefty bundles of cheap and mass-produced clothing and glamorizes overconsumption. At the height of this haul culture, Platform13 was tasked to create a global TikTok campaign for Dr. Martens 2021 sandals. We wanted to address this trend, so using Dr. Martens heritage of durability, we introduced #OneStopDocs – enlisting eight TikTok creators from across five countries to show us how a single pair of Dr. Martens can complement any upcycled outfit and how good-quality, durable footwear can help promote slow fashion solutions. The community-led styling challenge also gave TikTok users the chance to win a pair of Dr. Martens sandals by duetting the video with their own slow-fashion fits to complement the sandal – promoting positive virality and creating a counter-culture against wasteful consumerism, all in the language of Dr. Martens and the platform.

Thankfully in 2024, de-influencing as a counter to mass haul culture has gained traction as consumers start to think critically about both the environment and their sense of self (and personal expression). From an insights perspective, your audiences are already warning you with movements like #SecondHandSeptember – de-influencing and underconsumption are gaining traction. In August 2024, *Jing Daily* reported over 47 million TikTok posts dedicated to 'underconsumption'.[15] It's making an impact. The publication reports that, on social media platform Xiaohongshu, hashtags such as #minimalismlife (#极简生活) and #lowdesirelife – similar to 'underconsumption' – are racking up tens of millions of views as consumers move towards more conscious and simple living.

PETER SEMPLE

If we want people to really think about changing their consumption behaviour, we need them to be excited to do the second-hand thing rather than buying new. There isn't a silver bullet way to make people excited about it, but that's the brand world we're building. You can get things that are no longer available or things that are different from what's available in the first-hand market – uniqueness and individualism are things the second-hand market can provide – as well as low prices. And underpinning all of that is the sustainability impact. We look at sustainability and that kind of moralistic, underlying purpose bit as really important to people, but it isn't necessarily what's actually going to motivate them in the first place. It's more of a validator. So, we have to be at least as exciting as new fashion, and then underpin that with the fact that you're making a good choice. You can tell people to feel proud that they've made this decision to shop here or to sell or buy another thing here versus contributing just to the mass piling up of new stuff.

It works from a self-expression and individuality perspective too, and it's forecast to be big business. Japan, for example, was known back in my day as a place to buy hard-to-find vintage and archival fashion pieces, and has now, through TikTok, become the go-to place for second-hand clothes; this culture is likely to keep growing as the Yen recovers. More recently, in what would have traditionally been competition, Diesel and Lee Jeans united to create a collection of one-of-a-kind jeans fully constructed from fabric sourced from both brands' respective unsold stock.[16] The rise of resale and rental platforms like Depop, a circular fashion marketplace, and ByRotation, a luxury clothes hire service, also backs up a 2024 GlobalData report for ThredUp, which expects the global second-hand market to reach $350 billion by 2028, growing three times faster than the overall global apparel market.[17] Other new aspects to support and shift consumer behaviour can be seen through activities like shoppable looks from eBay's first preloved fashion show around the concept of the endless runway to celebrate the 40th anniversary of London Fashion Week.[18] The industry has a major influence too, with, for example, the newly opened Heinemann Pre-Loved Luxury store at Copenhagen Airport[19] and Selfridges incorporating new, second-hand and circular products as part of a seamless shopping experience, through their Reselfridges approach.[20] These are all telling signals of consumer demand and how brands can support us all on the journey. Brands are in the business of selling products, and, in this era of overconsumption and overproduction, a brand's product offering directly impacts responsible growth. And this works across generations too.

AI normalized

Whether we realize it or not, AI is increasingly providing personalized recommendations and affecting our brand experiences, for example Netflix's recommendation engine and Spotify's Discover Weekly playlists. AI algorithms analyse user preferences and viewing or listening history to recommend films, TV series, music and other content tailored to individual entertainment tastes. Once wearable AR, VR and AI technology become day to day, this will shift behaviours forever (as I talk about in the next chapter). At the same time, the consumer experience will become even more convenient, with AI user interfaces delivering a lot of value for what you want to be solved, rather than having to search for a product and compare prices and everything else. The companies that become the best at doing this will become a customer's first place for any needs-driven shopping journey, because they won't have to waste time 'searching'. The tools might also be linked into voice, so you won't even have to type, just speak. So, I think 'shopping' will be simplified and give people time back – perhaps to do those real-life activities I talked about earlier.

That's why I believe AI might be as impactful as the adoption of the internet and the smartphone.

Where the smartphone app helps us to do tasks, the current form of AI has shifted the way we do those tasks; and then, in the future, will do the task for us, almost like the perfect personal assistant that truly understands you and can predict what you need. Already Gen Z are using AI to manifest their dream lives, and then using it to plan the path to get there. As distrust in influencers and celebrities (and their product brands) grows, performance marketing reaches critical levels (and consumers switch off) and awareness of the true impact of overconsumption (highlighted in Chapter 9) is embedded in culture; things are changing fast. Soon, brand search through AI models in a world overrun by a seemingly unending choice of products and content across a plethora of platforms will become more challenging.

Media transformed

As mass media continues to decentralize and fragment, online platforms and social and new forms of media offer brands and communities of fans, consumers and employees real-time connection, participation and interaction with each other across a number of platforms at the same time, offering important opportunities to deepen the fan experience. This means platform-specific, cohesive planning between both brand and performance marketing and paid and organic social strategies need to be optimized for discoverability by fans by ensuring compelling cultural nuggets are embedded from insights to execution, from culture to content and everything in between.

Not only that, it's clear that simply passively viewing something is obsolete. This is why your above-the-line campaigns are as important as your social strategy and as important as your gaming strategy, with dedicated adaptable content and cohesive amplification across all relevant channels, coordinated to tell the full brand story. Ofcom's 2024 media report shows that broadcast TV's weekly reach fell from 79 per cent in 2022 to 75 per cent in 2023, marking a second consecutive year of record decline.[21] It also discovered that, for the first time, less than half (48 per cent) of 16–24-year-olds tuned into broadcast TV in an average week. All age groups, however, contributed to the overall downward trend – for example, children's viewing fell by 20 per cent in 2022 and 6 per cent in 2023, while 65–74s' viewing fell by 21 per cent in 2022 and 5 per cent in 2023.

New media innovators, self-taught and grown up on YouTube, are ripping up the rule book and significantly impacting how major broadcasters operate, reshaping the media landscape in terms of aesthetics, subject matter and talent. They give a voice to the under-represented, underscoring the importance of community, bridging the gap between fans and professionals, and promoting their causes through culture-first storytelling. It doesn't stop at the storytellers; even the professionals understand this new era. Footballer Jude Bellingham's *Out of the Floodlights* YouTube channel documents his off-pitch life, giving fans personal footage and leveraging his popularity through ownership of his narrative.[22] In addition, fans' appetite for discovery mixed with internet culture can create something new that can elevate subcultures, under-the-radar brands and niche interests into mainstream phenomena overnight. Kate Bush's 1985 hit 'Running Up That Hill' gained millions of views after a version of the *Stranger Things* clip in which it was used was reposted on TikTok.[23] The song was then used in over 500,000 videos – a new generation discovering it for the first time and playfully adopting it in their creations, and a lesson for brands around how this generation discovers things. Another good example is the explosion of user-generated content and coverage around sharpshooting in the 2024 Olympics, with all types of people and publications, including me, obsessing over South Korea's Kim Yeji. As a fan of sci-fi, riot grrrl and punk, her and China's marksmen duo Huang Yuting and Sheng Lihao's style, stance and precision, piqued my interest and made me discover their sport. Brands associated with or adjacent to it, showing up here credibly are in a great position to be discovered.

That is why culture-led creativity, as outlined in Chapter 4, is important, and, if it's effective, drives shareability of that creativity, ready to be discovered by your audiences. This is delivered through marketing, product and creative innovation, itself impacted by how audiences adopt new channels and technology. Culture-led transmedia content can navigate that difficult-to-achieve attention and what can easily become a sea of sameness in content, and, ignited by today's fan culture's ability to fan the flames of their passions, can drive incredible brand awareness and brand fame. We may see the end of household brands we never thought could disappear, so knowledge of what resonates on a variety of different platforms is essential for success. A brand needs to enter the audience's world with empathy; the less ad-like and the less trend-follower-like the better, while still being authentically recognizable as the brand. Creativity is the way a brand communicates its stories in ways to stop people in their tracks, stop their thumbs from scrolling and build shareable memories through connection with others. This is why relying solely on performance metrics as success measurements in a traditional, rigid campaign cycle becomes a problem.

Loyalty is the job

In a world where brands are becoming famous for one viral product or moment and other brands are already struggling with discovery on social channels and in online communities, the job now is in how they build communities and foster interaction and fandom to engage through culture and experiences sufficiently to drive conversion and loyalty. It's amazing once you get that attention, but to drive loyalty, you have to garner, retain and maintain interest, for your audience to advocate and tell each other about your brand, positively.

To unlock product and marketing innovation and brand loyalty, you need to enlist the cultural voices of the communities and fans of the cultures you are part of or want to be part of, across the cultural pipeline, and, ever more importantly, your brand superfans (those who love your brand and buy a lot of it). I described the importance of cultural agility when it comes to new markets in Chapter 2. It means brands having to relinquish that ownership and control to create an authentic two-way dialogue with these cohorts by delivering exclusive experiences, such as taking them on that influencer trip, creating that special only-if-you-were-there merch and finding ways that stimulate connection and participation between each other. Give them the licence to play with the brand they love, let them interpret the brand in their way… and share it. They understand what resonates for themselves and their communities; they are relatable to audiences and more personal too. They can help to identify the problems to solve, help solve them and then advocate and amplify the result, and defend it if necessary.

JAMES KIRKHAM

Where you see the brand misstep is when they want to buy a slice of the culture and then leave and say, 'in our deck...' The word culture comes from cultivate and nurture, so, if they're not in it for the long haul, the audience will smell it a mile off. And the brands would be quite annoyed because they'll insist, 'No, we're all right, we've got money to spend,' but I'd say, 'Yeah, but you're just trying to come in and do something, frankly, that's only going to be words and then leave again.' You have to give it that kind of opportunity to flourish and grow. And I think that's important. When brands know that audiences trust them and we all see it out there, they are wicked; they really get it.

This is what it takes to build your community and create a brand that goes beyond the category. Today, finding ways for your brand to garner that all-important relevance and loyalty becomes increasingly important, so that the brand name is used in prompts by those audiences. This means new metrics to measure your brand in AI datasets to understand the business impact of your strategies. While I can easily see how AI can help measure current brand-led activities more accurately, how do you measure the effectiveness of your marketing when AI assistants start to intelligently predict consumer needs and find the most relevant products, services and experiences autonomously and by scraping data from outside brand sites? Different from the market share of 20th-century growth, which was enhanced further by share of voice related to media spend, or the early-21st-century share of search using Google trends indicative of whether people were interested in the brand or activity, the next iteration to understand how these LLMs think about your brand will take some doing.

Cultural intelligence enables brands (and their products and services) to transcend their category, to double down on their unique offer, their cultural positioning and role in the world, innovating and impacting a mix of retail and shopping journeys, product creation and marketing, blending internet codes with through-the-line comms – using adaptable, culture-led, creative ecosystems.

Notes

1   Cokelaere, Hanne. 'It's Not Just Boomers, Young People are Voting Far Right Too', *Politico*, 29 May 2024, politico.eu/article/europe-young-people-right-wing-voters-far-right-politics-eu-elections-parliament (archived at https://perma.cc/4XR6-QSVJ).

2   Burn-Murdoch, John. 'A New Global Gender Divide is Emerging', *The Financial Times*, 26 January 2024, ft.com/content/29fd9b5c-2f35-41bf-9d4c-994db4e12998 (archived at https://perma.cc/99QK-4FY4).

3   Contagious. 'Cannes Lions 2024: Social & Influencer Winners', 19 June 2024, contagious.com/news-and-views/cannes-lions-2024-social-influencer-winners (archived at https://perma.cc/L4UQ-B59Y).

4   Kim, Sohee. 'TikTok Sees K-Culture Spend Doubling to $143 Billion by 2030', *The Japan Times*, 15 July 2024, japantimes.co.jp/business/2024/07/15/tiktok-k-culture-143-billion-2030 (archived at https://perma.cc/TUV2-QK4X).

5   Haidt, Jonathan. 'End the Phone-Based Childhood Now', *The Atlantic*, 13 March 2024, theatlantic.com/technology/archive/2024/03/teen-childhood-smartphone-use-mental-health-effects/677722 (archived at https://perma.cc/HK9A-XAAP).

6   Mzizi, Yola. 'What Fashion Needs to Know about Gen Alpha's Social Media Restrictions', *The Business of Fashion*, 7 October 2024, businessoffashion.com/ articles/marketing-pr/what-fashion-needs-to-know-about-gen-alphas-social-media-restrictions/?utm_source=newsletter_dailydigest&utm_medium=email&utm_campaign=Daily_Digest_071024&utm_term=EDGR4COCEVA2PGUF6CVLJI6C2A&utm_content=top_story_1_cta (archived at https://perma.cc/4277-TG2E).

7   AP News. 'Oxford University Press has Selected Its Word of the Year', Associated Press, 3 December 2024, apnews.com/article/oxford-word-year-brain-rot-b43d864aed7f7d9d039edbd9b8a19ffb (archived at https://perma.cc/J43G-HSPM).

8   Reddit. 'R/Dumbphones', 2024, reddit.com/r/dumbphones (archived at https://perma.cc/452E-E5FD).

9   Takanashi, Lei. 'Old-School Magazines Are Brands' New Favourite Marketing Tactic', *The Business of Fashion*, 8 October 2024, businessoffashion.com/articles/marketing-pr/fashion-brand-magazine-pring-resurgence/?utm_source=linkedin&utm_medium=newsletter&utm_campaign=LINewsletter121024 (archived at https://perma.cc/VYR2-D5LF).

10   DJ AG ONLINE, instagram.com/djagonline/?hl=en (archived at https://perma.cc/AP6F-SF3R).

11   The Offline Club, instagram.com/theoffline_club/?igsh=bTU1emw4ZXY2M29w (archived at https://perma.cc/UDG8-EEC3).

12   D'Arpizio, Claudia, and Federica Levato. 'Global Luxury Spending to Land near €1.5 Trillion in 2024, Remaining Relatively Flat as Consumers Prioritize Experiences over Products amid Uncertainty', Bain & Company, 13 November 2024, bain.com/about/media-center/press-releases/2024/global-luxury-spending-to-land-near-1.5-trillion-in-2024-remaining-relatively-flat-as-consumers-prioritize-experiences-over-products-amid-uncertainty/?share-date=17-11-2024 (archived at https://perma.cc/MZF9-FVMB).

13   Booker, Avery. 'China 2025 Luxury Market Forecast: Key Consumer Trends', *Jing Daily*, 31 October 2024, jingdaily.com/posts/china-2025-luxury-market-forecast-key-consumer-trends (archived at https://perma.cc/YW3R-BVWL).

14   Hill, Amelia. 'Counterfeit Goes Cool: High-End Brands Urged to Embrace Rise of #dupe', *The Guardian*, 20 May 2024, theguardian.com/media/article/2024/may/20/counterfeit-cool-high-end-brands-urged-embrace-dupe (archived at https://perma.cc/89U6-ZL7F).

15   Ryder, Bethanie. 'From Flex to Frugal: Gen Z Rejects Hyper-Consumption', *Jing Daily*, 3 August 2024, jingdaily.com/posts/from-flex-to-frugal-china-s-gen-z-rejects-hyper-consumption (archived at https://perma.cc/G4QL-CF6G).

16   Diesel. 'Diesel Loves Lee', uk.diesel.com/en/diesel-loves/lee (archived at https://perma.cc/N76B-567M).

17 ThredUp. *ThredUp Resale Report 2024*, https://cf-assets-tup.thredup.com/resale_report/2024/ThredUp_2024_Resale%20Report.pdf (archived at https://perma.cc/3GQS-LSTU).

18 Jackson, Clementina. 'Everything You Need to Know About eBay's First-Ever Pre-Loved London Fashion Week Show', *Elle*, 12 September 2024, elle.com/uk/fashion/a62168699/ebay-pre-loved-london-fashion-week-show (archived at https://perma.cc/Q6SY-9S74).

19 Rozario, Kevin. 'Pre-Owned Luxury Comes to Copenhagen Airport and Royal Caribbean Amid Faded High-End Demand', *Forbes*, 24 September 2024, forbes.com/sites/kevinrozario/2024/09/24/pre-owned-luxury-comes-to-copenhagen-airport-and-royal-caribbean-amid-faded-high-end-demand (archived at https://perma.cc/QQY9-6BY9).

20 Selfridges. 'Selfridges Opens Permanent Reselfridges Accessories Destinations in Every Store', 8 April 2024, selfridgespress.com/2024/04/08/selfridges-opens-permanent-reselfridges-accessories-destinations-in-every-store (archived at https://perma.cc/J87D-682H).

21 Ofcom. *Media Nations UK 2024*, ofcom.org.uk/siteassets/resources/documents/research-and-data/multi-sector/media-nations/2024/media-nations-2024-uk.pdf?v=371192 (archived at https://perma.cc/27Q7-T2DT).

22 Iluyomade, Simi. 'Jude Bellingham Just Launched a YouTube Channel', *Versus*, 6 September 2024, versus.uk.com/articles/jude-bellingham-just-launched-a-youtube-channel (archived at https://perma.cc/7MF9-DM4U).

23 Suciu, Peter. '"Running Up That Hill" – TikTok and YouTube are Giving Old Songs New Life', *Forbes*, 30 November 2022, forbes.com/sites/petersuciu/2022/11/21/running-up-that-hilltiktok-and-youtube-are-giving-old-songs-new-life (archived at https://perma.cc/W2UA-SKLL).

06

Integrating technology and culture

Adapting to transformations

In March 2020, as the Covid pandemic took hold of us all, I wrote an opinion piece for *The Drum* on Luxury Digital Transformation.[1] I noted that, although luxury brands were running excellent digital campaigns, the critical internal digital transformation was often sidelined, as big brands shied away from the disruption that true digital change brings. I put some questions forward for brands and businesses to ask themselves: Is your workforce agile and mobile? Can staff easily work remotely and collaboratively? How do you pivot and adapt plans without losing momentum? Within marketing and communications, do you have the right partners to ensure projects don't derail? I shared my opinion that brands, especially fashion brands, must tackle environmental impact head-on and that, even with internal resistance, digital transformation here can hugely benefit brand value and the bottom line. I discussed how brands need to be creative and flexible in response to unexpected changes, and brand success hinges on the ability to adapt swiftly to the ever-changing landscape in the short, medium and long term.

In fact, even then, I talked about how digital transformation is, simply, transformation.

Then, starting in June 2020, the long-awaited and much-needed conversations around systemic racism in all parts of society started to take place. I talk about this in detail in Chapter 8 and touch on how organizations and their leadership need to lead through new skills. For me and my culture stacks, it felt like an opened box that can never be closed again. There is still a long way to go in this area. I talk a lot about the importance of people's culture stacks in brands and business, so, with this at the heart of business transformation, this chapter presents a non-exhaustive outline of technological shifts and their impact on culture-led brands and business, and their audiences.

MICHELLE LAVIPOUR

Times of change in a business or brand are heightened times of scrutiny. I see it as the job of the Comms team to be the critical friend of whoever is leading a project, to ask questions and probe into areas which could land in a more challenging way with different stakeholder groups or consumer groups. Ahead of launch is the time to map out different scenarios and talk through how things might be perceived and our approach to manage any issues. The external world doesn't care if they see something from your marketing team, your corporate comms team or your employer brand team. They see something from the brand or business. Fundamentally, it's all about storytelling and it's about telling compelling stories that resonate with your audience and feel deeply linked to your brand or business. And that's what I think great comms teams care about.

A tech-powered future

While everyone seems to agree that AI transformation is needed or inevitable, no one has all the answers to the questions it raises or if it will actually be the game-changer we are being led to believe it might be. What we do know is that incorporating AI into the business cannot be approached in the same way as when computers became the norm in the workplace or when new systems need to be cascaded through a large organization. This shift was computers taking away mundane tasks or helping with new business or regulatory needs. I remember how hard it was integrating Sprinkler globally or cascading new policies like GDPR through the business. AI simply doesn't have the same effects because users input conversational prompts that work in an iterative way, with the AI model continuously learning what the user needs and wants.

MORDECAI

When you got your first mobile phone, it was often supplied by the company or institution, with a shepherding 'how to'. In essence, you were given permission and you participated, so companies and brands are used to being the front. With AI, you don't have that. You have everyone personally using it, looking at their brands, their consumer interactions, their companies that they work for and asking, 'Why am I not using this tool that I use on my phone in front of you?' So, if you don't see the importance of that cultural flip that is no longer in the driver's seat of technologies and experience opportunities, you are out.

Today, while AI is, without question, one of the most critical technological shifts happening right now, the business consultant I interviewed highlighted the many other transformative trends emerging under the radar. He mentioned, for instance, how extraordinary quantum computing was. His view was that, while AI tackles solvable, complex problems, quantum computing approaches the unsolvable – problems we haven't been able to crack until now. Interestingly, he was surprised how little it's being discussed, even in advanced business circles, given its potential. Another area he focused on was deep tech like molecular and biomolecular printing and genome editing. We discussed what it would mean to replace or even rewrite parts of our genomic sequence, and the profound questions it raises like 'Could we, and should we?'

Product creation: ESG- and AI-based

Like transformation, product creation is also on a spectrum – from incremental innovation to breakthrough products, be they B2B, B2C, FMCG or luxury. In my view, incremental innovation, like updated colourways, new-flavoured drinks or merch, serves a fundamentally different purpose and yields a different kind of commercial return versus breakthrough innovation that can carve out entirely new categories or subcategories. Incremental changes are about refining and expanding on what already exists; offering a safer, often predictable boost in engagement and sales. For me, one of the first steps in modern transformation for every business in the world is to urgently audit their product offer through one cultural lens – ESG. Add incoming AI productivity tools and this can become hyper-personalized and/or -customized and sustainable. Operationally, that directly impacts creation, marketing, distribution and, especially, production. For businesses, this means a comprehensive overhaul to make authentic, impactful changes right at the source of emissions – from energy use and manufacturing to supply chain logistics – all the way to opportunities for repair.

In 2023, the incoming EU-wide digital product passports (DPPs) – a blockchain-like digital record that stores key traceability data of that product, covering how the product is made, how it's used and what happens at the end of its life – were to be fitted to fashion and other consumer goods as early as 2026. Introduced to improve sustainability and drive circularity and decarbonization, this regulation should have a positively transformational impact on eco-design and product creation. Digital IDs or DPPs also play other essential roles – of building brand trust with their audiences through transparency and product authentication and deepening the user experience, especially when it comes to accessing services like resale and repair. They will, however, be challenging for big businesses to implement, needing transparent information from their own and other partners along the supply chain and scannable components on every product, connected to every part of the supply chain. This interoperability – when a company's systems all work together without manual intervention – is tough to scale, complex by nature, and needs quality data and strong data protection and privacy systems. It might be further challenged as different countries will have different legislations around this. Once implemented, however, this will help businesses with real-time analysis of supply chains, resulting in optimizing these processes, ultimately improving efficiency and driving cost savings.

Break the silos: cross-functional collaboration

Sometimes, what's needed is not necessarily trying to fix the old, but evolving to the new. This can also be phased in an iterative sustainable way of remodelling the organization by refining and refreshing what works and reducing what doesn't. Blending new AI models with modern human-oriented working systems, like cloud and quantum computing,[2] is an exciting move, shifting brand evolution and business transformation even faster and in more ways than we thought possible. We have an opportunity to create operations and productivity with redesigned workflows and processes that can and must address the key challenge of the siloed way of working in big companies, many of which were set up in the 20th-century as product-led organizations built for category leadership.

This time, companies need to completely rethink their end-to-end processes, redesign for human–machine and cross-functional collaboration. This will require business-wide AI literacy and organizational transformation across all parts of the business. This type of organizational change is hugely disruptive for businesses created in the 20th century, both from an operations perspective and for the workforce, so businesses need innovative approaches to facilitate reskilling, upskilling and job transitions.

Good data: better customer experience

While multichannel involves marketing across various channels without connection, and cross-channel links these channels for more cohesive experiences, they may still lack full integration. Omnichannel bridges this gap by integrating all online and offline marketing channels, offering a unified consumer view, empowering brands to deliver real-time, personalized content, enhancing customer engagement across all touchpoints.

In Chapter 5, I talked about new shopping paths, mentioning the rise of retail media. This is when retailers offer data, access and advertising like traditional media and publishers, but helped with AI models at that critical moment of consumption, which is a big consideration. A *Campaign* article in August 2024, revealed that Meta, Amazon and Alphabet were on track to take up more than half of the global ad market by 2028, according to the latest analysis by WARC.[3] It predicts the trio's share of the global ad market to be 43.6 per cent in 2024, rising to more than 46 per cent by 2026 (caveated that it depended on many variables). Further, WARC indicated that retail media (up 21.3 per cent), social media (up 14.2 per cent) and search (up 12.1 per cent) are set to lead digital growth in 2024, with these three sectors alone accounting for more than 85 per cent of online spend and almost three in every five (58.7 per cent) incremental dollars spent on advertising worldwide this year. This is further compounded by retail media's opportunity when combined with connected TV (CTV). Meanwhile, Digiday highlighted how these can work together in terms of scale, targeted advertising, data-driven insights and personalization.[4] For organizations set up for traditional B2B business, data strategies must now include a retail or commerce media approach, a necessary key strategy for growth, bridging media, consumer insights and the retailer or business customer. As always, metrics and measurements should be carefully scrutinized to ensure the right return on investment.

Success here will depend on that breaking-of-silos transformation highlighted at the beginning of the chapter. This is where brand data and AI really come into play, unifying consumer, product and sales data, and giving you the best understanding of your consumer needs and wants. It is also an opportunity to identify why a consumer is no longer engaging or interested in your product or service. Using AI to analyse the vast amounts of a business's big data and identify patterns can enable evolving multichannel and cross-channel approaches and processes to deliver truly personalized, relevant experiences no matter where consumers interact with the brand – a clear competitive advantage for the business. From a customer experience perspective, Vodafone and Booking.com, for example, now use AI conversational chatbots on their websites or apps to answer customer questions, provide information about products and services, and guide users through processes such as booking appointments or making purchases. This human-like customer service can detect emotion, especially frustration and intent, in the dialogue and can respond accordingly. Done well, this can deepen and improve customer satis-faction, especially as it becomes difficult to achieve high levels of customer service across the multitude of consumer entry points and channels.

Operationally, this can only work if your data is prepared. As with any data transformation, most organizations will face a monumental challenge in curating, cleaning and integrating all unstructured data for use in AI applications. This means applying metadata – data about the raw data – to help it to be discoverable and reusable. It is important to ensure the data is as clean and high-quality as possible. In a 2023 chief data officer study, with a survey of 334 respondents with CDO or equivalent titles and positions, including qualitative interviews with 12 leading CDOs, nearly half (46 per cent) of CDOs pointed to data quality as a significant challenge.[5] And data quality is not the only aspect to drive customer satisfaction. Importantly, all audiences increasingly demand privacy and protection, which I talk about in detail in Chapter 10.

Connected commerce: shopping journey evolution

While the Covid pandemic normalized online shopping via desktop and mobile, brands focused on seamless shopping journeys and omnichannel marketing for everyone. Those viral social trends that enable discovery needed a smooth path to shop on a retail or brand e-commerce site. Algorithms now optimize content and trends for you... and you buy again. Where the seamless experience can take you easily from communications to conversation and improve the customer experience (CX), the frictionless onward path removes any barrier to purchase.

Social commerce – the process of selling products and services directly through social media – is leading the charge. This is different from e-commerce as it happens within the social platforms with your consumers going instantly and directly from discovery to purchase. In 2023, TikTok Shop brought shoppable content to its app,[6] and Amazon Live launched an interactive and shoppable channel on Prime Video and Amazon Freevee, where customers can easily add items to their shopping cart and complete their purchases in just a few clicks or taps without ever leaving what they're watching.[7] These capabilities have changed shopping behaviour for ever, and TikTok Shop has duly announced a dedicated fulfilment centre, cement-ing its commitment to 21st-century commerce.[8] YouTube is not hanging around either. According to its newsroom, in 2023, people watched over

30 billion hours of shopping-related videos on YouTube helping make connections between shopping creators and their fans deeper, easier and more fulfilling, and, in 2024, it expanded its affiliate programme with Shopify.[9] In 2023 and 2024, Amazon partnered with Meta, TikTok, Snap and Pinterest, with users linking their social profiles to their Amazon accounts.[10] This enables discovery on the social platforms and searching, and buying, straight from Amazon (and potentially that fast delivery on Prime). Cohesive, social-first comms planning is key for success. A 2024 report from Deloitte found that brands with a social-first strategy were eight times more likely to have exceeded revenue goals by 25 per cent or more in their B2C lines of business.[11]

Additionally to social commerce, in China, platforms like Taobao Live, Douyin and WeChat reach half of the population. McKinsey has suggested that live commerce using live streaming to products and audience participation through chat-type systems are exploding.[12] For brands, this can be useful for real-time feedback, insights that drive product and marketing innovations and/or instant conversion. In 2024, Roblox announced Shopify as its first commerce integration partner, shaping the future of immersive commerce.[13] Users will be able to shop physical products like clothing, accessories and collectables designed by their favorite creators and brands, all within Roblox, powered by Shopify. This gives Roblox creators a brand new avenue to entrepreneurship, and a new path for Shopify brands to engage and sell to a massive audience of nearly 80 million daily, highly engaged Roblox users.[14] Further, as Roblox transitions its forums from Groups to Communities, this starts to reflect a more social aspect for gamers, and fandom. Already, entertainment and fandom is driving new forms of commerce – viewers of the Netflix show *Emily in Paris* can scan her outfits via Google Lens.[15] A 'Pause ads' feature takes fans to a shopping page where they can purchase the looks. Set up in 2017, Google Lens solved a pain problem by enabling a way for shoppers to identify and find products online, in stores or on the street without knowing their brand or name. In 2024, according to *Glossy*, it was upgraded to enable specific product information, including price comparisons across retailers and user reviews.[16]

We are seeing commerce that is fan-culture-based and entertainment-content-driven happen in real time. While this feels like it's answering a consumer need, what does it mean for impulse buying and overconsumption? An article by *Vogue Business* in 2024 raised an important point: from a sustainability and overconsumption point of view, friction can also be a safeguard against impulse purchases – those items that people buy on a whim but will likely never actually wear, or thought would fit but don't.[17] This is not only one of the key behavioural drivers of overconsumption today, but is directly connected to consumer culture, outlined in Chapter 9. There is still some hesitation as new-generation consumers' awareness around their data privacy on the big platforms is unearthed, but this is behaviour that won't go backwards in terms of consumer expectations. These behaviours are becoming normalized, and businesses not ready or prepared to transact in these new formats may find themselves obsolete.

Transactions innovation: business model evolution

Payments are the basis of any business of any size: through sales of your product or service to consumers, whether paid immediately or not; purchasing of products or services for your business; or payments for business-related transactions including tax and salaries and so on. Technological innovation in payments is at the heart of shaping business going forward and one of the key drivers of business transformation. As a consumer, I clearly remember the move from tills to POS (point of sales) systems in the early 2000s. If the POS system were connected to nascent online commerce systems, I can only imagine how that would have transformed retail business systems and operations. This would have evolved the stock inventory process, enable the brand to judge which products worked or not and changed the consumer experience for ever. One example was being able to buy something online and collect it in the store.

Things have progressed dramatically since then.

Early in this chapter, I talked about brands and creating seamless to frictionless paths to purchase to deliver better CX. The combination of traditional, fintech and PayTech that your business implements is one of the foundations of your business model and therefore a key driver in business transformation. In 2022, EY published a report on the rise of PayTech, identifying seven innovations with significant influence over today's payments landscape: open banking, real-time payments rails (RTP), buy now, pay later (BNPL), digital wallets and super apps, embedded payments, digital currencies and cross-border payments.[18] Today, BNPL through fintech like Klarna, embedded payments through, for instance, Uber or Spotify, digital or more specifically, mobile wallets and contactless payments, are the norm. It's easy to see how these types of businesses came to dominate certain industries and drive behavioural changes for consumers. I remember my irritation when contactless went offline at a large national grocer – it took me almost five more seconds to insert my card. Just imagine the inconvenience! Digital wallets are to be innovated again with Apple's 2024 iPhone iOS 18.1 announcement that it's opening up its NFC chip and Secure Element through APIs, enabling developers to offer in-app contactless transactions for in-store payments, car keys, closed-loop transit, corporate badges, student IDs, home keys, hotel keys, loyalty and rewards cards and event tickets, with government IDs to be supported in the future, once again changing behaviour.[19]

In Chapter 2, I covered cultural agility in a world of globalization, changing population trends and economic power shifts that are happening in real time. As businesses move to new markets, besides the mindset and behavioural shifts that need to happen internally and from a societal perspective, there are also key business operations around transactions to address. Mobile payments and mobile money were game-changers in non-Western countries – from text-based payments through M-PESA in Kenya and payments by QR-code in China via Alipay, to UPI in India and Pix in Brazil. Today, the proliferation of online transactions feels like an inevitable move towards a cashless society. While this has driven global financial inclusion, and enabled cross-border transactions in emerging markets, not everywhere in the world has the infrastructure needed for a purely cashless society, and, even within industrialized countries, there are still pockets of society who would not benefit.

For businesses today, digital currencies could support cross-border transactions and help to prepare for global and market opportunities and challenges. As more human-like, conversational types of personalized and customized interaction continue to become more and more part of daily life, consumers will also expect this type of contact with brands and businesses. From a brand perspective, as phygital experiences and technology become part of the retail landscape, the shopping experience becomes even more personalized. And for those enabling AI-powered wearables interacting with text, audio and video, this life is becoming easier to imagine. In 2023, Meta partnered with Ray-Ban to launch a generation of smart glasses. The glasses connect to a smartphone app, allowing the wearer to interact with Meta AI much as they would with Alexa, Google Assistant or Siri. They can snap photos, capture videos, stream live to Instagram, and double as Bluetooth speakers for music and phone calls. In less than a year, these glasses have the added ability to 'see' and analyse the content captured by their cameras. Branded as 'Meta AI with Vision', this feature enables wearers to ask the AI for outfit advice by simply looking at a piece of clothing or seeking feedback on their outfit in the mirror.[20]

Brands need to find ways to show up in the response. As the technology continues to advance, consumers will likely see AI integrated into more aspects of their daily lives, driving another evolution of behaviour and more challenges for big brands just getting used to the digital landscape. This puts a sharp focus on the super-apps areas of the EY report (such as WeChat and even TikTok). This is where services such as search, messaging, social networking, payments and shopping happen in one place only – and are attractive to this generation's mobile-first behaviour. While difficult to implement, super apps, embedded with AI, are, in theory, an opportunity for a frictionless user experience, supercharged personalization and integrated social commerce.

AI for creative production: the experimentation phase

The pace of technological acceleration is itself impacting creative production. From 3D products for virtual try-ons to spatial computing – techniques that are perceived by users as taking place in the real world, in and around their natural bodies and physical environments – delivering mixed-reality presents significant potential for deep experiential immersive storytelling, and marketers need to know how to create for each medium's strength. This is where those dynamic brand universes become even more important in unlocking incredible creative possibilities across any medium, from traditional channels to immersive platforms, delivering the brand narrative, the brand story, the message and products in unexpected and/or increasingly phygital formats.

There is much to be done in this area.

Early in 2024, the furious debate around the Under Armour ad featuring Anthony Joshua was a sign of our times.[21] The original directors of the 'remixed' footage weren't credited until the brand and its ad director were called out – highlighting a moral and ethical issue. As budgets are cut, and brands expect work faster than ever, the future of ad production and the roles of directors and DOPs in the face of agency-generated creativity bring up tough questions about the human and artistic toll. When production project contracts are signed, creatives often unknowingly give up significant rights, adding another layer of complexity to this new conversation. Is AI just a new form of sampling, and where does it leave the art and craft of creativity? Which parts of the process are inherently human and must remain so, and which ones can we train AI to handle? How do they then work as partners? We know that this shift in the industry is inevitable, but we must find a way forward that embraces innovation while preserving the integrity of creativity.

PETER SEMPLE

On the creative and the marketing side, we use AI sporadically. We use it sometimes for copy generation, and I think we haven't done it a great deal, but someone once told me that they used it to think about CRM editorial topics. There are lots of interesting, generative-spark things that we can do. And I guess at times we use it on the spark end, at times maybe for longer form copy. As we become more familiar with the tools, they can help us in many ways. And then as we become more familiar with their incredible potential, then I think maybe we can be more directive about the ideas we can use them to manifest.

While multiple AI learnings are happening that will revolutionize content supply chains, AI can already enable rapid concepting and multichannel content creation, real-time creative iterations and campaign analysis and automated reporting and measurement, whether in traditional or retail media. In 2024, Instagram launched its Trial Reels, where creators or anyone with a business account can test their content with non-followers before they share to their audiences.[22] Enhanced by AI tools, feedback loops on content are supercharged, driving creativity to another level. This could be pretty transformative for traditional and performance marketing, freeing up time for that all-important brand-marketing thinking and planning for the incoming generations' particularities.

21st-century transformation means culture-led brands

Redesigning how the organization works through the culture stacks means constantly reviewing and innovating the product offer and marketing strategies in the cultural pipeline. Using AI models to innovate around productivity, efficiency and effectiveness can transform the business. This may seem counterintuitive for big brands that thrive on rigid processes to do big business. The number of times I've heard, 'it's like turning an oil tanker' as a corporate shortcut for, 'it's difficult and will take a long time to do', at best, or, 'let's not challenge the status quo', at worst, and everything in between, are too many to count. This can be a problem because, to be a modern, culture-led brand, adaptable ecosystems and flexible solutions with a networked and collaborative business structure need to be in place to address business-critical challenges at pace, without compromising on the values of the brand. For legacy brands, it doesn't have to be negative. It doesn't mean you throw away all those years of work. But, I think we can all agree that business transformation/reinvention/evolution/expansion/revitalization needs to be addressed to stay relevant. I think we can also agree that all transformations are not equal. It does mean holding a mirror up to ourselves and our businesses to identify what works and what doesn't – all the way from decision-makers' views on the world, insights to product development, marketing to supply chains – to decide what should be iterated, adjusted and disrupted, while maintaining stability.

In an uncertain world, with monumental shifts happening on multiple fronts, transformation today means that some departmental budget needs to be allocated for test and learn, which could be phased. Importantly, it would require there to be an understanding that experimental test and learn activities need to be seen as a value, not as a cost, and that comfort with failure (within reason) is accepted as part of the journey. There should also be a top-down acceptance that not everything that's done will have a sale directly and immediately linked to it. For example, in marketing, we know that the long tail of marketing activity is ineffective. Internally, we all know about the scramble to spend excess budget at the end of the fiscal year to ensure you have the same or more budget for the following. For brands in transformation, imagine if that non-effective budget was put to work at the beginning of the year, to support emerging cultural scenes or experimenting on new platforms or new technology in a proactive, not reactive manner. Then, year on year, by evaluating the impact of each input on audience behaviour, sales and ROI, budgets can be reallocated to new priorities and/or new experimental areas. This way of working is vital for brands to credibly engage and introduce the brand to audiences through a multitude of entry points.

This is relevant for other parts of the business too. As the diversity of talent pools expands, both within organizations and in collaborations with external teams and partners, exploring new hiring and procurement policies could open up the business positively. From an insights perspective, developing your cultural intelligence channels could be a good starter; while, from a strategy perspective, that allocation could be used to uncover your brand's cultural positionings. From an innovation perspective, what could it mean for your product offer in terms of new or evolved products? In creative, that budget could be used to evolve your brand world into a brand universe playbook to open up creativity in incredible ways; and commercial teams could start reworking assortments and distribution channels while exploring digital commerce, and so on.

As mentioned in Chapter 5, your cultural positioning, or the role that only your brand can do in the world, helps decision-makers mitigate risk, both strategically and in implementation across all parts of the business. This will mean new, agile business systems and teams all working cohesively, fed by ongoing cultural intelligence, filtered through your cultural positioning. So, AI-powered operations (both internally and customer or consumer facing) need to be primed to respond and adapt to multiple and interconnected cultural shifts, enabling a business and brand to be as ready as possible for what's just around the corner.

Notes

1   Fataar, Leila. 'Luxury Brands Have Perfected Digital Campaigning – Now They Must Transform Internally', *The Drum*, 26 Mar. 2020, thedrum.com/opinion/2020/03/26/luxury-brands-have-perfected-digital-campaigning-now-they-must-transform (archived at https://perma.cc/TG5W-9DG8).

2   Vallance, Chris. 'Google Unveils "Mind-Boggling" Quantum Computing Chip', BBC News, 9 December 2024, bbc.co.uk/news/articles/c791ng0zvl3o (archived at https://perma.cc/UP8T-R8HP).

3   Farey-Jones, Daniel. 'Half of Global Adspend to Go to Meta, Amazon and Alphabet by 2028', *Campaign*, 22 August 2024, campaignlive.co.uk/article/half-global-adspend-go-meta-amazon-alphabet-2028/1885848 (archived at https://perma.cc/E8CN-MLHT).

4   Dinichert, Ed. 'How Advertisers are Connecting CTV and Retail Media to Add Value', Digiday, 24 September 2024, digiday.com/sponsored/how-advertisers-are-connecting-ctv-and-retail-media-to-add-value/?utm_source=&utm_medium=email&utm_campaign=Digiday+International+Newsletter+10042024&utm_content=Digiday+International+Newsletter+10042024%2BCID_aff5722 53e4667562ceff923f2951618&utm_term=READ+MORE (archived at https://perma.cc/79WW-A775).

5   Davenport, Thomas H. et al. *CDO Agenda 2024: Navigating Data and Generative AI Frontiers*, AWS for Data, 2023, d1.awsstatic.com/psc-digital/2023/gc-600/cdo-agenda-2024/cdo-agenda-2024.pdf (archived at https://perma.cc/7Z5E-ZFSJ).

6   TikTok. 'Introducing TikTok Shop', Tiktok Newsroom, 12 September 2023, newsroom.tiktok.com/en-us/introducing-tiktok-shop (archived at https://perma.cc/TV98-KK88).

7   Amazon. 'Amazon Live Introduces an Interactive and Shoppable Channel on Prime Video', 16 April 2024, aboutamazon.com/news/entertainment/amazon-live-free-channel-prime-video-freevee-shopping (archived at https://perma.cc/R3RY-TKAG).

8   TikTok. 'TikTok on Linkedin: Fulfillment by TikTok Shop', LinkedIn,
     27 August 2024, linkedin.com/posts/tiktok_fulfillment-by-tiktok-shop-ugcPost-
     7234108267331788801-3iQe/?utm_source=share&utm_medium=member_ios
     (archived at https://perma.cc/UPH8-S749).

9   Karnawat, Suyog. 'Supercharge Your Sales with Shopify and the YouTube
     Shopping Affiliate Program', YouTube Official Blog, 20 August 2024, blog.
     youtube/news-and-events/shopify-expansion (archived at https://perma.cc/
     K9VH-PSUE).

10 TikTok. 'Shop Select Amazon Ads on TikTok Without Leaving the App',
     TikTok for Business, 8 August 2024, ads.tiktok.com/business/en-US/blog/
     amazon-ads-native-checkout?ab_version=experiment_2&agp_template_
     id=7400238737994547218 (archived at https://perma.cc/8C5C-DLPA).

11 Gold, Kenny, and Christina Kavalauskas. *Driving Resilience and Revenue
     through Social Business Transformation*, Deloitte Digital, 2024, deloittedigital.
     com/content/dam/digital/global/legacy/documents/offerings/offering-20231023-
     state-of-social-charticle.pdf?id=us:2el:3dp:wsjspon:awa:WSJCMO:2023:WS
     JFY24 (archived at https://perma.cc/35PM-4582).

12 Arora, Arun et al. 'It's Showtime! How Live Commerce is Transforming the
     Shopping Experience', McKinsey Digital, McKinsey & Company, 21 July
     2021, mckinsey.com/capabilities/mckinsey-digital/our-insights/its-showtime-
     how-live-commerce-is-transforming-the-shopping-experience (archived at
     https://perma.cc/S55A-8T7E).

13 Shopify. 'New Quest Unlocked: Shopify and Roblox', 6 September 2024,
     shopify.com/news/shopify-roblox (archived at https://perma.cc/9AEJ-JTZU).

14 LinkedIn. 'Shopify', linkedin.com/company/shopify (archived at https://perma.
     cc/U6R3-NN8K).

15 Steinberg, Brian. 'Netflix, Google Team-Up Lets "Emily in Paris" Fans Shop for
     Her Clothes', *Variety*, 15 August 2024, variety.com/2024/tv/news/netflix-
     google-advertising-emily-in-paris-shopping-1236108223 (archived at https://
     perma.cc/BU5Y-GK8V).

16 Zwieglinska, Zofia. 'Google Updates Lens to Streamline the Path to Purchase',
     Glossy, 3 October 2024, glossy.co/fashion/google-lens-takes-shopping-to-the-
     next-level-with-new-updates (archived at https://perma.cc/CC4M-U8QG).

17 Webb, Bella. 'Overconsumption: Can We Ever Put the Genie Back in the
     Bottle?', *Vogue Business*, 29 August 2024, voguebusiness.com/story/
     sustainability/overconsumption-can-we-ever-put-the-genie-back-in-the-
     bottle (archived at https://perma.cc/U9SC-RRER).

18 EY. *The Rise of PayTech: Seven Forces Shaping the Future of Payments*,
     EYGM, 2022, ey.com/content/dam/ey-unified-site/ey-com/en-gl/insights/
     payments/documents/ey-the-rise-of-paytech-seven-forces-shaping-the-future-
     of-payments-final.pdf (archived at https://perma.cc/HDE2-5SGU).

19 Apple. 'Developers Can Soon Offer In-App NFC Transactions Using the Secure Element', Apple Newsroom, 14 August 2024, apple.com/uk/newsroom/2024/08/developers-can-soon-offer-in-app-nfc-transactions-using-the-secure-element (archived at https://perma.cc/CLG6-AWXX).

20 Meta. 'New Ray-Ban / Meta Smart Glasses Styles and Meta AIi Updates', Meta Newsroom, 23 April 2024, about.fb.com/news/2024/04/new-ray-ban-meta-smart-glasses-styles-and-meta-ai-updates (archived at https://perma.cc/Z7QY-DWZX).

21 Landymore, Frank. 'Advertisers Horrified by Under Armour's AI-Generated Commercial', *The Byte*, 19 March 2024, futurism.com/the-byte/under-armour-ai-generated-commercial (archived at https://perma.cc/P43E-YZE8).

22 Hutchinson, Andrew. 'Instagram Launches Trial Reels for Audience Sampling', *SocialMediaToday*, 10 December 2024, socialmediatoday.com/news/instagram-launches-trial-reels-audience-sampling/735136 (archived at https://perma.cc/2MLZ-JFJB).

07

The new rules of influence

Harnessing the power of cultural voices

There is a growing and seismic shift of people's mindsets and priorities when it comes to how and who they are influenced by today. Pre-internet, or even before broadcast media expanded, influence was attached to accomplishments, in sports, arts, innovations and the like, and was often local to a specific culture and community. Fast-forward to the 20th century, and the roots of contemporary celebrity culture can be linked directly to mass media, when these influential people went global. And brands, in that era of consumption, jumped onto that aspirational influence to be endorsed, drive desire and, ultimately, sell more products. Then, the paparazzi gold rush of the early 2000s was a turning point for people famous for being famous – the start of the celebrity culture we know today. We began being fascinated by people without a specific talent or recognized accomplishment. We couldn't get enough of their personal lives – tragic or not. This fascination was compounded by reality-TV franchises like *Big Brother* and *The Bachelor*,[1,2] continuing when, for example, Paris Hilton and Nicole Ritchie took to our screens with their reality TV show, *The Simple Life*, in 2003.[3]

The rise of blogging, vlogging and social media changed the effect of 'influential' people even further.

A significant cultural and behavioural shift began with the launch of YouTube in 2005, introducing user-created media for the first time, while the rise of blogging from 2007 created a new form of journalism – both heralding an exciting era of communications. This coincided with a time when big brands were struggling to connect with their core and new audiences. A *Harvard Business Review* article from 2005 opined that the methods previously taught to traditional marketers around segmentation and understanding customers were broken, even quoting Procter & Gamble CEO A.G. Lafley about the need for a new model for consumer marketing as brand distrust grew and consumers became advertising savvy.[4] Brands had to find new ways to reach consumers, to find a way to sell their products without it feeling like a hard sell, to be 'authentic' by using real people whose followers trusted them – the perfect means to catalyse what became known as 'influencer marketing'.

With this landscape as the backdrop, the mid-2000s were an era when brands and marketers tried to understand and connect with a new generation – millennials, aka Gen Y, – of digital natives, the first cohort with full access to online communications technology, with sharing behaviours so different from the generations before them. They were heavily active on mobile social media, especially Instagram and Snapchat, where, for the first time, traditional marketing activity such as advertising had diminishing power to control brand narratives and consumer connections. In adland, these platforms drove a groundswell of realization that traditional media was starting to fragment and democratize amid a new understanding of the power of the internet and new consumer behaviours. So, brands started to build their own channels as media hubs in this emergent stage of internet culture.

RIP influencer marketing, long live influence

The mid-2010s marked the height of brands' influencer marketing, which had only started gaining traction in 2015, and which, before 2016, wasn't even included on dictionary.com. The wave of paid ads and sponsorships drove some influencers to create bots to gain fake followers, automating likes, following and unfollowing to get their numbers up and get those brand sponsorships in. The problem became so widespread that, in 2018, Keith Weed, then CMO of Unilever, announced at Cannes Lions that the company would not work with influencers with bought followers.[5] As one of the world's biggest advertisers and, importantly, himself influential in adland, this carried weight.

As someone who has worked closely with cultural voices and culturally influential people since the beginning of my career, I felt strongly that, for some big brands, this new description of and way of working with these 'influencers' was no different from traditional celebrity endorsement. It was and still is based on follower count, which is where my problem lies. Don't get me wrong, a celebrity or social media influencer could absolutely be a cultural voice, but it's important that they have skin in the game, that they truly represent that culture and be a voice of and for that community. This should by no means take away from the fact that there is a role to play in traditional celebrity or influencer endorsement as part of a through-the-line campaign.

But let's be clear, and call it what it is.

For me, the conflation happened because 'influencers' were usually procured through traditional media companies or newly formed talent agencies touting the same talent for multiple brands, with success measured in the same way as a media buy – meaning that reach (number of followers) over engagement was the key deciding factor. Using people who may not care about your brand and/or the culture you are trying to be part of, selected mainly because of their follower count, briefed to deliver your message and assets in a brand-out way, still feels really inauthentic. This stems from mass-broadcast ways of doing things and the long-term industry belief that the bigger the numbers, the better.

I was at Diageo during this time and, even before I launched Platform13, it was already obvious that marketers were driving an oversaturation of influencer marketing and, worse, were nowhere near measuring and optimizing the right data on social media. This was confirmed by a WARC report at the time and the clear stats that 84 per cent of brand conversations were happening in 'dark social' (for example on messenger and WhatsApp) with 90 per cent of marketing investment, deployed by traditional media companies, on public social.[6] This meant that brands were not engaging authentically and were missing out on important conversations and insights about their brands. I was personally frustrated with the algorithmic feeds becoming overwhelmed by generic visuals featuring the ubiquitous #ad tag.

I launched Platform13 in 2017 with a challenge, intention and call to action: 'RIP Influencer Marketing, Long Live Influence'. I set out to break the mould of this new version of influencer marketing, determined to create a company that delivered thumb-stopping creativity. I wanted to make brands reconsider what true 'influence' is and to challenge them to look beyond only the online 'platforms' to find additional ways to engage with their consumers. In fact, I used the word 'platform' as a direct response to online platforms and their influencers – for me, a platform is where people and communities gather, whether online, offline, virtual or other. I wanted to make sure that brands understood that culture, the stuff of real life, encompassed music, fashion and art, and included behaviour-changing aspects such as politics and technology, and that there were global communities who connected around these mindsets. I wanted to reiterate that, within these cultures, there are people with influence, shaping and representing these communities, creating stories that were original and creative that told those stories in new ways. I wanted to ensure that marketers and 'adland' understood the importance of credibly and respectfully collaborating and working with these influential people. I wanted to ensure brands knew that, by including experts from the category and the relevant culture and community, deep insights and nuances would be baked in on the input, delivering culturally relevant work that resonates.

In keynotes and on main stages in the first two years of Platform13, I used the Pepsi ad from 2017 as an example of what *not* to do.[7] I felt that this ad was symptomatic of how brands wanted to be in conversation and to be culturally relevant, but showed the flaws of ticking a box possibly seen on an annual marketing trend report that may have highlighted Black Lives Matter as an important topic to reach millennials. It then ticked the 'influencer' box by using a 'protesting' celebrity handing a can of Pepsi as a peacemaker to a policeman at a rally. Of course, the whole ad in the brand colourways was really something to see. The backlash was so immense that the ad was pulled one day after airing.

Now here is the context. The year before, in September 2016, American football star Colin Kaepernick began taking the knee during the national anthem in a peaceful symbolic protest against the oppression of his community – Black people and People of Colour in the US. For me, this was an act of true influence that resonated deeply with people in and beyond the sport. The ripple effect was powerful. Taking the knee became a symbol for protest against racial inequality and was adopted by athletes from Megan Rapinoe to Lewis Hamilton and even superstars like Stevie Wonder.[8,9,10] No one on social media or anyone reading the news could have missed it, so it shows that, if someone in the agency or at Pepsi had the nous to recognize the impact of their ad in the face of this cultural movement, had challenged and checked it, the result might have been different.

Brand wise, Nike did it just right. In 2018, it featured Kaepernick (whom it already had a long association with) in its global campaign titled 'Dream Crazy', alongside other sports legends including LeBron James and Serena Williams, cultural voices who have also helped advance social and political issues. Amid the support, Kaepernick had faced huge backlash and was ousted from the NFL. However, even newly inaugurated President Trump's vocal opposition of Kaepernick's action didn't stop a sales surge of 31 per cent for Nike post-campaign.[11]

Creators over influencers

Scrolling the carefully curated and staged Instagram aesthetic of influencer sameness at the end of the 2010s started to get boring and repetitive as the challenges with traditional influencer marketing and the algorithmic nature of the feed became apparent. So, it made sense when TikTok really took off in 2020, its growth accelerated by the virality of the platform, with entertainment and discovery the way for us to pass the time in lockdown. This new platform was driven by a generation creating their own authentic content in their niche interests with hyper-engaged audiences – today, the difference is even more pronounced. Now, the follower count of Instagram has become less of a criterion for investment. New types of creators, like life-hacker Khabane Lame, illusionist Zach King, performer Charli D'Amelio, baseball star Khalil Greene delivering history lessons and Big Manny teaching science in the new format of 'edutainment', ushered in a new era. This new type of creator is experimenting with platform editing tools, enabling a quickfire raw style of content creation. Using entertainment, trend-jumping and truth-telling in an unfiltered way causes a shift from brands being able to dictate what audiences consume to brands vying for hard-to-achieve attention.

Culture-led brands understand that they may not be the audience or even understand their language, and that's ok. Having the right hires or partners to help you navigate such cultural shifts before or as they happen is a solution. For brands, this new generation of creators had the ability to drive sales in a more authentic way. And yet, some brands continued to work with creators in the same way as they had with 'influencers'. This included briefing influencers to share social cut-downs from their ATL campaigns or to create content in the brand style in the brand world.

JAMES KIRKHAM

The reality is that it cannot be overly prescriptive. It really needs to be driven by them, their character, their personality. The reason the [Marcus] Rashford campaign took off was his own origins and his very public upbringing and his love and devotion of his mum in a single parent house. It's all legit. It was just as legit, actually, that Idris Elba was fronting a knife crime campaign, because Idris, and we know, actually, he knows a bit about that space. There is authenticity. It has to come from the character and the personality and who they are and an origin story or whatever that might be.

> The old brand would say, 'Hey, mate, love your good-looking face. Can we stick you on a box of cornflakes for as much money as is needed until you say yes?' Now it's like, 'Tell me about you. We think we know about you, which is why we're so excited and interested in you, but...' Really getting under the skin of who they actually are, what actually drives them. Because storytelling is vital and the stories will always be able to be told.

Today, creators are found on all digital platforms – from LinkedIn to YouTube to Instagram, TikTok, Twitch and Roblox, all adding updated features. And platforms we don't even know yet are coming, both inside your business and externally. These creators have widely ranging follower numbers, but, today, they use their online platforms to share and/or monetize their expertise or niche to their highly engaged audiences. Some creators are savvy enough to understand that they no longer even need to promote traditional brands to survive. They can create their products in any category because, as long as the product aligns with *their* brand, it will sell.

With creators and cultural voices, their credibility and power is in *how* they create their content. The most successful brand–creator partnerships no longer 'brief' these creators, rather they collaborate with them. Co-creation ensures their brand shows up credibly on a platform – from visual podcasts on YouTube to the aesthetics-focused lifestyle content on Instagram to the unfiltered, on-the-fly entertainment of TikTok. It might be a bit scary for marketers to hand over some control, but getting the best results will mean managing these relationships in a collaborative and co-creative way, similar to the culture stacks over a transactional approach as a media buy. Let's be clear; while these people must be paid, as 'influencers' are, it's their type of influence and their credibility that makes the difference to whether your brand is truly relevant or not. Traditional influencers may drive a short-term spike in attention-grabbing noise and can even drive short-term sales, but this is not necessarily enough for ongoing sustainable growth. According to a 2024 report by Deloitte, 9 in 10 consumers say they trust creators they follow as sources of information.[12] Recent complaints of an employee 'breaking the employee handbook rules' by creating content to advocate for their employer feel set in 20th-century processes.[13] Rather, businesses should embrace employee influencers as humanizing. The best way to do this is to ensure employee audiences are as invested in as your consumers. Utilized well, UGC (user-generated content) and EGC (employee-generated content) can do more for your brand than traditional paid and sponsored ads.

The age of the truth-tellers

Back in the 20th century, businesses could control their brand narratives with ease. This changed drastically with the advent of user-created and social media and the new truth-tellers. This power shift, from consumers and employees, has produced long- and much-needed accountability and transparency in those leaders and businesses that impact our lives.

The 2020 Covid pandemic was a challenging time for brands. Using traditional celebrity or influencer strategies to simply sell more products felt tone deaf and performative. Such sentiment only heightens as tensions rise in conversations around identity and heritage, whether at home or in the diaspora, and around propaganda, colonialism, global inequality, international law, human rights and democracy. Shareable Instagram-ready resources and political TikTok analysis drive the scale of awareness and discovery, spreading globally faster than ever. (I talk about this in detail in Chapter 8.) At the same time, centralized media and the newsfeed that has always influenced us at scale is under pressure as social media breaks down the traditional media gates. This is driving people to think critically about what they see and hear on traditional broadcast channels, delivering previously unknown insights into who is really behind the media narratives as ugly truths from the source are revealed, livestreamed and shared.

There is still much to be done, however, around ensuring verification and credibility of what is being shared online.

We know social moves faster than the facts.

We should always question where and how we get our information from, with deeper understanding of mis- and disinformation, propaganda, censorship and so on.

In 2023, YouTube briefed Platform13 to create a culturally relevant way to engage 13–15-year-olds in the UK about the importance of digital literacy. Its insight was shocking: only 2 per cent of young people online have the critical literacy skills to tell if a story is real or fake. It was important to find a way to enable critical thinking and develop the online skills they urgently need to navigate life online, especially in a world where they can easily fall into dangerous places, as outlined in Chapter 5. We held a month-long sprint, collaborating with a cross-functional YouTube team and the Institute of Strategic Dialogue, to deep dive into YouTube's existing programme, *Be Internet Citizens*. This had already rolled out in schools and youth centres, targeting the unique needs of this audience. Our research included upwards of 10 focus groups with the target audience and over 20 one-to-one interviews with cultural voices across impact, education and youth culture spaces, and used a bespoke impact measurement framework for the project. This allowed us to better understand how this audience learns and what they are and aren't receptive to online. The result was an audience-first platform, an 'edutainment' strategy called YouTube Reframe designed to complement the existing *Be Internet Citizens* curriculum.[14]

We brought this to life in a 10-part series on the official YouTube UK channel, with our playlist tackling important topics and issues facing young people online today. We ensured the target audience played a central role in development, with everything from naming to emojis and scripts, and creatively tested with 13–15-year-olds from across the UK. Importantly, we worked closely with the Institute of Strategic Dialogue on official 'learning outcomes'. The series featured the target audience and relatable creators and cultural voices with relevant, lived experience of the topics. It was important to explain the concept of echo chambers, both in real life and particularly in an algorithmic social media landscape. This is defined by Dictionary.com as an environment in which a person encounters only, and repeatedly, beliefs or opinions that coincide with their own, so that their existing views are reinforced and alternative ideas are not considered. This has become an increasing consideration in a world where listening to the other side can drive better understanding and empathy, but there are many environments that shut down what are perceived as dissenting views. Other topics included free speech versus hate speech, the impacts of online abuse and how to tackle it, mental health, how to balance your online-offline life, misinformation and disinformation, bias and stereotyping, and conspiracy theories.

In 2024, there were many studies on the impact of the algorithmic platforms that were designed to drive views and engagement, even if harmful, to be attractive to brand media spend and that age-old obsession with reach at any cost. On the other hand, we have also seen countless examples of the positive power that social media can wield to share truths and build bridges. I know what I would rather see. Today, as well as being content creators on platforms such as YouTube, TikTok and Twitch, late Gen Z and incoming Gen A are already on the move, this time to immersive and gaming platforms and new private online communities like Discord. Gaming today connects communities through identity and interests, some of the lenses of the culture stacks. For this generation, a 2024 report by Fandom found that 60 per cent of gamers feel that their online personalities are an important form of self-expression and identity, but 80 per cent admitted that this differs from their real-life identity.[15] The report states that 64 per cent feel that gaming and new immersive platforms are safe spaces for them. These are key considerations for brands wanting to enter these spaces, both from an influence and engagement perspective, but also from a product extension or innovation opportunity.

The power of cultural voices

The past few years have shown vividly the chasm that exists between those with money and those without, the double standards applied to people's lives dependent on fame and privilege, and the devastating impact of over-consumption on the planet and people, especially in the Global South. It's impossible to separate celebrity culture from capitalism and consumption, driving problematic, unrealistic and unattainable norms of beauty and life-style for the rest of us. Today, people take the time to ensure that celebrities know that they can see through virtue signalling and are putting them on notice. Some of these high-profile celebs and influencers are losing their shine for consumers, meaning that brands that work with them need to be clear on the risks attached.

JAMES KIRKHAM

In these troubled times when young people are so disenfranchised, disassociated, absolutely at odds with anyone's leadership,.. my belief is they've turned to talent. Who are the athletes, the artists, the DJs we might have once had on our bedroom walls, and they even become increasingly culturally symbolic in that time. So, the obvious example, what Marcus Rashford did, changing actual policy in education. But there's many more within football, actually. Raheem Sterling was anointed by fans really, as a figurehead against racism because he was so vilified by a horrific tabloid newspaper that spent its time trying to... It was very quasi-racist, frankly. There's a guy called Troy Deeney who's done some brilliant work within the school curriculum. Of course, in music, you have Stormzy. You've got a huge amount of incredible work going on at Angel FC in the States. What I believe is, you've got some interesting stuff going on. With talent and realizing, 'Oh, that's actually quite a good thing to do.' Hey, they also like doing it. A lot of them do it. There's a guy called Max Kilman who is a Wolves defender who's half Ukrainian. No one knows him. And he builds playgrounds in the Midlands, just putting back because he's a normal guy.

For me, cultural voices – people, creatives, collectives, companies, films, channels and events – with true influence along the cultural pipeline differ vastly from endorsement celebrities, paid social media influencers and even content creators, in a very pointed way. Ultimately, true influence, where you

have earned the right to be a voice of a culture and community you represent, is what I will always champion over the number of followers. It feels
as though, since 2024, an appreciation for expertise has once again started
to rise. This is not about age and the gatekeeping of old, but about knowledge sharing and lived experiences, about insider context and curation in a
world of excess.

At the end of the day, brands want their consumers to be emotional about
their brands, to connect in an 'authentic' way. As always, I believe that
capturing that hard-to-get attention can be disproportionately multiplied by
working with voices credible in that culture and that community. But a
brand needs to have collaborated respectfully with those people for them to
advocate for your brand. By involving cultural voices directly from ideas to
the final output, ensuring their voices are platformed (and heard) while
giving them the most authentic and distinctive brand experience builds true
cultural resonance (and the priceless word of mouth, now amplified in
minutes via social media). This ensures your unique cultural positioning has
the cultural nuggets of gold that only comes from those who have both lived
and professional experience and who shape, represent and influence culture
along the cultural pipeline. For me, the right input reflects output with creativity that resonates as built in, not bolted on. The creativity falls out of this
input, especially if the creatives used are also part of that community. They
know how to talk about and to their community in the places where their
culture gathers, usually amplified across selected social media, and the effect
ripples outwards (Figure 7.1).

FIGURE 7.1 The cultural ripple

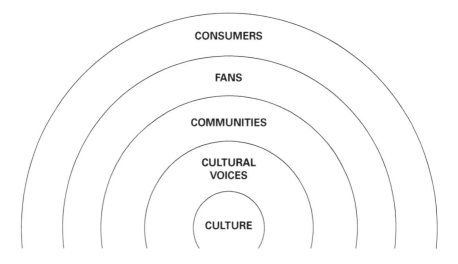

It feels today that we are finally coming full circle – celebrating new icons for their achievements, and the game-changers, cultural voices and truth tellers. Look a bit deeper and you can see how their culture stacks have shaped and motivated them. Take sports, for example. In 2024, the *Financial Times* highlighted marathons as the new fashion weeks.[16] For me, this connection to style and music was already happening in 2007 with Run Dem Crew in London, set up as a running club for people who don't consider themselves runners. Then the game was changed for ever when Run Dem Crew founder Charlie Dark, and Mike Saes, founder of NY Bridge Runners, joined forces to create Bridge the Gap – a movement to connect the dots between running culture, lifestyle, music, art and creativity with events around the globe where diverse crews come together to meet and run together. Other run clubs include Paris Run Club, Patta Running Team in Amsterdam, Black Roses in New York, Berlin Braves, Harbour Runners in Hong Kong and NBRO from Copenhagen.[17] Today, you will still find Run Dem Crew competing and, at Mile 21 at the London Marathon, cheering people on. For brands who had identified and collaborated with Run Dem Crew by this stage, there was a distinct early-mover advantage.

Meanwhile, there has been an incredible rise of women's sports, with clear roles for brands to partner, support and drive culture forward. In tennis, although 2024 saw greats of the past few years retire, this kicked off a new era and a reinvention of the game with players like Coco Gauff, Naomi Osaka and Carlos Alcaraz at the forefront.[18] In August 2024, Osaka played the US Open in a one-of-a-kind day-and-night kit, made up of statement bows, ruffles and tulle detailing. Designed for Nike in collaboration with Yoon Ahn, founder of Tokyo label Ambush, Osaka brought her self-expression on court and to our feeds. Women's football and basketball globally is a joy to see. Beyond representation, it's about challenging stereotypes, driving quality and building communities from players to referees to commentators to fans, and each other. I talk about a Platform13 project close to my heart in the next chapter: Guinness' 'Never Settle', part of which included female representation in rugby.

It was the 2024 Olympic Games that really brought home how much this influence has changed for me, for the better. So many of us watched this via multiple screens and creators, including the actual Olympians on their personal channels. While previous-generation icons usually felt untouchable, today's Olympians seem more relatable, creating content on their channels that spreads like wildfire. Let's admit, in the nicest way possible, that the 2024 Olympic Village was ultimately an Olympic brand creator house enabling us all to get closer to these world-class athletes. The Olympians too understand their influence beyond sports. A great example is that of champion US gymnast Sunisa Lee, using the Rhode phone case to apply her lipstick – who knows if it was a paid partnership or she is simply a fan. This Olympics also continued conversations by athletes like Ilona Maher and Emily Campbell around what body shapes should look like, or Imane Khalief and Katie Ledecky facing untruths about their genders. We saw athletes show off their cultural style, from nail art on Sha'carri Richardson to grillz on Jordan Chiles. We also saw the first all-Black gymnastics podium with Simone Biles, Rebeca Andrade and Jordan Chiles winning silver, gold and bronze respectively for their floor routines. That was already enough, but it was the bow from Biles and Chiles to Andrade for achieving the gold that dominated our feed, and our hearts. From an influential perspective, Simone Biles has already done *a lot*. A study by the Female Quotient found that, in being vulnerable, sharing her struggles with mental health and shocking the sports world by taking a break from competing to pay attention to that, she has inspired over 60 per cent of women in the US to also take action in bettering their mental health.[19] Biles returned to the Paris Olympics stronger than ever.

Cultural voices as brands

Influence, through the culture stacks, has always happened across other influential cultures. For brands, whether created by cultural voices or hand in hand with cultural voices connected to the cultural pipeline, influence is one of the foundations of a culture-led brand.

Rihanna, for example, redefined motherhood, while casually smashing beauty and music business glass ceilings and inspiring an entire generation. On a personal note about the game-changing multitude of skin tones in her Fenty Beauty brand, what I loved most was that it took into account women like me, who don't fit societal norms of beauty or any kind of stereotypes of traditional beauty. I never engaged with traditional beauty brand communications, whereas I felt that Fenty both related to me and reflected me, and that's something that I hadn't seen before. Additionally, Rihanna's campaigns don't feel like the category norms at all and, as a practitioner, that also speaks to me.

Another example is the late (and great) Virgil Abloh. He broke barriers in the traditional luxury space through founding of his own brand, Off-White, his raft of incredible brand partnerships from IKEA to Nike and through tenureship at Louis Vuitton from 2018 to his passing. He was a master at crossing the cultures of architecture (he was a trained architect), art, skateboarding, music, luxury and streetwear, and he opened the gates for a generation of people who previously had no access to these spaces, all the while generously sharing his knowledge online and offline for his community to progress. I once suggested that he take the helm as creative director for Johnnie Walker while I was at Diageo.

More recently, we see the impact of amazing music artist Stormzy, from the launch of his Merky Foundation in 2018,[20] committing £10 million over 10 years to fight for racial equality and justice reform, including the Stormzy Scholarship with HSBC to support Black students to go to Cambridge University, to headlining Glastonbury in 2019 – after only one critically acclaimed album. In a Union Jack bullet-proof vest (designed by Banksy), playing a speech by a prominent politician about the injustice of the criminal system and including a powerful performance by a Black ballet company, that performance brought tears to my eyes. In 2024, he launched his football academy, Merky FC with adidas, giving players hope for a better future.

In the US, one of my favourite designers is Latino Willy Chavarria, who has been using his shows and collections for political expression since 2015. He finally broke into the mainstream in 2024 with his SS25 show entitled 'America'. It was timely in that voting year for the US that he focused on workwear and uniforms, celebrating the people who built the country, taking inspiration from the United Farm Workers Movement of the 1970s, and opening his critically acclaimed show at New York Fashion Week with a live mariachi band.[21]

In an era of fake news and clickbait, we all need to be careful about what and where information and mis- and disinformation spreads. With so much on offer and tech that is supposedly helping us make the right brand or product/service choices, a trusted voice, whether by word of mouth, advocacy online or curated by the people we follow, is still one of our biggest influences.

In this time of transformation, brands have an opportunity to themselves become cultural voices of their categories, bringing their values to life in exciting and new ways. I call this convergence communications – where corporate and consumer activity become one. This is how a brand transcends category leadership and attains cultural leadership.

Notes

1   Venn, Lydia. 'Big Brother Timeline: When Did the Series Last Air?' *Cosmopolitan*, 4 Oct. 2023, cosmopolitan.com/uk/entertainment/a45441054/big-brother-timeline (archived at https://perma.cc/H7MS-MZP5).

2   Yuan, Jada. 'A History of the Bachelor, by the People Who Lived It', *The Cut*, 2015, thecut.com/2015/12/history-of-the-bachelor-c-v-r.html (archived at https://perma.cc/YLE5-QBR3).

3   Time. 'The 50 Most Influential Reality TV Seasons of All Time: The Simple Life', Time.com, 4 August 2022, time.com/collection/reality-tv-most-influential-seasons/6197762/the-simple-life (archived at https://perma.cc/2KYV-4BZ4).

4   Christensen, Clayton M., et al. 'Marketing Malpractice: The Cause and the Cure', *Harvard Business Review*, December 2005, hbr.org/2005/12/marketing-malpractice-the-cause-and-the-cure (archived at https://perma.cc/6EPC-55LW).

5   Pearl, Diana. 'Unilever to Crack Down on Influencers Who Buy Fake Followers and Use Bots', *Adweek*, 18 June 2018, adweek.com/brand-marketing/unilever-to-crack-down-on-influencers-who-buy-fake-followers-and-use-bots (archived at https://perma.cc/S8ZD-KAVM).

6   Warc. 'The Rise of "Dark Social" and Chat Apps to Impact Marketers – Warc Toolkit 2017', Warc press release, warc.com/Images/WARCSiteContent/PressReleases/The_rise_of_dark_social_and_chat_apps_to_impact_marketers_-_WARC_Toolkit_2017.pdf (archived at https://perma.cc/64BQ-92YR).

7   Victor, Daniel (2017): 'Pepsi Pulls Ad Accused of Trivializing Black Lives Matter', *The New York Times*, 5 May 2017, nytimes.com/2017/04/05/business/kendall-jenner-pepsi-ad.html (archived at https://perma.cc/9JQ4-22M9).

8   Rapinoe, Megan. 'Megan Rapinoe on Taking a Knee: "White People Were Mad. Whew, Were They Mad"', *The Guardian*, 20 November 2020, theguardian.com/football/2020/nov/20/megan-rapinoe-taking-knee-white-people-were-mad-book-extract-usa-womens-football (archived at https://perma.cc/S2QG-D2WS).

9   Elson, James. 'Lewis Hamilton Explains Why He'll Keep Taking the Knee before F1 Races', *MotorSport*, 25 March 2021, motorsportmagazine.com/articles/single-seaters/lewis-hamilton-explains-why-hell-keep-taking-the-knee-before-f1-races (archived at https://perma.cc/4RJT-LKSW).

10 Bryant, Kenzie. 'Stevie Wonder Took a Knee "for America" at the Global Citizen Festival', *Vanity Fair*, 24 September 2017, vanityfair.com/style/2017/09/stevie-wonder-takes-knee?srsltid=AfmBOopESiWHmJvianTq7MeFQCNVgAeKNjQWeqhQ7h8M7EtadrEwhN8C (archived at https://perma.cc/SZ8A-LTSW).

11 Pengelly, Martin. 'Nike Sales Surge 31% in Days after Colin Kaepernick Ad Unveiled, Analyst Says', *The Guardian*, 8 September 2018, theguardian.com/sport/2018/sep/08/colin-kaepernick-nike-ad-sales-up (archived at https://perma.cc/E9W9-F2PP).

12 Deloitte. *Driving Resilience and Revenue through Social Business Transformation*, Deloitte Digital, January 2024, response.deloittedigital.com/ stateofsocial (archived at https://perma.cc/M6JP-KDA5)

13 See, for example, tiktok.com/@mirithesiren/video/7358287026812128555? lang=en (archived at https://perma.cc/2Y3S-9WB2).

14 Fataar, Leila. 'YouTube: Reframe', Platform13, www.platform13.net/ p13thedepot/youtube-reframe (archived at https://perma.cc/FY6D-GQX2).

15 Fandom. 'Fandom Explores the Growing Importance of Gaming & Self-Expression in 2024 Inside Gaming Report', 20 May 2024, about.fandom.com/ news/fandom-explores-the-growing-importance-of-gaming-self-expression-in-2024-inside-gaming-report (archived at https://perma.cc/395J-68GU).

16 Cook, Grace. 'For Runners, Marathons Have Become the New "Fashion Weeks"', *The Financial Times*, 17 April 2024, ft.com/content/b63eb47a-1602-4fc3-8c3b-42f8427ac507 (archived at https://perma.cc/NA6K-YB4J).

17 Elgersma, Joey, and Stephan Wever. 'Bridge the Gap – The Story', Vimeo, 24 April 2014, vimeo.com/92826333 (archived at https://perma.cc/CU4W-QYRH).

18 Fendrich, Howard. 'It's Not Just Rafael Nadal: Retirement is in the Tennis Air as the French Open Starts', AP News, 25 May 2024, apnews.com/article/ french-open-2024-nadal-murray-retirement-3f992e4838b6b44b67e5fb1c155 a6c71 (archived at https://perma.cc/6T5P-SRUV).

19 Suzy Research / The Female Quotient, *Empowering Women's Wellness: Addressing Stressors and Creating Supportive Brand Partnerships*, 2024, engage.suzy.com/hubfs/Female-Quotient-Whitepaper.pdf?hsLang=en (archived at https://perma.cc/6CWU-T52A).

20 #MERKY Foundation, merkyfoundation.org.uk (archived at https://perma.cc/ C2MC-LC42).

21 Cardenas, Cat. 'It's Willy Chavarria's America, and We're Just living In It', *Los Angeles Times*, De Los, 4 October 2024, latimes.com/delos/story/2024-10-04/ willy-chavarria-america-nyfw-yahritza-y-su-esencia-united-farm-workers (archived at https://perma.cc/YWS8-A6A2).

08

Diversity and inclusion

Not just a policy, but a brand imperative

Historically, socio-political change tended to happen gradually, with direct lobbying of policymakers and legislators as a crucial strategy, especially when the activities or demands go against existing laws or challenge the status quo. Things move forward and evolve through protest and resistance, usually in the face of policies that divide or marginalize people. A non-exhaustive list includes the feminist movement from the early 20th century to today, the US civil rights movements in the 1950s and 1960s, climate justice from the 1960s, LGBTQia+ rights after the Stonewall Riots of 1969, the Soweto Uprising in 1976 and the ultimate fall of South African apartheid in 1994, the Arab Spring of 2010, Occupy Wall Street in 2011, the Hong Kong Protests in 2019, Black Lives Matter resurgence in 2020 and the ongoing Palestinian crisis. Each era-changing movement builds on another, enabling collective understanding and encouraging us all to think ever deeper about the global status quo of exclusivity and inequality. These realities are deeply ingrained in our culture stacks, going beyond ethnicity, and are the lenses through which we make decisions.

They naturally extend into the workplace and our work.

As someone who has never officially worked in D&I, but with personal and direct experience of apartheid, the impact of colonization, and deep inequality written in law, I will always stand with marginalized people. I was born and raised in a system specifically and legally set up to segregate and discriminate by the colour of our skin and ethnicity. It was and will never be a concept I condone or even understand. Having seen incredible talent in my own and historically marginalized communities that had no or limited access to industries at all, both by law and through our history under apartheid, this has always been a deep, unspoken motivator for me as my career developed. I will always advocate for pathways into industries to be as open as possible to people like me by challenging the industry about what constitutes the right career experience and to find new ways to widen the gates. It is simply how I see the world. In the places and spaces that I can do this credibly, I will always lend my voice, share my knowledge, open any gates I can and exchange credible evidence to reframe narratives.

Within the context of global cultural shifts that impact all our realities, how brands react is absolutely reflected in whether they are relevant to us, and how we engage, work for, advocate for or buy brand products and services. To mitigate risk around call-out culture and genuinely resonate with all their audiences, brands must authentically earn their place within diverse and global cultures or communities. For brands and business, people have simply never fitted into neat demographic boxes. I wrote about this in Chapter 4, and it can be seen from interviews in the *New York Times* describing Gen Z as America's most diverse generation.[1]

The problem with typical D&I

In businesses today, diversity and inclusion are usually paired together or conflated, and 'lumped in' with equity. In theory, it's true, they are connected. In practice, they definitely need to be approached in different ways to ensure long-term success and actual, tangible change. It starts with understanding the differences. Diversity is directly connected to the inherited culture stack, describing people and their identity on their range of experiences and backgrounds, based around characteristics including gender, socio-economic background, cultural upbringing, religion, education, sexual orientation, disability, ethnicity and/or neurodiversity.

Inclusivity is ensuring that people are not only represented, but also thriving because of their unique differences. This happens if people feel that they belong, and is manifested in equality in opportunities, resources and treatment. This also extends beyond the workplace to the choice of external partners. Organizations talk about taking action, but, at the end of the day, a person's values and unconscious biases affect their professional life and those around them. Your company may be on the way to being more diverse, but personal mindsets to foster inclusivity (and equity) are not a given. Beyond the corporate initiatives, it is not the job of marginalized communities in the workplace to teach everyone else. There are countless tools, books, podcasts and other resources available to self-educate on how to practise inclusivity in your everyday actions. For those who want to be allies, it's about listening and asking how you can support, and sometimes that means not being involved. No one expects you to have the right answers if you aren't from a specific community.

In the workplace, it is well documented that we still have to navigate white-male-dominated leadership, which has been the case since… forever. The past decades have seen huge impact made by people and organizations who have gained ground on what was, for a long time, seen as corporate diversity – the single issue of gender – but it is still a hard fight today. From a future work-force perspective, this 'drop to the top' can also be more pronounced in STEM occupations than in non-STEM roles, giving women a double disadvantage with regards to technological and workforce transitions. In areas where gender parity is increasing, like in AI, progression is slow. A 2023 article in *Vogue Business* confirmed that, of the top 30 luxury brands in its business index, only 8 of the 33 creative director roles were held by women, of which only one is of colour, but we will come to intersectionality later in the chapter.[2]

The uncomfortable truths around systemic racism exploded recently, from the upsurge of the Black Lives Matter movement in 2020 to the Palestinian crisis from 2023. In 2020, black squares dominated our feeds in what started as a day of solidarity, reflection and protest, originally organized within the music industry in response to the murder of George Floyd and other innocent victims of racial police brutality in the US. Now, however, it has become seen as corporate virtue signalling and performative allyship. I say this because, since around 2022 to 2023, it's been disheartening to see the deprioritization of what could have been those game-changing corporate D&I pledges.

A June 2024 report from the Center for an Urban Future found that of nearly 70,000 advertising employees in New York, less than 8 per cent were Black, about 11 per cent were Asian and under 15 per cent were Latino.[3] Over 58 per cent of employees were women, but most of them white. At that time, the scale of race-oriented DEI activity meant we could only assume that the gap was massive.

It also feels like the remit translates 'DEI' into simply 'adding' more people of colour into the business and brand and using an increased number of diverse people in the business as success metrics. For the limited POC who were and are put in DEI positions, the lack of empowerment to decolonize old-world policies on hiring, progression and procurement while being placed in these positions for the optics leads to a potential for burnout after fighting the good fight and not necessarily getting anywhere. At the other end of the spectrum is the placement of POC in positions of power because they reflect the traditional structures and are able to maintain the status quo.

When the memes around this topic go viral, you know it's a live conversation. Black Americans are taking this into their own hands with creatives, intellectuals, business leaders and political voices coming together for the 2024 Chief Diversity Officer Summit, to find solutions, for them, by them.[4]

This is why traditional solutions and measures of success around single issues, while hugely significant and important, can also feel underdeveloped. So, while there has been good progress in diversity, the fully inclusive bucket at brands, companies and agencies is where work still really needs to happen across all levels, especially when it comes to progression.

Intersectionality matters... a lot

We cannot address D&I without understanding the impact of intersectionality.[5] The term was coined by Kimberlé Crenshaw in 1989 as the intersection and overlapping of people's characteristics, for example a queer, working-class, Black woman versus a woman. It compounds the contexts that could be used to discriminate through unconscious, and sometimes conscious, bias and stereotypes. Unconscious or implicit bias is everywhere. We all have it. While the culture stacks are the lenses through which we view the world, they can also trigger our brain to make quick stereotypical judgements with significant influence on our attitudes and behaviours. These can be negative or even dangerous, especially when they are towards other people and can influence decisions in the workplace that contribute to inequality, for instance in hiring, appraisals or promotion.

I penned an article for Highsnobiety on BlackOut Tuesday in 2020, focused on how brands cannot simply talk about racism; they have to actually take anti-racist action.[6] I asked brand leaders to reflect on their personal biases (which we all have) and associated privileges, to examine the make-up of their executive leadership, to audit their hiring and procurement policies, and address the day-to-day microaggressions and assumptions that under-represented people have always experienced. I outlined how unconscious bias and stereotypes easily enable people of colour being collectively labelled as 'difficult' or 'aggressive' if we challenge the status quo, or are regarded as not being a 'team player' if we share different reference points. The same goes for people of non-binary genders, or who are neurodiverse or have a disability, or any combination of 'differences'. We want to be in these positions not as tokens of DEI, but as a true representation, regardless of whether we look different, act differently, think differently, talk differently and don't fit the 'ideal company profile'. Believe me, being your authentic self in spaces not set up for you means that you feel like you have to constantly prove yourself to justify being there.

It's exhausting.

Intersectionality also includes country- or territory-specific societal layers. It's important to take this into account. In the UK, Dr. Martens has a long association with alternative music through its punk heritage and protest roots, known for breaking the norm and advocating for progress. To ensure its new global music activity was informed by credible and authentic insights, Platform13 was tasked to unpack the challenges faced by those who are under-represented in the music industry globally, and to unlock a credible recommendation for how the brand could make a positive impact in music. While the music industry is globalized, we didn't assume that the challenges and barriers are the same everywhere. Our global research team designed a unique methodology – across Japan, Germany, the UK and the US – that respected and reflected the important cultural nuances, including age, gender, race and class, and how they intersect. Then, speaking to a broad and representative mix of local communities and individuals at different stages of their music journeys, either getting into or already in the industry, meant that we were able to better understand this vast audience's needs, local landscapes and challenges.

Thankfully, there is a deeper understanding of this multi-layered and interconnected system of intersectionality. Especially since 2020, the E in DEI begins to rise. Equity recognizes that people's intersectional experiences and cultural backgrounds differ vastly and that this inequity can impact their starting points, can be a shortcoming and can move us all backwards instead of forwards. It's important to appreciate the context before attempting a solution. This means understanding that a lot of people were *never* given the opportunities to even be at that 'equal and inclusive' stage, so it is important for companies to acknowledge that and create equity-driving initiatives through their businesses and in their industries for training, fair access, opportunity and advancement.

Progressive advertising is simply advertising

For a brand's audiences, from consumers to employees to partners, diverse representation in advertising is no longer a differentiator; rather, it's expected.

JAMIE GILL

If you think of what innovation is, in layman's terms, innovation is bringing new ideas to the table. If you think about fashion design, you're innovating by reinterpreting something that we've seen before, whether it's in a new colour and new fabrication, and bringing it with the relevancy of what's happening in the world and culture right now. And I think that's the exact point. Innovation comes from fresh perspectives. We are a tragically under-represented industry that's reliant on a global consumer base that's very diverse, so diversity is a huge opportunity for us. It's about bringing in perspectives that we currently lack, which is essential for driving innovation. The ideas are there, but we're missing the people to execute them. Bringing in the right talent should be straightforward: they are out there, just working in other industries right now.

While I was in-house at Diageo, bringing Smirnoff's inclusivity positioning to life in culture was a joy. For Pride 2016 in Belfast, where, at the time, same-sex marriage was illegal, the 'Love Wins' activation involved pasting onto a five-story building on the march route the image of a same-sex couple (who had travelled to the US to get married), kissing, in tribute to the city's mural culture.[7] This continued into 2017, and my first project for my new company, Platform13, went live. Smirnoff wanted to bring its inclusive mission statement of a good-time brand to life in its 'Labels are for Bottles, not People' ad campaign. The message was to show that the more diverse people come together, the better the good times are.

Our job was to oversee the cultural approach and ensure the right gender non-conforming talent for the campaign. At that time, at the peak of influencer marketing, an easy option would be to use the biggest YouTuber we could find. Instead, our approach was to root the campaign in nightlife, a credible occasion for Smirnoff. For us, that meant working with people who were cultural voices in nightlife, so we identified people from that scene who have championed and been part of, and represent and reflect, what gender non-conforming means today to form a Platform13 committee. This committee was instrumental in the decision-making, from the talent to the story narrative to the creative to the music, making the ad land positively both for the community and the wider world.

> ### ETE DAVIES
>
> There's a reason why creativity and creative thinking is supercharged in certain communities and that's because those communities have had to basically hack biased and prejudicial systems, day in, day out.

In 2017, I penned an article for *Campaign* on music as a global connector of culture.[8] I talked about how music transcended tunes, that it was about the lifestyle, the politics, the issues in the community. It's the same for food. They both reflect people's reality so it's emotional and connects global communities. Take Harlem's ASAP Mob or the Bronx's Ghetto Gastro – they showed us another way to build a brand, look, style and following. These independent entities are rooted in the power of their own brand and have a deep understanding of the culture it moves within. In the article, I challenged brands to rid themselves of the safety net of only taking bought views as a measure of success, and put forward an alternative idea: what if that 20 per cent KPI was used to make a long-term cultural contribution or achieve cultural relevance? I asked what brands would do as the data over-takes media, and today I continue to ask questions around what if, and do, we build and create a legacy for our brands? Thinking in this way drives meaning for both internal and external audiences, while also challenging the category and societal norms, breaking stereotypes and driving a new-world narrative in the way only these brands could.

Diversity drives success... and sales

In the same year, 2017, the Unstereotype Alliance was founded, led by UN Women and Unilever, with other multinational companies. It is a thought and action platform that seeks to eradicate harmful stereotypes in all media and advertising content. At Cannes Lions 2024, I was invited to meet them by the wonderful Ali Hanan, founder of Creative Equals. It was great to hear about their findings, including the world-first study to test if progres-sive advertising drives sales and growth. This is important because, up until this groundbreaking study, advertising with inclusivity baked in may have been seen as the dreaded 'purpose marketing', and as a nice-to-have.

The study, conducted by Oxford University's Saïd Business School academics Dr Felipe Thomaz and Prof Andrew Stephen, used data from Unstereotype Alliance members Bayer Consumer Healthcare, Diageo,

Kantar, Mars, Mondelēz and Unilever.[9] The report analysed advertising and sales data for 392 brands across 58 countries, from 2020 to 2023, across consumer health, snacks and confectionery, alcohol and beverages, pet care and consumer packaged goods. The findings were clear. Progressive advertising drives significant sales impacts, showing an uplift greater than less-progressive ads of 3.46 per cent in the short term and 16.26 per cent in the long term. The study also found that brand equity is improved, with a strong multiplying impact. High-scoring brands on progressive advertising indicators are 9.8 per cent more 'meaningful' and 11.8 per cent more 'different' (key drivers of brand equity as scored by Kantar BrandZ). It noted that brands are crucial intangible corporate assets that, when they hold value and are strong, provide future income streams and help protect companies from economic downturns and other challenges, and that progressive advertising must be seen as a vital element of corporate strategy. It is a way for brands to strengthen the value of their assets, which in turn pays off with higher customer value and, ultimately, sales performance. The study also found that loyalty (intent to repurchase) is 1.29 times higher, strong purchase consideration is 1.43 times higher, and pricing power is 1.52 times higher.

I think it's safe to say that a progressive brand is simply a culture-led brand.

One of my favourite (progressive) ads has to be Apple's 'The Greatest'. The inspiring ad celebrates the company's accessibility features through the stories of the disabled cast. Apple has incorporated accessibility into its products for a while, working with community groups to develop features that make a real impact on people's lives, so this felt like a completely credible area for them to play in. I also love that Virgin Atlantic announced that its staff can choose their uniforms, no matter their gender, and it makes perfect sense for a brand that has always championed individuality, both internally and externally.[10]

Another proud example for me is the long-term inclusivity programme that Platform13 created for Guinness. In the UK, an immediate association of the brand is as a long-established stronghold and influence within rugby. The sport's and brand's presence are huge and far reaching, with drinkers, pundits and players across the world celebrating their own connections. However, the perceived core audience for both the brand and the sport are overwhelmingly white, heterosexual, able-bodied, affluent males, with inequality and intolerance rife. We were tasked with uncovering actionable insights and executions to focus on those not currently being spoken to by the brand and the sport. Our deep research yielded clear results. While, for some, the sport is a symbol of community and national pride, there are many others who feel excluded from this narrative, through an obvious lack of diversity within rugby, and instead are faced with the sexism, homophobia, transphobia and institutional racism which plague the sport. Our response was a new long-term initiative for Guinness Rugby: 'Never Settle' – our action-led platform that uses the brand's media power and sponsorship weight in rugby for good.[11] The brand made a commitment to *never settle* until *everyone* who loves the sport feels that they belong.

This work was so well received internally that Platform13 was invited to collaborate on the global strategy for Diageo's new 'Fair Sport' framework with its global agency. As Guinness is a product that is best consumed after it settles, we felt this ownable platform name would work well for the long term. And it did – kicking off with an award-winning launch of the Women's Six Nations (W6N) in 2021, restarting an important conversation around the lack of visibility of women's sport in the media. This included a creative idea from Platform13 to demonstrate visually how little women's sport is actually covered in the press and an all-important (unfortunate) strategy against online abuse/trolling.

In 2022, we built on 'visibility' to drive inclusivity, with 'Never Settle' going through the line for the Men's Six Nations. We led and advised how the platform could credibly integrate into all the plans from a strategic and impact perspective. This included updating the original brief to bring 'Never Settle' upstream, on par with the business objectives. Executed by Guinness agencies, this meant that the platform impacted everything from media and comms, including the TV spot, OOH, PR and social, in stadium activation, nationwide experiential, industry and rugby union partnerships and sponsorships, and in grocery and in-the-home activity.

For W6N in 2022, 'Never Settle' continued to be the platform that anchored all activity driving inclusivity. In addition to leading and advising the brand and rostered agencies from a strategic and impact perspective, Platform13 identified and outreached to cultural voices such as Black Girls Ruck, activated by the brand during the season. In 2023, Six Nations Rugby and Guinness announced a new long-term partnership that will see the women's event renamed the Guinness Women's Six Nations as of 2024, alongside the extension of the title partnership of the Guinness Men's Six Nations.

When doing such work, it is assumed that powerful and culturally relevant activity like this will probably lose *some* customers to the 'Go woke, go broke' brigade. A striking example is the now-infamous 2023 Bud Light partnership with Dylan Mulvaney, a trans woman.[12] The brand partnership outraged its core audience who labelled the brand 'woke', boycotted it, posted anti-Bud and anti-trans activity and toppled Bud Light's status as the number-one US beer. The brand did nothing to defend itself nor Mulvaney, and she felt totally abandoned amid a dangerous transphobic backlash. The brand's actions all round were so offensive to the community, that the country's largest advocacy group for LGBTQ+ rights suspended its benchmark equality and inclusion rating for the whole company.

So, if being inclusive lines up with your brand values, you may at first lose some consumers. But that's ok, because you can be sure your employees and the right and new customers will come to your defence and advocate for you. Brands who have come under fire and not only weathered the storm but flourished because of it include Disney for a host of 'transgressions' including casting Halle Bailey as the Little Mermaid and adding LGTBQia+ characters to their shows, LEGO for adding characters that represent children with disabilities and, as I have talked about earlier, Nike and Kaepernick.

A win for inclusivity is a win for everyone

On a positive note, and in a sign of progression, since 2020, businesses, especially corporate structures, have been grappling with their gaps in diversity and the reasons for this. It's deep, complex and nuanced, and part of the process is asking yourself the hard questions and facing and addressing the uncomfortable truths about yourself and the business you are part of. Finally, at an unprecedented scale, people are holding a mirror up to their *own* actions, and seeking to educate themselves, with an immediate mobilization via social media across communities. Despite some examples of performative activism by brands, influencers and celebrities, there is no denying that things feel different. Those engaged with the movement have scrutinized the brands they follow, asking new questions around how the brands have engaged with the movement, if their words are supported by actions, how inclusive their teams are (at all levels), who their investors support and so on.

And in a world of profound change, with the need for radical imagination ever greater, I was excited to read a Gartner statement in 2024 which predicts that, by 2027, 20 per cent of sales organizations within Fortune 500 companies will actively recruit neurodivergent talent across conditions like autism, attention deficit hyperactivity disorder (ADHD) and dyslexia *to improve business performance*.[13]

It was great to learn from Rachel Lowenstein, Global Head of Inclusive Innovation at Mindshare, who helpfully shared a neuroinclusive communications guide.[14] It covers areas around clarity on the types and methods of communication at the beginning of a work project, including offering options for independent work, email communication or meetings based on people's preferences.

I honestly feel like this way of working would make a positive difference for us all.

As post-pandemic survival and the reality of actually doing the anti-racist work set in, some companies have reverted to traditional cost savings and profitability-driving across the business. As departments that cannot and should not be focused on short-term profits and performance, this would have been a cost line on a budget sheet easily removed. Unfortunately, this is what seems to have happened. I do believe one of the reasons is because businesses used their traditional ways of addressing 'problems' and created DEI as a function in a siloed vertical within the business.

This results in DEI activity such as updating your company logo with a rainbow flag during Pride Month or holding a series of talks during Black History Month. While we can use these moments as focus times, brands that matter in culture are inclusive *as standard, all year round.* This type of work shouldn't only happen during a campaign spike or a DEI calendar moment. If embedded in the brand and business, it drives continued positive conversations, engaging and attracting multiple audiences, resonating with people whether they are the ones targeted or not. It was good to see Kantar's brand inclusion index of 2024 created by talking to 20,300 respondents across 18 countries and 5 regions, in 11 languages, and covering 28 different categories.[15] It highlighted some of the key areas covered throughout this book that brands can affect: aspirational beauty, body inclusivity, authentic representation, local representation and marginalized communities.

Inclusive brands are growth brands

Culture-led brands understand and recognize that *people* build brands and businesses, and that true representation, intersectionality and language matters… *a lot.* This has to happen, crucially, in senior-level decision-making to impact everyone meaningfully. This is because a diverse and inclusive organization fosters resilience and a sense of belonging, enabling even the (previously) most marginalized employees to thrive, making all consumers feel fully considered and represented, and using its weight to tackle inequality in its industry is how everyone benefits. An inclusive organization attracts top-tier talent and decreases employee turnover, in turn directly impacting a company's bottom line by driving creativity, performance and innovation for your brand, business and industry. With the ear of the masses at scale, brands have the responsibility and obligation to champion and drive positive change, challenge stereotypes, change historical narratives and, especially, tackle harmful societal norms, so driving externally resonant, meaningful and representative work across the board. We have seen many examples of tone-deaf campaigns and brand experiences, as an activation, in retail and online, which can alienate global core consumers and potential new ones, for whom fairness and real inclusivity are standard and non-negotiable. This in turn directly impacts consumer mindsets and behaviour, so authenticity in this area can lead to positive, responsible, good growth.

As leadership evolves, there is an opportunity for corporate iteration on those 20th-century workplace structures and policies. Culture-led brands need to be driven internally by cultural leaders, hand in hand with new-world agencies and partners, with diverse teams to build legacy projects that ensure true resonance with their communities, and ultimately, durable business growth. It starts with acknowledging that ticking the diversity boxes, whether in outward-facing work or internally, is not the same as building an inclusive organization or putting equity-driving policies and programmes into place. Ensuring companies are set up for a truly diverse workforce and world, for today and to future-proof the business for incoming generations, starts at the leadership level, which sets the tone for the organization and is crucial for both accountability and deployment. I talk about this throughout the book, particularly in Chapter 3. It does mean embedding inclusivity upstream as part of the brand values and business strategy, and being clear on your specific definition of inclusivity and goals, both internally and for your consumers, and then tracking it.

JAMIE GILL

Data shows a clear correlation between companies with robust DEI strategies with the satisfaction of all employees at all levels. In businesses that focus on DEI and invest in it, employees tend to stay with the business longer, are more likely to recommend people to work there and it leads to higher retention rates. When you consider the savings from retaining staff for four years instead of just two, the financial benefits are clear. A reduction in recruitment fees and repeating lengthy onboarding processes can save significant sums of money alone. But the benefits of longer service, greater knowledge, more efficiency and growing talent is where the real money is made. From our UK fashion DEI census, the data shows that respondents who worked for organizations with a clear DEI strategy and dedicated resources towards DEI felt a strong sense of belonging within the workforce. And that's not just diverse groups, that's from everyone.

But, don't take only mine and Jamie's word for it.

In its fourth edition of *Diversity Matters Even More* (2023), McKinsey found that companies with diverse leadership teams continue to be associated with higher financial returns.[16] The research, spanning 1,265 companies, 23 countries, 6 global regions and multiple company interviews, shows this is true across industries and regions, despite differing challenges, stakeholder expectations and ambitions. It also found that companies with more women on their boards are 27 per cent more likely to outperform, while those with people of colour are 13 per cent more likely to outperform. Firms in the top quartile for both gender and ethnic diversity in executive teams are on average 9 per cent more likely to outperform their peers. Meanwhile, those in the bottom quartile for both are 66 per cent less likely to outperform financially on average, up from 27 per cent in 2020, indicating that lack of diversity may be getting more expensive. I was happy to see that the report, for the first time, focused beyond the relationship between diversity and financial performance and explored the 'holistic impact' of diversity on communities, workforces and the environment.

This indicates a clear shift in reframing business success.

Biases in AI

As part of this, and in the face of wide industry and workplace AI deployment, brands and businesses need to take AI bias seriously.[17] We know that AI is only as good as the data it's trained on, and, as it starts to bleed into our everyday lives at scale, embracing it also means understanding the inherent real-world biases in the massive datasets it operates with. The public internet holds vast amounts of personal data, where these biases – data that already discriminates against marginalized groups – are already present. While it's fun to play with fantastical imagery and video using AI generators, there is growing awareness that these models have been trained on Western data, leading to these products delivering stereotypical and harmful imagery. The impact of this is wide reaching, reflecting and perpetuating historical stereotypes and biases, and tackling this will be as difficult as removing systemic real-world issues. In the US, a 2021 report by ACLU outlines that AI, built by humans, is deployed in programmes and institutions such as legal systems, housing, workplaces and financial systems with deeply entrenched discrimination, and it called on the Biden administration to bring civil rights and equity to the forefront of its AI and technology policies.[18] So, it was disappointing to see a post from POC in Tech sharing that the recently formed AI advisory council for Meta was made up entirely of white men.[19] It clarified that this council was different from Meta's board of directors and its oversight board, which have more diverse gender and racial representation, but seemed to be made up of business executives, with no ethicists.

From an inclusivity perspective, brands must be accountable to ensure their AI models are as free from bias as possible. This means diverse AI development teams are crucial, with continuous observation essential through organizational transformation and process, as outlined in Chapter 6. Done right, this can foster inclusivity and accessibility for everyone, enhance transparency and trust through the business and help create inclusive product and marketing innovation. This encourages the dismantling of current processes that block inclusivity, and addresses the underlying factors for success to make a positive impact on your employees, in culture and for communities, socially and financially. Different from the typical 2020 DEI activity, this inclusive way of working stretches and cascades throughout the business from the C-suite and impacts all functions – from hiring to procurement, to product creation, to innovation, to supply chains and sustainability, and all the way to marketing. For us within brands, or as external partners, while we need and appreciate mentorship, we urgently need championship – advocating for us in the places and spaces we aren't in.

We all need to drive positive change with deliberate intent, purpose, courage and empathy. Embedding inclusive strategies through the business, leveraging the power of the diverse communities that define the world and using their globally renowned status and weight, big brands can evolve outdated narratives and transform industries to shape a better future for people, the planet and themselves.

Notes

1   Adriana Ramic et al. '900 Voices From Gen Z, America's Most Diverse Generation', *The New York Times*, 22 March 2019, nytimes.com/interactive/2019/us/generation-z.html?smid=pl-share (archived at https://perma.cc/ZBA5-RPH8).

2   Francombe, Amy. 'Why are So Many Creative Directors White Men?', *Vogue Business*, 6 October 2023, voguebusiness.com/fashion/why-are-so-many-creative-directors-white-men (archived at https://perma.cc/V9KL-M27Z).

3 Neches, Rachel, and Jonathan Bowles. 'Expanding Access to Advertising Careers in NYC', Center for an Urban Future, June 2024, nycfuture.org/research/expanding-access-to-advertising-careers-in-nyc (archived at https://perma.cc/79GQ-ETZC).

4 Martha's Vineyard CDO Summit, mvcdosummit.com (archived at https://perma.cc/B6QH-8FBR)

5 'Intersectionality', *Encyclopædia Britannica*, britannica.com/topic/intersectionality (archived at https://perma.cc/6WRZ-4FQE).

6 Fataar, Leila. 'How Brands Can Actually Take Anti-Racist Action', Highsnobiety, 3 June 2020, highsnobiety.com/p/lessons-brands-inclusive-workplace-poc-bame (archived at https://perma.cc/6GFT-9LW5).

7 Wong, Curtis M. 'Artist Creates Stunning, 5-Story Mural to Support Same-Sex Marriage', *HuffPost*, 4 August 2016, huffingtonpost.co.uk/entry/joe-caslin-love-wins-mural_n_57a355dae4b0104052a179ec (archived at https://perma.cc/2VB2-VUKV).

8 Fataar, Leila. 'How Brands Can Use Music to Keep in Tune with Consumers', *Campaign*, 11 December 2017, campaignlive.co.uk/article/brands-use-music-keep-tune-consumers/1452503 (archived at https://perma.cc/A28H-GC6D).

9 Stephen, Andrew, et al. 'Global First Study Proving Progressive Advertising Can Drive Sales and Growth, Revealed at Cannes Lions', Saïd Business School, University of Oxford, 18 June 2024, sbs.ox.ac.uk/news/global-first-study-proving-progressive-advertising-can-drive-sales-and-growth-revealed-cannes-lions (archived at https://perma.cc/VB7D-PD6E).

10 Ormesher, Ellen. 'Virgin Atlantic Pilots Inclusive Campaign to Celebrate Its Updated Gender Identity Policy', *The Drum*, 28 September 2022, thedrum.com/news/2022/09/28/virgin-atlantic-pilots-inclusive-campaign-celebrate-its-updated-gender-identity (archived at https://perma.cc/FR3Q-PRJU).

11 Guinness. 'Never Settle: Celebrating Diversity in Rugby', guinness.com/en-gb/sport/never-settle (archived at https://perma.cc/Y2VL-VU2A).

12 Riedel, Samantha, et al. 'Everything You Need to Know About the Bud Light and Dylan Mulvaney Fiasco', *Them*, 14 August 2023, them.us/story/dylan-mulvaney-bud-light-drama-explained (archived at https://perma.cc/T6GZ-47GL).

13 Stamford, Conn. 'Gartner Predicts 20% of Sales Organizations in Fortune 500 Companies Will Actively Recruit Neurodivergent Talent to Improve Business Performance by 2027', Gartner, 29 February 2024, gartner.com/en/newsroom/press-releases/2024-02-29-gartner-predicts-20-percent-of-sales-organizationsi-in-fortune-500-companies-will-actively-recruit-neurodivergent-talent-to-improve-business-performance-by-2027 (archived at https://perma.cc/4YW5-J587).

14 Lowenstein, Rachel. 'Neuroinclusive Communications: Best Practices on Communicating with Your Neurodivergent Colleagues', Canva, canva.com/design/DAF96ik4QHs/-kN4l6OZP2NqtOh48_xlJg/edit (archived at https://perma.cc/53ZV-RWCB).

15 Piaggio, Valeria. 'Brand Inclusion Index 2024', Kantar, 2024, kantar.com/campaigns/brand-inclusion-index (archived at https://perma.cc/UH7T-2DYJ).

16 Hunt, Vivian, et al. *Diversity Matters Even More: The Case for Holistic Impact*, McKinsey & Company, 5 December 2023, mckinsey.com/featured-insights/diversity-and-inclusion/diversity-matters-even-more-the-case-for-holistic-impact (archived at https://perma.cc/S9B3-6DML).

17 Libby, Kristina. 'Four Solutions to Tackle AI Bias for a More Effective AI Strategy', The Shutterstock Blog, 6 July 2023, shutterstock.com/blog/four-solutions-to-tackle-ai-bias (archived at https://perma.cc/47TJ-QW5C).

18 Akselrod, Olga. 'How Artificial Intelligence Can Deepen Racial and Economic Inequities', American Civil Liberties Union, 13 July 2021, aclu.org/news/privacy-technology/how-artificial-intelligence-can-deepen-racial-and-economic-inequities (archived at https://perma.cc/AW9N-Q53Z).

19 POC In Tech, instagram.com/pocintech (archived at https://perma.cc/PZB9-GMR5).

09

Environmental consciousness

Aligning brand strategy with climate action

Humanity and our world are, and will be forever, deeply affected by climate change. According to the US National Institutes of Health, microplastics can be found everywhere in the environment – lakes, rivers, seas, drinking water, the food we eat and even in the air we breathe; they are all around us.[1] There are countless studies about how we got here and where we are now, and many resources and sources of advice on what needs to be done from a packaging and retail point of view. So, I am focused here on mindsets, behaviours and the role of brands and their products.

The Intergovernmental Panel on Climate Change (IPCC), which imputed the scientific information for the 2015 Paris Agreement, and whose findings were formally approved by the world's governments in 2018, has been clear: emissions must be halved by 2030 to limit global warming to 1.5°C.[2] The Paris Agreement meant that nations around the world committed to control warming to no more than 1.5 degrees above pre-industrialization levels.[3] This would mean countries need to reduce emissions by 45 per cent by 2030 and reach net zero by 2050.

By 2021, the UN had declared that the evidence is irrefutable: greenhouse-gas emissions from fossil-fuel burning and deforestation are choking our planet and putting billions of people at both immediate and long-term risk. It adds that global heating is affecting every region on Earth, with many of the changes already irreversible, calling it out as 'Code red for humanity'.[4] At the closing of the Climate Change Conference COP28 in 2023, UN Secretary-General António Guterres reaffirmed the need for drastic reductions in global greenhouse-gas emissions in this decade, stressing the need to transition away from fossil fuels, that the era of fossil fuels must end, and, further, that promised plans need to deliver climate justice to those on the front lines of the crisis.[5]

That was then.

In 2024, COP29 was mired in controversy. An open letter by climate experts stated that these talks are no longer fit for purpose and there is an urgent need to shift from negotiation to implementation, asking the COP to deliver on agreed commitments and ensure the urgent energy transition and phase-out of fossil energy.[6] Further, importantly and once again, there was shown a clear divide between the economically rich and the economically poorer countries that are literally on the front lines of the climate crisis. Some delegates of the latter walked out in protest as the climate finance offer of an annual $300 billion (about £240 billion) of a requested $1.3 trillion (£1.08 trillion) they will receive by 2035 is not enough to make meaningful progress towards decarbonizing their economies when they are already suffering the effects of the climate crisis. The frustration and anger are understandable; after all, the economically wealthy countries are where 75 per cent of the growth in emissions has occurred in the past decade. (I talk about this in more detail later in the chapter.)

Beyond code red for humanity

Unfortunately, in 2024, Guterres stated that greenhouse-gas emissions had hit new highs and that the world is heading for a temperature rise far above the Paris Agreement goals unless countries deliver more than they have promised.[7] This means that, without urgent action to stop fossil-fuel use, these extreme weather patterns, like heatwaves, droughts and flooding, will become more common, longer lasting and even deadlier. This was further confirmed by the European Union's Copernicus Climate Change Service reporting that 2023 was the hottest year and 22 July 2024 was the hottest day since such records began in 1940.[8] The report attributes these high temperatures largely to greenhouse-gas emissions from fossil-fuel-based industries like Big Oil.

There was *some* good news, however. According to the think tank, Ember, in 2023, renewable sources accounted for 30 per cent of global electricity, driven by growth in solar and wind for the first time, giving us a glimpse into what's possible and more achievable than we seem to think.[9] Ember identifies five fast-growing technologies that are already noticeably contributing to electricity demand, accounting for over half of the world's demand growth in 2023: electric vehicles, heat pumps, electrolysers for green hydrogen, data centres and air conditioners. It highlights the need for a strong focus on efficiency to avoid wasteful demand growth in a world of limited clean electricity.

These approaches are crucial for what looks like a computing-powered future.

While AI does feel like an opportunity to help us find solutions for climate change, paradoxically, its own environmental impact is huge due to the amount of electricity, water and land needed to build and run AI systems. A 2024 NPR article shows Big Tech under pressure when it comes to emissions statuses.[10] The article highlights Google's and Microsoft's 2024 sustainability reports telling us that the former's greenhouse-gas emissions climbed 48 per cent over the past five years because of the surge to its data-centre energy consumption and supply chain emissions. Similarly, Microsoft's emissions have grown by 29 per cent since 2020 due to the construction of more AI-focused data centres.

As the AI wars heat up, so will the planet.

The rise of extreme weather

The increase of 'unprecedented' weather we see raging across the globe is becoming too regular for that title. Across Asia in April 2024, Reuters reported 15 days of record-breaking heat that affected billions of people, killing hundreds in related illnesses.[11] Schools closed, affecting the workforce, crops failed, electricity supply was shut down in the Philippines, and communities across the region were devastated. In South and South East Asia, where much of the fast-fashion industry supply chain is – and already under pressure from less-than-ideal working conditions – things became dangerous for workers and workplaces. For many people in the Global South, not being able to work means immediately not being able to support your family, which means generational inequality continues.

Extreme weather is not only affecting the Global South. A 2021 *Financial Times* article 'Learning to live with 50C temperatures' highlights people's experiences across the socio-economic spectrum in cities in the Gulf states.[12] Al Jazeera reported in June 2024 that more than 130 million people in the US are under threat from a long-running heatwave that had already broken records with dangerously high temperatures – scorching heat felt from coast to coast, persisting across south-western parts of the US, Mexico and the northern countries of Central America.[13] Canada and Australia suffer repeated wildfires; and, in Europe, searing heat is increasingly commonplace in summer months across Italy, Spain, Portugal and France as wildfires like those in Greece in 2023 and 2024 seem more regular.

Some cities are able to respond, as outlined in an opinion piece on Monocle that highlighted the need to evolve the 20th-century urban infrastructure that was created in a different climate landscape.[14] It showcased heat action plans: Seoul and Santa Fe resurfacing buried rivers, lowering temperatures significantly; Medellín, Montréal and Milan making efforts to connect their existing green spaces, creating a tree-canopy network that supports walkability.

Climate change looks to reshape our living environments affecting our behaviours too. Short-term solutions are not enough. We need radical ideas like Barcelona's *superilla* (superblocks), created in response to excessive pollution and noise levels.[15] The idea was that clusters of inner-minor streets in the city are closed to through traffic, becoming public spaces. Cars, in one direction only, are allowed primarily for accessing residences and for disabled people, with access given for public transport, emergency vehicles and bicycles for recreation. This comes with a multitude of challenges, but we need more of this type of thinking in big cities. As temperature rises become normal, we look to Singapore's Green Plan,[16] with its five pillars that will influence all its citizens' lives: City in Nature – building liveable and sustainable homes; an Energy Reset – cleaner energy sources across all sectors; Sustainable Living – consuming less, recycling more and using public transport; the Green Economy – harnessing sustainability as a competitive advantage; and a Resilient Future – preparing for the next century.

Otherwise, the outlook for business is bleak – if we continue the way we are. A World Economic Forum report from August 2024 finds that more than 70 per cent of the global workforce is at risk from death or injury due to extreme heat.[17] It highlights that, in Africa, nearly 93 per cent of the workforce is exposed to extreme heat. On the Arabian peninsula, over 83 per cent of workers face excessive heat. In Europe and Central Asia, the risk to workers from extreme heat is increasing faster than anywhere else in the world, having risen by more than 17 per cent since 2020. This means that more than 2.4 billion workers are at risk from excessive heat at work, and the WEF urges new policies to protect workers from heat stress. It highlights a UN finding that people are being endangered by 'increasingly severe heat waves driven largely by a fossil-fuel charged, human-induced climate crisis'.[18] The ILO (International Labour Organization) outlines simple and effective measures to mitigate the dangers of excessive heat in the workplace, such as ensuring adequate hydration and providing cool and shaded rest areas.[19] It also challenges obsolete regulations and stresses the need for those to be updated, with clear extensions of worker protections beyond periods officially classed as heatwaves.

As mentioned throughout this book, solutions should include the people impacted, so, involving workers in developing heat-stress policies will be crucial for success. Your cultural positioning can help define your unique role so the need to compete at all costs with competitors can be reduced. These learnings then could be shared across industries and borders to speed up progress on global policies and protect billions of workers from the growing threat of excessive heat. Collaborating with but challenging your industry and category by leveraging your brand power to act in all our interests is a game-changer. It's not only workers; interest cultures, directly connected to brands in the culture stacks, are affected too. Use cultural intelligence to analyse what is happening in subcultures and emerging cultures connected to your industry and category and collaborate with those cultural voices.

As Paris prepared for the 2024 Olympics, the *Rings of Fire* report, insti-gated after the Tokyo Olympics in 2020, and published a month before Paris, outlined that climate change should increasingly be viewed as an exis-tential threat to sport, and, in fashion, the unpredictable and changing climate is upending both shopping habits and inventory management.[20]

Regulations force change

Actions have always spoken louder than words. Merely stating that a brand is committed to a particular goal by 2030 or 2050 isn't sufficient. It's more crucial than ever to transparently and tangibly act on those corporate poli-cies and promises. Brands have much to do in building trust with audiences after countless cases of, at best, greenwashing (in some cases unintentional, in others very intentional) and, at worst, greenhushing – keeping silent in the hope that sustainability is moved out of the spotlight.

With time running out, long-needed regulations could be the only way to force change and make business leaders, brands and industries accountable. According to a 2024 LSE report, at least 230 new global corporate climate cases have been filed since 2015, the year of the Paris Agreement.[21] These include 'climate-washing', which has grown in recent years, with 47 cases filed in 2023, bringing the recorded total to more than 140. More than 70 per cent of completed cases decided in favour of the claimants. There have also been 30 cases in 'polluter pays', which seek to hold companies accountable for climate-related harm caused by their activities. The report also found that litigants continue to file new 'corporate framework' cases, seeking to ensure companies align their group-level policies and governance processes with climate goals. 2024 has seen a new category of 'transition risk' cases, which includes cases filed against corporate directors and officers for their (lack of) management of climate risks. Nearly 50 of the 230-plus cases filed in 2023 did not align with climate goals. Some cases challenge climate action, others are more concerned with the way in which climate action is implemented. These include: ESG backlash cases, which challenge the incorporation of climate risk into financial decision-making; strategic litigation against public participation (SLAPP) suits against NGOs and shareholder activists, which seek to deter them from pursuing climate agendas; just transition cases, which challenge the distributional impacts of climate policy or the processes by which policies were developed, normally on human rights grounds; and green versus green cases, which concern potential trade-offs between climate and biodiversity or other environmental aims. Individuals are also driving change through other legal channels. In 2023, a group of activists won a landmark lawsuit against the US state of Montana for violating their constitutional right to a 'clean and healthful environment'.[22] In 2024, Puerto Rico sued Big Oil companies of fraudulent marketing for over $1 billion, for climate-induced hurricanes that devastated the island's resources and shorelines.[23]

On the other hand, industry and government *cooperation* gives hope. One clear opportunity is that of digital product passports or digital product identities (touched on in Chapter 6). Here, brands are able to authenticate their products, both new and, importantly, resale or second-hand, and deliver traceability product information for consumers and producers all along the life cycle, from production to after sale.

Shifting CSR into ESG

This is a world where all your audiences – investors, regulators, industry-leaders, NGOs, employees, fans and consumers – expect accuracy and transparency and who also want to see evidence and traceability of this positive impact. This means a definitive shift incorporating CSR into ESG, the outcome less about reporting and more about operational input, industry collaboration and product innovation.

Brands and businesses must understand the subtle differences between these. In a nutshell CSR is an initiative created internally to fulfil a corporate purpose, rooted in corporate philanthropy. This is manifested in company culture policies like DEI, sustainability and practices such as volunteering days off and community programmes. ESG goes one step further, providing insights into ethical practices, sustainability and CSR. It reflects a company's impact on society, attracts investors and can support performance. A robust structure can mitigate risk when it comes to regulations, litigation and reputation; it can reduce waste and encourage energy efficiency, with employee wellbeing reducing staff turnover. It is impacting consumers too. *ESG Today* reported that ESG has become a top-three key purchasing criteria for more than half of consumers globally, from a survey of nearly 200,000 consumers in four countries and nine consumer categories.[24] Additionally, *ESG Today* reports that consumers are personally 'divesting' from brands with poor DEI and social track records.[25] For example, 33 per cent of the Gen Z consumers (aged 18 to 24) in the US say they would boycott a brand with bad labour practices.

Culture-led brands must incorporate ESG strategy upstream into business strategy. Your unique role, unlocked through cultural positioning work, defines your ESG strategy specific to your industry and your brand – impacting reputation, global operations, product and marketing innovation and evolving the supply chain. This is where the CFO role and skills are perfectly set up to evolve the traditional cost/benefit analysis that makes business decisions, to find ways to calculate profitability based on ESG impact. It also makes sense for the CFO to lead regulatory compliance, monitoring and reporting, while bringing investors along on the journey. Businesses need to supercharge this approach as, according to a 2024 Accenture study, only 22 per cent of CFOs are well prepared.[26] No one expects your brand to solve everything alone, but ESG can power innovation and growth positively through new business models where success is measured by brand impact versus profit and cross-industry collaboration thrives.

It is important to ensure that each of the E, S and G are not conflated. Like DEI, while connected, they must also be treated separately.

The role of colonization, capitalism and consumption

From a culture-lens perspective, to move forward, it is important to understand the context and connections through the culture stacks. This sits directly in the impact on people's inherited culture; the legacy at the intersection between colonization, capitalism and consumption still survives today. Colonization has been happening since at least ancient Greek times, and according to *National Geographic*, civilizations such as the ancient Romans and Egyptians gained power by extending their borders into surrounding areas as far back as 1550 BCE.[27] Fast forward to the Western Christian world and the first wave of modern colonialism, the so-called Age of Discovery, was on the seas. From the 15th to 17th centuries, Portugal and

Spain led and were followed quickly by the other main powers of Western Europe. This empire-building interlinked world systems and lay the foundations for globalization and international trade. Also fondly known by many in the West as the Age of Exploration for 'God, Gold and Glory', its leaders were hailed as explorers and heroes.[28] For God because there was a belief that Christianity was the saving power for the 'natives'; gold is obvious – the exploitation of resources for economic gain; and there was 'glory' in conquering a country or winning it in battle against other colonizers.

The fact that there were indigenous people – with centuries-old eco-stewardship, who see the Earth as a gift passed on from generation to generation, with their own rituals, customs and traditions – already living in these 'discovered' places was a bit of a footnote at the time. Today, these are the same displaced people, with deep knowledge of sustainable solutions from their ancestors, who have nurtured and protected the Earth for generations locally, and who, collectively, can help us all globally. The 2024 Davos meeting convened 22 innovators, activists and indigenous leaders whose communities are most impacted by decisions made by others, who were finally being appreciated by global leaders in business and governments.[29] These cultural voices are essential to help identify innovative pathways to help fix the food system and use respectful regeneration and rewilding towards a long-term systemic approach to a net-zero and nature-positive world by 2050.

The second wave of colonialism began during the 19th century and is known as the Race or Scramble for Africa. Once ships from the West reached the coast of Africa, and word of the interior's vast raw materials and resources to fuel the new industrialization reached the colonizing countries, they began to lay claim to Africa. I say 'lay claim' because that was how it was done. At a Berlin conference called by German chancellor Otto von Bismarck in 1884, the US, the Ottoman Empire and 12 European countries divided up most of the African continent between them. There were no African representatives. By 1914, 90 per cent of Africa was controlled by seven European countries, and trade began to be controlled in earnest as the colonizers constructed railways and steamships to get along rivers and into the interiors. By 1919, the British Empire was the largest in the world. A not-so-fun fact from the Royal Museums in Greenwich is that, at that time, 'the sun never set on the British Empire', meaning that, during a 24-hour day, there was never a moment at which it was not daylight somewhere in Britain's territories.[30]

This industrial revolution meant that business owners (capitalists) started to organize labour in the factories of the Global North to drive output and profitability, vastly different from the craft and guild systems before, with products made by machine instead of hand. There were many advantages, of course – efficiencies, and employment for some, driving people to cities and bringing with them city infrastructure and innovation. On the other hand, that relentless chase for maximum profitability drove terrible working conditions for most and horrendous living conditions in overpopulated and polluted cities, and profound behaviour changes. Over time, companies from the Global North, still pulling raw materials from the Global South, began to move production of these products there as well, exploiting cheap labour, and where the impact of the original imperialism compounded by the climate emergency connected to overconsumption (and related waste), is still deeply felt today. Meanwhile, as workers in the Global South followed these companies to the cities, both these and the abandoned rural areas are even more vulnerable to climate change and its devastating effects. Hence, there is an urgent need to evolve the supply chain systems put into place from colonialism, which are still alive and kicking and deeply impacting people's lives.

The rise of climate justice

In 2013, in an intersection of systemic issues all connected to the culture stacks, five separate garment factories in one building collapsed. At least 1,138 people died at the Rana Plaza in Bangladesh, including several rescue workers, and a further 2,500 were injured or disabled, leading to a groundbreaking and legally binding accord between global brands and trade unions to improve workplace conditions for garment workers in the country. According to *Vogue Business*, as of 2023, at least 150,000 safety hazards had been identified in Bangladesh through the accord, of which more than 95 per cent were remedied.[31] This framework is now being rolled out to Pakistan, with 117 brands including Gap and adidas joining, which means its safety initiatives are set to expand to 484 factories and 539,697 workers in the country.

So, we know collaboration can work.

In summer 2018, Greta Thunberg, aged 15, held the first School Strike for Climate outside the Swedish parliament. By 2019, inspired by her, young people across Europe skipped school to demonstrate about climate change, demanding that politicians act before it is too late. In that same year, the European Parliament declared a climate emergency, igniting a new appreciation of the planet. Greta's message to world leaders at the 2019 UN Climate Action Summit was clear and stark: 'We'll be watching you.' In 2020, deeper awareness of the interconnectedness of business, climate and ingrained racial and social inequalities went mainstream and global. The movement was led by Gen Z climate activists who turned their attention directly to companies who they saw as shifting the blame to the end consumer instead of taking responsibility for it.

And this voice of protest is not going away.

The role of brands in (over)consumption

In the 20th century, consumerism moved from a need state – food, home, clothing – to a want state, closer to where we are now. The mass production resulting from industrialization and global distribution was only possible and maintainable if a company's products were selling to as many people as possible.

This soon meant that companies had to create a demand for their products… and then continue to create demand for new or updated versions of their products through planned obsolescence (the designing of products to last only for a short period of time). In the 1920s, the target audience for these brands sat directly in the places that could afford it, in the industrialized world – the West or the Global North. More spending meant more business, resulting in both economic growth of that area or country and more job opportunities for people, within hierarchies of power and privilege. People's disposable income – remaining wages after their basic needs have been met – was ready to be spent on items they wanted but didn't really need; items usually only available to those with wealth, items that, at first, felt like luxuries. This made a person feel upwardly mobile, and being seen to own these and other 'things' became a prominent measure of success. It became the aspiration. Alongside, business strategy focused on maximizing profitability, and more profit meant bigger bonuses and, often, better opportunity for promotion and higher salaries, making the corporate ladder very attractive.

Capitalism and the relentless pursuit of profit became the dominant economic system and meant that businesses needed to ensure that their brand was front of mind, ramping up marketing and advertising to keep driving demand. The media of newspapers, then radio and then TV developed mass communication. For brands, this gave unprecedented access to people, and they were able to showcase and associate their products visually, connected to these new aspirational lifestyles, at scale. This all meant that the variety and amount of products manufactured to meet human desires of consumption went into overdrive, with brands competing for their category leadership, fuelling consumer culture. The result is vast, unsustainable and continuing overproduction and 'disposable' consumption. *National Geographic* reported in 2023 on how fast-fashion garments are incinerated in South Asia and Africa or dumped in places like Chile's Atacama Desert – reports of 39,000 tonnes illegally per year – nicknamed the great fashion garbage patch (in reference to Great Pacific Garbage Patch of litter and plastic in the oceans; and in Ghana, there are reports of a landfill which is 60 per cent clothing and 65 feet high.[32]

Today, marketing and advertising are responsible for escalating consumer desire globally, driving widespread demands for more and more goods, and building the now-expected 'always on' approach. With online the key channel for these communications, this also meant a *huge* amount of digital marketing – we have all seen the uptick since 2020. According to earth.org, this translates to the need for more powerful and energy-consuming infrastructure to support the amount of digital traffic.[33] Earth.org highlights a study which found that online advertising 'consumes vast amounts of energy' and contributes around 10–20 per cent of the total internet infrastructure's consumption.[34] Then, a 2024 WARC report finds the global advertising market is on track for a major leap, with ad spend expected to rise by 10.5 per cent, topping $1 trillion for the first time.[35] It confirms that ad spend has more than doubled worldwide over the last decade, with just three companies – Amazon, Alphabet and Meta – accounting for more than 70 per cent of this incremental spend. This upward trend seems set to continue and, by 2026, global ad spend is projected to hit $1.23 trillion – an 80 per cent increase from pre-pandemic levels in 2019.

Without a doubt, overconsumption – and the encouragement of it – are inextricably linked to climate change because it pushes overproduction of everything. And we all know it. A rebalance is needed.

Sustainability is not a trend

I curated a roundtable at Highsnobiety in 2021 to discuss overconsumption, exploring whether we need events like Black Friday.[36] We talked about the need for supply chain disruption and regulation, the opportunities around digital and circular fashion, 3D printing and upcycling, the challenge with wealth inequality driving fast and cheap fashion, how new generations are creating new ecosystems of commerce, the need for brand transparency, the myth of hype and that it can be a way to drive better consumption, and the misunderstandings surrounding recycling. We all agreed that, while we *don't* need calendar moments like Black Friday, people will continue to shop, so how could brands use these moments to help them shop better?

The current approach to consumerism drives how we create, buy, sell and promote goods and services. While today's are the most consciously aware generations, many of us avoiding single-use plastics, using paper straws and definitely taking our own bags for our shopping, the continued impact of materialistic values and influencer/celebrity culture cannot be overlooked. Shaming people, especially Gen Z who have grown up with a cost-of-living crisis, and algorithmic and fast fashion will not change behaviour.

It sits directly in the responsibility and obligations of brands and businesses to be part of the solution in enabling consumers to make the right and informed choices. And it doesn't have to be preachy or boring.

Some are already taking the lead from Miu Miu Upcycled, which, interestingly, has been one of the only brands to buck the luxury slowdown trend.[37] According to *Vogue Business*, Miu Miu's revenues have more than doubled recently, up 105 per cent in the third quarter year-on-year and up 97 per cent in the first nine months of 2024.[38] Meanwhile, Massive Attack held a mini music festival, Act 1.5, in 2024 summer.[39] It brought to life the result of a piece of research the band commissioned in 2019 to explore opportunities for significantly reducing the emissions associated with live music touring, and finessed in 2021 with the Tyndall Centre – a partnership of universities bringing together researchers from the social and natural sciences and engineering to develop sustainable responses to climate change.[40] Another great example is Potato Head Beach Club in Bali and its commitment to regenerative hospitality, adopting a circular approach, by managing waste responsibly.[41] This includes creatively upcycling waste it produces into furniture, amenities, art and more. Another loved brand with a cult and loyal following (and a shortcut for Scandi cool) on the circularity journey is fashion label Ganni. In its 2023 sustainability report,[42] co-founder and CEO Nicolaj Reffstrup is clear: 'The journey towards sustainability will cost you, and brands need to pay the premium, as consumers won't and shouldn't.' He talks about modest growth in 2023, and, reading between the lines, he is ok with that because the outcome of the transition is a carbon decrease of 7 per cent in absolute terms from a 2021 baseline during a period in which the company grew 18 per cent on average from 2021 to 2023. Reffstrup mentions materials innovation (and the public-facing communication around this), living wage, company-wide cross-functional carbon reduction, solar-panel installation for renewable energy and, importantly, the tying of bonuses to carbon targets, and also importantly, hope and resilience.

There must be something in the water in Denmark. During the pandemic, ECCO approached Platform13 to help steer into existence a new bag brand concept – Ecco Leather Goods – to be part of the ECCO group, but standing apart with its own distinct audience and identity. We started by interviewing several senior stakeholders to identify the company's challenges and needs. We followed with a global target consumer research project to answer the questions: Does the world need another bag brand? Who could the target audience be? How can it be launched in a pandemic world? Our research covered the brand's key markets of China, Russia, UK and Germany to understand the functional, social and emotional needs of a potential target consumer in a pandemic and post-pandemic climate. Our answer was, no, the world doesn't need a new bag brand. But, if we were to do it, we recognized that the new consumer does need brands that are considerate of the planet and people. Our cultural and strategic positioning and recommendation included a radical approach to the business rooted in the company's unique leather by-products materials and with a three-year actionable road map to launch the brand credibly, including educating consumers on ECCO leather innovation and its role in sustainability.

As brand and business leaders, we have a clear role to play in redefining consumer culture and capitalism. Existing culture-led shifts should be a clear warning signal to brands and companies that they have to contend with consumers simply buying less all together. When they do buy, the brand needs to show authenticity and innovation that supports people and the planet and find a balance in driving positive growth.

Ensuring your brand and business are part of the people-and-planet solution is essential for your survival. By embracing ESG initiatives beyond the tick-box and pilot modes, cascading this through the whole business led by the C-suite, being radically transparent about almost-guaranteed challenges and failures on the journey, sharing and collaborating with others, we can encourage our consumers to buy less and/or better through exciting product and marketing innovations. We must embrace the responsibility to help consumers navigate this by encouraging personal expression and individuality, informing and educating them on the harms and remedies in their language, places and spaces, providing alternative product options that are marketed in an aspirational way. The possibilities are endless and there for us to grab.

Notes

1 Ziani, Khaled, et al. 'Microplastics: A Real Global Threat for Environment and Food Safety: A State of the Art Review', *Nutrients*, 15(3), 25 January 2023, doi: 10.3390/nu15030617, pmc.ncbi.nlm.nih.gov/articles/PMC9920460/#:~:text=Microplastic%20particles%20can%20be%20found,they%20are%20all%20around%20us (archived at https://perma.cc/J4U9-WH8W).

2 Masson-Delmotte, Valérie, et al. *Global Warming of 1.5°C: An IPCC Special Report on the Impacts of Global Warming of 1.5°C Above Pre-Industrial Levels and Related Global Greenhouse Gas Emission Pathways...*, ipcc.ch/site/assets/uploads/sites/2/2019/06/SR15_Summary_Volume_Low_Res.pdf (archived at https://perma.cc/2ZSG-5RAP).

3 United Nations. 'The Paris Agreement', 2015, un.org/en/climatechange/paris-agreement (archived at https://perma.cc/98MW-FPNQ).

4 United Nations. 'Secretary-General Calls Latest IPCC Climate Report "Code Red for Humanity", Stressing "Irrefutable" Evidence of Human Influence', UN press release, 9 August 2021, press.un.org/en/2021/sgsm20847.doc.htm (archived at https://perma.cc/4DCD-92NR).

5 Guterres, António. 'Secretary-General's Statement at the Closing of the UN Climate Change Conference COP28 Secretary-General', *United Nations*, United Nations, 13 Dec. 2023, www.un.org/sg/en/content/sg/statement/2023-12-13/secretary-generals-statement-the-closing-of-the-un-climate-change-conference-cop28 (archived at https://perma.cc/Z62X-NAKX). Accessed 16 Dec. 2024.

6 Club of Rome. 'Open Letter on COP Reform to All States that Are Parties to the Convention, Mr. Simon Stiell, Executive Secretary of the UNFCCC Secretariat and UN Secretary-General António Guterres', The Club of Rome, 15 November 2024, clubofrome.org/cop-reform-2024 (archived at https://perma.cc/YU4X-7MCU).

7 Sommer, Lauren. 'How Is the World Doing on Climate Change? Not Great', NPR, 24 October 2024, npr.org/2024/10/24/nx-s1-5157789/climate-change-emissions-greenhouse-gases-united-nations (archived at https://perma.cc/5UYR-FFAH).

8 Copernicus. 'New Record Daily Global Average Temperature Reached in July 2024', Copernicus Climate Change Service, 23 July 2024, climate.copernicus.eu/new-record-daily-global-average-temperature-reached-july-2024 (archived at https://perma.cc/WH74-97YH).

9 Wiatros-Motyka, Malgorzata, et al. *Global Electricity Review 2024*, Ember, 8 May 2024, ember-energy.org/latest-insights/global-electricity-review-2024 (archived at https://perma.cc/MQ6B-W2UJ).

10 Kerr, Dara. 'AI Brings Soaring Emissions for Google and Microsoft, a Major Contributor to Climate Change', NPR, 12 July 2024, npr.org/2024/07/12/g-s1-9545/ai-brings-soaring-emissions-for-google-and-microsoft-a-major-contributor-to-climate-change (archived at https://perma.cc/UW73-H5CF).

11   Reuters. 'Asia's Extreme April Heat Worsened by Climate Change, Scientists Say', 14 May 2024, reuters.com/business/environment/asias-extreme-april-heat-worsened-by-climate-change-scientists-say-2024-05-14 (archived at https://perma.cc/4NYG-28G9).

12   Cornish, Chloe. 'Learning to Live with 50C Temperatures', *Financial Times*, 28 August 2024, ft.com/content/d5a5bc1f-e225-4397-b99f-56c62b00366d (archived at https://perma.cc/ME66-7DTK).

13   Al Jazeera. 'Record-Breaking Heatwave Threatens 130 Million People in US', 7 July 2024, aljazeera.com/news/2024/7/7/record-breaking-heatwave-threatens-130-million-people-in-us (archived at https://perma.cc/3L4F-5HR3).

14   Myrivili, Eleni. 'As Cities Heat up, Urban Life Needn't Become Unbearable. Sometimes, the Simplest Solutions Can Be the Most Effective', *The Monocle Minute*, 30 July 2024, monocle.com/minute/2024/07/30/?utm_source=Klaviyo &utm_medium=email&_kx=OQU3Kn0CqfomMF9vIHJkC9lexlOfIhB4AJbXz OmHB38ThqqloD7EIRTmeg5hbN59.WEFNwV#as-cities-heat-up-urban-life-needn-t-become-unbearable-sometimes-the-simplest-solutions-can-be-the-most-effective (archived at https://perma.cc/4G6D-9DKH).

15   Postaria, Ronika. 'Superblock (Superilla) Barcelona – a City Redefined', Cities Forum, 31 May 2021, citiesforum.org/news/superblock-superilla-barcelona-a-city-redefined (archived at https://perma.cc/ADA5-WKWV).

16   Green Plan. 'A City of Green Possibilities: What is the Singapore Green Plan 2030?', Singapore Green Plan 2030, 3 December 2024, greenplan.gov.sg (archived at https://perma.cc/4YDE-WAAQ).

17   Torkington, Simon. 'More than 70% of the Global Workforce is at Risk from Severe Heat – Report', World Economic Forum, 8 August 2024, weforum.org/stories/2024/08/extreme-heat-workers-climate-health (archived at https://perma.cc/HKF6-38BY).

18   United Nations. 'Secretary-General's Call to Action on Extreme Heat', July 2024, un.org/en/climatechange/extreme-heat (archived at https://perma.cc/GAP4-DAAB).

19   ILO. *Ensuring Safety and Health at Work in a Changing Climate*, International Labour Office, 2024, ilo.org/publications/ensuring-safety-and-health-work-changing-climate (archived at https://perma.cc/5D95-GXLS). ISBN: 9789220405079.

20   Basis / Front Runners, *Rings of Fire: Heat Risks at the 2024 Paris Olympics*, basis.org.uk/wp-content/uploads/2024/06/Rings-of-Fire-FINAL.pdf (archived at https://perma.cc/5SUV-WJZZ).

21   Setzer, Joana, and Catherine Higham. *Global Trends in Climate Change Litigation: 2024 Snapshot*, Grantham Research Institute on Climate Change and the Environment, London School of Economics and Political Science, 2024, lse.ac.uk/granthaminstitute/wp-content/uploads/2024/06/Global-trends-in-climate-change-litigation-2024-snapshot.pdf (archived at https://perma.cc/V7QS-3XW8).

22 UN OHCHR. '"This Is about Our Human Rights": U.S. Youths Win Landmark Climate Case', 29 August 2023, ohchr.org/en/stories/2023/08/about-our-human-rights-us-youths-win-landmark-climate-case (archived at https://perma.cc/YD54-C96T).

23 Clark, Lesley. 'Puerto Rico Files $1B Climate Lawsuit Against Oil Companies', *E&E News*, 16 July 2024, eenews.net/articles/puerto-rico-files-1b-climate-lawsuit-against-oil-companies (archived at https://perma.cc/C7AF-25LY).

24 Segal, Mark. 'CEOs are Deprioritizing Sustainability as It Becomes More Important to Consumers, Corporate Buyers: Bain Survey', *ESG Today*, 10 September 2024, esgtoday.com/ceos-are-deprioritizing-sustainability-as-it-becomes-more-important-to-consumers-corporate-buyers-bain-survey (archived at https://perma.cc/W83X-R3FE).

25 Segal, Mark. 'Only 22% of CFOs Are Ready for Climate Reporting and Assurance Requirements: Accenture Survey', *ESG Today*, 2 July 2024, esgtoday.com/only-22-of-cfos-are-ready-for-climate-reporting-and-assurance-requirements-accenture-survey (archived at https://perma.cc/8USU-DGFV).

26 Segal. 'Only 22% of CFOs are Ready for Climate Reporting and Assurance Requirements.

27 Blakemore, Erin. 'What is Colonialism? The Subjugation of Indigenous People – and the Exploitation of Their Land and Resources – Has a Long and Brutal History', *National Geographic*, 16 August 2024, nationalgeographic.com/culture/article/colonialism (archived at https://perma.cc/Y3J4-HQXB).

28 Encyclopedia.com. 'Gold, God, and Glory', 2 December 2024, encyclopedia.com/social-sciences/applied-and-social-sciences-magazines/gold-god-and-glory (archived at https://perma.cc/9XUD-UXCW).

29 Pierce, Natalie, and Lindsey Prowse. 'Meet the Young Leaders Driving Solutions for Nature and Climate in Davos and Beyond', World Economic Forum, 25 January 2024, weforum.org/stories/2024/01/global-shapers-nature-climate (archived at https://perma.cc/3ZXR-JZKS).

30 Royal Museums Greenwich. 'The Size of the British Empire: Did the Sun Never Really Set on the British Empire?', rmg.co.uk/stories/topics/size-british-empire (archived at https://perma.cc/K68W-ZDQM).

31 Mayer, Aditi. 'How Learnings from Rana Plaza Are Being Rolled out in Pakistan', *Vogue Business*, 24 April 2024, voguebusiness.com/story/sustainability/how-learnings-from-rana-plaza-are-being-rolled-out-in-pakistan (archived at https://perma.cc/26LF-CRYN).

32 Bartlett, John. 'Fast Fashion Goes to Die in the World's Largest Fog Desert', *National Geographic*, 5 March 2024, nationalgeographic.com/environment/article/chile-fashion-pollution (archived at https://perma.cc/W7PD-4U54).

33 Walker, Simon. 'The Environmental Impact of Advertising', Earth.Org, 13 March 2023, earth.org/environmental-impact-of-advertising (archived at https://perma.cc/Q9PQ-QG87).

34 Pärssinen, Matti, et al. 'Environmental Impact Assessment of Online Advertising', *Environmental Impact Assessment Review*, 2018, researchgate. net/publication/328665574_Environmental_impact_assessment_of_online_advertising (archived at https://perma.cc/JTS6-HLWS).

35 WARC. 'Global Ad Spend Outlook 2024/25', WARC Media, 2024, page.warc. com/global-ad-spend-outlook-2024-25.html?utm_campaign=global-ad-spend-outlook&utm_medium=social&utm_source=linkedin&utm_content=nocontent &utm_term=noterm (archived at https://perma.cc/2EER-TK9G).

36 Morency, Christopher. 'A Brutally Honest Conversation on Black Friday Consumerism', Highsnobiety, 2021, highsnobiety.com/p/black-friday-consumerism-roundtable (archived at https://perma.cc/85JV-CW8G).

37 Miu Miu. 'Miu Miu Upcycled', miumiu.com/gb/en/collections/miu-miu-upcycled/c/10515EU (archived at https://perma.cc/U4ES-NM9H).

38 Shoaib, Maliha. 'Miu Miu Sales Spike 105% as Prada Group Bucks Slowdown', *Vogue Business*, Vogue Business, 30 Oct. 2024, www. voguebusiness.com/story/companies/miu-miu-sales-spike-105-as-prada-group-bucks-slowdown (archived at https://perma.cc/LS7D-PJGL). Accessed 16 Dec. 2024.

39 Corner, Adam. 'Act 1.5: Inside Massive Attack's Bristol Blueprint for the Future of Sustainable Live Music', *NME*, 29 August 2024, nme.com/features/music-features/massive-attack-act-1-5-sustainable-live-music-3788505 (archived at https://perma.cc/KD8K-EMT3).

40 Jones, Chris, et al. *Super-Low Carbon Live Music: A Roadmap for the UK Live Music Sector to Play Its Part in Tackling the Climate Crisis*, Tyndall Centre, University of Manchester, 2021, documents.manchester.ac.uk/display. aspx?DocID=56701 (archived at https://perma.cc/546D-4VM4).

41 Potato Head. 'Potato Head Bali Sustainability Practices', seminyak.potatohead. co/regenerate (archived at https://perma.cc/3GEM-ASFA).

42 Ganni. *2023 Ganni Responsibility Report: The 2025 Vision*, ganni.com/en-es/ responsibility/2023-report-2025-vision.html (archived at https://perma.cc/ HKU9-ZZT6).

10

The future of privacy

Brand responsibilities in data ethics

The Privacy clause or Article 12 of the 1948 *Universal Declaration of Human Rights* states: 'No one shall be subjected to arbitrary interference with his privacy, family, home or correspondence, nor to attacks upon his honour and reputation. Everyone has the right to the protection of the law against such interference or attacks.'[1]

The necessity for privacy became apparent with Web2 and Big Tech dominating our lives. Privacy is even more relevant in today's digital age, as our online lives mean that our behaviours and movements are easily collected, tracked and used – sometimes with our knowledge, sometimes with our permission, and, up until what feels like quite recently, usually not. Lack of data protection can mean susceptibility to hacking. This then increases the probability of people's identity being stolen, people being scammed, phished, bullied online and even geolocated in real life.

Privacy importantly protects us from being controlled, discriminated against or manipulated by those who have access to our personal information. We see this through feed algorithms serving us, at best, perfectly selected personalized content and a system that opens us up to new and like-minded communities, or, at worst, feeding our consumer addiction, sharing mis- and disinformation, and delivering echo chambers and conspiracy theories, some of which I highlighted in Chapter 7. Additionally, there is surveillance capitalism – a term used by Shoshana Zuboff to describe how privacy is not private, amid the delusions we had around free services like search and social, and that we did not realize that we (or at least our personal data) were the commodity. Her words from a 2020 *New York Times* article have stayed with me.[2] She highlights that, while we think we use search engines, they search us; while we think we use social media to connect, we are learning that the connection is how social media uses us.

The cookie crumbles

Businesses traditionally collected consumer data from different sources – first (1P), second (2P) and third (3P) parties – in order to understand their consumers better, provide better CX (as outlined in Chapter 6), and, importantly, to be able to target them with brand updates, new products and more. First-party data is the most valuable as it is from a brand's own consumers or those specifically interested in the brand, collected through its own activities, such as from the website, social media and subscriptions, and usually stored on a variety of CRM tools and the like. Second-party data is bought through trusted partners with the objective to share audience insights; in other words, sharing both companies' 1P data, such as a hotel booking site and a hotel group. Third-party data is collected by businesses with no connection to your company or even your industry. For 20th-century businesses obsessed with mass reach, 3P data is the most interesting as an opportunity to reach new and potential consumers. But, a word of warning, both 2P and 3P data are extremely varied in quality (and consent) and limited by the browser or website they are attached to, and they can be blocked or deleted.

Data is collected through cookies – a weird name for it to be sure. Created in the early 1990s, when the internet was in its infancy (Web1), cookies had a clear objective: to enable browsers to remember basic actions like putting things in your basket or login details. Early in the 21st century, following the first banner ad in 1994, and specifically in 2012, things changed.[3] Apple introduced its IDFA – like a cookie for devices, created for targeting and evaluating advertising – which has now been updated so users can consent to be tracked. Then tracking pixels (sometimes known as spy pixels) went one step further – a tiny piece of code created to work seamlessly across various platforms and devices that can be embedded in websites, emails and digital ads, traditionally used for hyper-targeting. Because this tracking is unobtrusive, it can also feel sneaky and can cause a loss of consumer trust.

Updated privacy laws

These types of actions by Big Tech drove the rise of digital marketing, with 3P cookies changing the game for marketers, allowing advertisers to track users' browsing habits and target them with ads. Fast forward and we have seen an explosion of conversations around privacy, especially as it pertained to data used for advertising targeting. In the EU, this intrusive activity resulted in the 2003 e-Privacy Directive, created to regulate cookies and deliver greater privacy by ensuring users had to opt-in to cookie usage.[4] So, when we do knowingly share our data by giving consent, we want to ensure that it is kept as private as possible. Unfortunately, misuse of data and the conditions and opaqueness of consent haven't lessened privacy concerns, meaning consumers increasingly want privacy and protection around their personal data. That early ePD has been updated in line with our digital usage and new platforms, and the basis for EU-wide regulations, like GDPR in 2018, which was about getting explicit consent *before* adding cookies to a user's browser – different from implied consent just because a person once bought something from your website. This also meant that businesses had to show their privacy policies on their website and enabled users to remove cookies. Becoming GDPR compliant was a huge but necessary undertaking for all businesses. I remember it well when I was at Diageo.

So, it was big news when Google announced in 2020 that it would remove all 3P cookies from its Chrome browser by 2022. As the leader in search, these plans were delayed and delayed, mainly due to push-back from the advertising industry and regulators. By 2024, it had made a complete U-turn, eventually evolving its Privacy Sandbox.[5] This aims to use technologies that both protect people's online privacy and give companies and developers tools to build thriving digital businesses by reducing cross-site and cross-app tracking while helping to keep online content and services free for all. It appeared to be a win for users and businesses. Unfortunately, according to *The Drum*,[6] the Competition and Markets Authority – the UK's anti-trust enforcer – had flagged 39 unique concerns in January 2024, upped to 79 by July, and also found research indicating that Google's Privacy Sandbox terms might, in fact, *violate* privacy laws.[7] In August 2024, Google's search engine was declared an illegal monopoly,[8] a significant victory for US regulators, and, in September 2024, the US Department of Justice brought the tech giant back to federal court, accusing it of controlling the majority of online advertising.

The outcomes of these cases could change the internet as we know it. For brands, there could be a massive impact on the online ad space, as well as setting a precedent for future anti-trust cases in Big Tech.

The value exchange

Preparation for the demise of the 3P cookie, and the 2020 announcement, have increased privacy concerns by consumers and resulted in less personal information shared. Meanwhile, in the walled garden ecosystems of retail media, social media, search and even music apps, savvy, culture-led brands would have been exploring alternative targeting, such as contextual advertising that places ads depending on the content rather than the user or shoring up their 1P and zero-party data strategies. Different from 1P data, zero-party data is information *willingly* given to businesses, as opposed to the data being collected through cookies, even if that is 1P through owned channels. To get that extremely valuable zero-party data, brand activities and experiences need to be so valuable that audiences *want* to share their data, meaning brands need to build real, trusted relationships with their consumers, which hopefully drives towards those sought-after loyalty and brand-prompts in an AI-powered world.

PETER SEMPLE

The evolution of digital in our worlds made everyone addicted to digital tracking and digital visibility and digital footprint, all the rest of it, and that eroded some focus on brand and cultural intention. Then you have these grand shifts like privacy effectively removing all of the consistency of digital visibility, and then everyone's leaning back on brand.

It sounds very similar to how brands need to engage fan culture through cultural intelligence, covered in detail in Chapters 4 and 5 respectively. A successful exchange ensures activities have privacy as part of data collection and through its whole life cycle, not as an afterthought. Loyalty programmes are easy methods for this important value exchange – brands get quality zero- and first-party data, enabling consumers to receive personalized and enhanced customer experience. Privacy-first activity is where new-generation loyalty activities can really shine, but it doesn't have to stop there. Take the IKEA Place app, which allows customers to use AR technology to virtually place IKEA furniture in their own homes, and with it a jargon-free privacy policy, designed to protect user privacy and data, and to enable users to control their personal information.[9] When, as a business, you do process personal information, it should be the minimum amount needed for your purpose, kept for the minimum time needed for that purpose and be as up to date and accurate as possible.

In a world where consumers expect personalization, and businesses need personal information to deliver that personalization, a mix of data ethics, proprietary data and zero-party data is an exciting prospect. Without audience trust, however, this is nearly impossible. And with so much choice, trust and loyalty can definitely ensure your brand stands out.

The AI innovation paradox

More recently, the idea of proprietary data – data that is unique to a company and can be used to create a competitive advantage – is once again raising its head. This is data owned by the company but not public facing; linked to what only your brand/business can do in the world, as outlined in Chapter 2. As AI and big data converge, the race to dominate AI is on. Leading in AI has the capacity to build a country's GDP and therefore its economic power and global influence – an attractive mission for the world's superpowers. This is a problem, as mentioned in Chapter 1, because AI innovation is moving faster than the regulations, so, it will take brands self-auditing and ensuring data ethics cascades through the business as information is shared globally and across multiple platforms, internally and externally and in real time. This means that what brands (and the data subjects that intertwine and determine the innovation paradox) feel are the right trade-offs are where evolution and revolution intersect.

Consider blockchain when it comes to data protection and data ownership. While we know these terms are mainly connected to crypto, blockchain – with cloud computing and other technologies – is in essence a decentralized ledger or database that stores data off-site. This means it is not stored in one place, changing how organizations store their data. The main benefit of this is that, once a record is created, it cannot be changed or deleted because records are made up of blocks: once filled, they are sealed and connected to the previous one, making up a chain. If you have access to the blockchain, you are able to see the history of transactions. This is so useful for the technology for the digital product passports mentioned in Chapters 6 and 10, but this is also where it pushes the privacy laws against seeing anyone's personal history and GDPR's 'right to be forgotten'. Thankfully, this is being addressed with products like zero-knowledge proofs, a way to verify claims without revealing the information itself, and smart contracts, which automatically execute a contract according to a predetermined set of rules. These smart transactions are expected to reach $73,773 million by 2030.[10] Both zero-proof and smart contracts enable transparency without giving away sensitive information.

For us all, ownership of our own personal data feels like an obvious next step, and tech like blockchain and smart contracts could also mean our personal, unique identities can be encrypted and we can manage this across universal systems. Web3 is built on technologies like this and where new-generation consumers are learning a new way of living. For them, this is not about hiding their data, rather about having agency across their personal data and making their own choices about what they want to share. This generation understands the value of their personal data, especially when it comes to marketing, and these new immersive platforms are also teaching them how to monetize it instead of it simply being used for the benefit of the platforms. While NFTs may have a bad reputation, in essence they are unique digital assets, powered by blockchain, giving ownership to the creator.

So, while this challenge may feel connected only to technological advancements, brands and businesses need to understand that this is a generational movement of behaviour, mindsets and expectations, and an opportunity. As the volume and variety of data increases, amid advancing technology, data analysts will need to find ways to create actionable insights that can help solve real-world issues: healthcare innovation versus medical data privacy, fraud detection versus financial data analysis, education evolution and student performance data, the list goes on.

But that means that we must focus on the way we move forward.

Data ethics: legal and/or moral

All day, every day, we are sharing vast bits of information about ourselves via, for example, DNA testing, smart products, social media platforms, and buying habits in an increasingly cashless society. These reveal everything from our genetics to demographics to our political and moral leanings, and our biases. All this is then pooled through algorithms and now AI, and fed back to us in ways that we may still not even be aware of. We need to consider the privacy around this metadata or small bits of what seem to be harmless data that AI is trained on and then the impact on privacy as AI is implemented. Regulators will have a tough job to introduce laws around data privacy that can adapt to heavily invested technological innovations. Further, as AI becomes used in day-to-day outputs, an article in *Vogue Business* in 2024 outlines key considerations around disclosure and transparency of AI system training data. This is particularly concerning around chatbots and when content, especially that using human likenesses, has been AI generated and there is potential copyright infringement.[11] It was

interesting to read a 2024 *Raconteur* interview with a cybersecurity strategist about the concerns around human error, unknown risks and the
complexity of AI.[12] Operationally, safeguarding personal information and
addressing threats to digital privacy and bias detection need to be prioritized and addressed by everyone in the business.

Cognizant defines data ethics as 'a branch of ethics that evaluates data
practices – collecting, generating, analyzing and disseminating data, both
structured and unstructured – that have the potential to adversely impact
people and society'.[13]

Distribution of information by only a few is inherently dangerous, harking back to the historical, political and brand influence of media narratives
discussed in Chapter 1. After all, those who control the flow of information
can shape conversations, drive (in)equality and even threaten democracy –
but now, globally, in seconds. Amnesty International defines toxic algorithms
as those deliberately designed to prioritize engagement above all else, calling
out the fuelling of the UK's 2024 riots firmly at the hands of Big Tech.[14] On
the other hand, we have seen the power of social media to raise awareness
and support for issues, sustaining positive movement and mobilizing people.
A good example is the on-the-street response to racist riots in London. On
a personal level, right through my culture stacks, my posts directly from my
LinkedIn account on the night before the London riots explain:

> I immigrated to London, after being born and raised in apartheid South Africa
> precisely for the incredible mix of people. It's what makes this city feel like
> home, like I belong, where I have met the most wonderful people and made
> lifelong friends from all walks of life, where I found myself. It's where I met my
> husband, I had our child and created two businesses. Stay strong, London. Stay
> safe, friends.

The social response was incredible. Thousands gathered to protect the
streets of London in a direct response to the mass of racist posts mentioning
when and where the riots would take place. The London community exem-
plified the exact reasons I moved here. This is a great example of the climate
we are currently in. Social media made a direct call to action and the community responded.

Today, with highly developed, and still developing, information technology, there are countless horror stories of harmful content, identity theft,
fraud and online safety abuses like doxxing (when private personal information such as names and addresses is published publicly online),
harassment and cyberbullying, especially for young people. A study by
University College London and the University of Kent looked into how the

processes of social media platforms circulate and present material appealing to young men's activities and interests, and of the impact of these on individual behaviours.[15] It is concerning. *The Guardian* also covered this in detail, determining that algorithms used by social media platforms are rapidly amplifying extreme misogynistic content, which is spreading from teenagers' screens and into school playgrounds where it has become normalized.[16] The study argues that harmful content is presented as entertainment through algorithmic social media processes. Toxic, hateful or misogynistic material is 'pushed' to young people, with, for example, boys who are suffering from anxiety and poor mental health at increased risk. This is extremely worrying, particularly for the increasing gender divide mentioned in Chapter 5.

In the UK, the Online Safety Act became law in 2023, and put the onus directly onto companies to protect children from harmful content, whether legal or illegal. Where it gets tricky is on messaging platforms like WhatsApp – which are end-to-end encrypted, so the company has no access to user info – where examining encrypted messages violates existing privacy policies. In the US in 2024, Instagram rolled out 'Teen Accounts',[17] guided by parents, with built-in protections that limit who can contact them and the content they see, providing new ways for teens to explore their interests. TikTok has announced restrictions on beauty filters for users under 18 over mental health concerns.[18,19] It's the same over at Roblox, which, in November 2024, rolled out a raft of new safety features for under 13s.[20] In November 2024, Australia announced a world-first ban on social media for under 16s, stating that tech companies could be fined up to A\$50 million (£25.7 million) for non-compliance.[21] It still begs the question about whether the Australian ruling is too broad and sweeping, dismissing the positive role that social media can play for this age group and for global communities.

I do believe it is all our responsibility to clear the path for future generations, so, while these are all steps in the right direction, there is still a lot more to be done. Take wearables – as they become more normalized, the opportunity for doxxing and misuse becomes increased. This was evidenced by two Harvard students who adapted Meta's glasses as facial recognition glasses to prove privacy risks.[22] Meanwhile, in 2023, members of the Hollywood entertainment industry went on their longest strike ever, in part protesting around provisions for consent and compensation from the use of AI replicas. Still, into 2024, *Rolling Stone* magazine finds that more than a dozen SAG-AFTRA union members, many of them actors and screenwriters, find that, in particular, the creation of digital replicas are a threat to their livelihoods.[23] Thankfully for some of us, while realistic and believable deepfakes are created in minutes and credit card hackers are more advanced than ever, greater regulations of data protection are incoming, and rightly so.

Privacy by design and default

An IAPP privacy and consumer trust report in 2023, based on a survey of nearly 5,000 consumers from 19 countries, found that nearly 68 per cent said they were somewhat or very concerned about their online privacy, and only 29 per cent of consumers said it was easy to understand how well a company protects their personal data.[24] Interestingly, as AI begins to become normalized, while 57 per cent of global consumers view the use of AI in collecting and processing personal data as a significant threat to privacy, a majority of consumers preferred their data being processed by a combination of humans and computers. This is further backed up by a Pew Research report in 2023 focused on US consumers.[25] Findings include 85 per cent of Americans believe the risks of data collection by companies outweigh the benefits, and 76 per cent feel there are little to no benefits from these data processing activities. Other stats back up the increasing concerns: 67 per cent say they understand little to nothing about what companies are doing with their personal data, up from 59 per cent. They also found that 81 per cent of Americans familiar with AI believe that the information companies collect will be used in ways that people aren't comfortable with, and 80 per cent say it will be used in ways that were not originally intended.

Consumers feel unsafe.

A 2023 Deloitte article notes that 67 per cent of smartphone users worry about data security and privacy on their phones, and 62 per cent of smart-home users worry about the same on their smart-home devices – up 13 and 10 per cent, respectively, from 2022.[26] Almost half (48 per cent) of smart-watch/fitness-tracker users are concerned about data security and privacy on those devices – a jump of 8 per cent from 2022. The article suggests a number of ways consumers could protect themselves – from using two-step authentication to turning off location and Bluetooth connections, to installing security software, but 27 per cent of respondents feel that companies can track them no matter what they do, and 17 per cent feel hackers can access their data no matter what actions they take. Of particular relevance to this book is people's growing distrust of companies' 'hacking and tracking', with only half of respondents feeling that the benefits they get from online services outweigh their data privacy concerns – a drop of 9 per cent from 2021. There are other signs of eroding trust. Only 41 per cent think it has become easier to protect their online data in the past year, and a mere 34 per cent feel companies are clear about how they use the data they collect from online services. Each of those findings shows a double-digit percentage drop from 2021. Lastly, 9 per cent of respondents said they bought a device in the past year that doesn't track them. It's a small cohort, but a notable jump of 5 per cent since 2022 and potentially an incoming shift.

Privacy is connected to human rights

For Amnesty International, data protection is understood as a series of safeguards designed to protect personal information that is collected, processed and stored by 'automated' means or intended to be part of a filing system.[27] Data protection principles are rooted in an understanding of human rights principles, including international human rights standards regarding privacy, due process and remedy. Amnesty says that effective and just data protection, in any context, must align with standards of human rights. However, a lack of comprehensive and well-enforced data protection regulation around the world, as well as the powerful reach of many private actors whose business model is dependent on this data, can result in violations of the rights to privacy, non-discrimination and more.

A key area to explore is the incoming legal and regulatory changes. Take the Big Tech anti-trust cases mentioned earlier. While some are about monopoly status, they are also about the unprecedented access to our personal data by a few very influential players. A December 2024 article by Digiday outlines a number of scenarios, from the least likely being that nothing is done about it, to what it believes is probable – that platforms will need to become more transparent.[28] I think a lot depends on new governments' agendas. Digiday considers, for example, whether the areas involved need to break up and separate, and, from a privacy perspective, could they innovate and offer new services like paid tiers of data protection – a bit like paying more not to see ads – with the obvious impact on socio-economic divide, and therefore types of data.

The following questions are non-exhaustive, but, what would the impact be on your business or brand in terms of your relationships with those platforms, from access to that data and how and where you communicate to shared audiences? How would your business need to be set up in terms of both data collection and data protection? What about how the shopping journey might be disrupted or evolved again? Even with AI, how do we continue to innovate while regulations are evolving in real time, still globally fragmented? Or, let's look at privacy through your consumers' lens. In Chapter 5, I outlined a global shift towards rebalancing the use of technology, where consumers are also finding in real life the spaces to connect with their communities. Not only do we need to be aware of this happening, but how does it connect with the value exchange discussed earlier in this chapter – a clear need for consumers? Or, on the other side, do people simply understand the trade-off of privacy for convenience and personalization? From a societal perspective, as we gain a better understanding of the surveillance capitalism mentioned at the beginning of the chapter, do we all, from employees to consumers, want to own our data and manage it as we see fit? As mentioned in Chapter 5, the new generation already understands the importance of this. What does that mean for your brand or business?

As privacy becomes more and more regulated and demanded by consumers, there will be an expectation for brands and businesses to be much more transparent and responsive to users' requests to be removed, deleted or opted out of databases. Additionally, there will be added rigour around things like consent, especially when it comes to recognizable personal data, and much more business compliance around these regulations. The American Privacy Rights Act (APRA), announced in April 2024, comes into effect in 2025, putting people directly in control of their own data, enforced by the FTC and placing the responsibility directly on businesses to ensure their systems are set up to comply.[29] To mitigate risk in data-driven decision-making, embracing data ethics is one of the cornerstones of the data transition from legacy systems, ongoing data management and AI-powered business transformation outlined in Chapter 6.

Importantly, data ethics is deeply intertwined with brand ethical behaviour and a belief (and company culture) around what's right and wrong, even if legally you can get away with it. For me, this is directly linked to a brand's cultural positioning, its leadership and its audience's culture stacks, and how it acts in the cultural pipeline that it is moving along. **Remembering that your audiences are humans and not just 'data' is a good start.**

Privacy affects us all, so, brands and businesses that take their audience fears and concerns seriously, and actively do something about it, will be the ones that survive the next era. There are obviously clear benefits to data ethics. Integrity drives trust by all your audiences – internally and externally – and can deliver employee satisfaction and quality data from happy consumers that is helpful to use safely and ethically for innovation, and this can drive growth and resilience as I talk about in the next chapter. How would your brand restructure as a privacy-first model, where all activities have privacy embedded by design and default? Or, if that feels too extreme a transformation, initially identifying which parts of the business are crucial for privacy to be collaboratively and creatively embedded in, not simply an afterthought, could be a start. This culture-led approach is a key pillar in safeguarding a brand's reputation and trust (focused on in the next chapter), and builds much-needed loyalty (as outlined in Chapter 5). For me, this is directly linked to company culture and its leadership, as part of an audited and standard cross-departmental operational process, not an afterthought. This and legal compliance lead to strong brand reputation. Together, as we know, they enable relevance and loyalty – both internally and externally – also directly linked to positive growth.

Privacy is about personal choice and sharing information about ourselves on our own terms, enabling us to enjoy other rights and freedoms, connected deeply into the culture stacks, and extremely important in our AI-powered future. The importance of privacy cannot be overstated and is directly related to the value of your brand in the world we live in. Just one data breach or mishandling of personal data can be the downfall of your business. The need to build trust with audiences and promote transparency and fairness mean that robust and integrated data privacy and protection will become a distinct competitive business advantage.

Notes

1   United Nations. *Universal Declaration of Human Rights*, un.org/en/about-us/universal-declaration-of-human-rights#:~:text=Article%2012,against%20such%20interference%20or%20attacks (archived at https://perma.cc/66WN-D7GX)

2   Zuboff, Shoshana. 'You Are Now Remotely Controlled: Surveillance Capitalists Control the Science and the Scientists, the Secrets and the Truth', *The New York Times*, 24 January 2020, nytimes.com/2020/01/24/opinion/sunday/surveillance-capitalism.html (archived at https://perma.cc/5V93-QPRK)

3   Digiday. '"The Beginning of a Giant Industry": An Oral History of the First Banner Ad', 8 November 2017, digiday.com/media/history-of-the-banner-ad (archived at https://perma.cc/57AK-WH84)

4   Legislation.gov.uk. 'The Privacy and Electronic Communications (EC Directive) Regulations 2003', legislation.gov.uk/ uksi /2003/2426 (archived at https://perma.cc/HU4Y-5YVN)

5   Privacy Sandbox. 'Protecting Your Privacy Online', Google, 2024, privacysandbox. com/intl/en_us (archived at https://perma.cc/742G-B8SN)

6   Barnett, Kendra. 'In Shock Decision, Google Abandons Third-Party Cookie Deprecation Plans', *The Drum*, 22 July 2024, thedrum.com/news/2024/07/22/ shock-decision-google-abandons-third-party-cookie-deprecation-plans (archived at https://perma.cc/468H-HJCP)

7   Barnett, Kendra. 'Google's Privacy Sandbox Terms May, Ironically, Violate Privacy Law, New Research Says', *The Drum*, 15 July 2024, thedrum.com/ news/2024/07/15/google-s-privacy-sandbox-terms-may-ironically-violate-privacy-law-new-research-says (archived at https://perma.cc/UM5L-QBUT)

8   CourtListener. *Case 1:20-Cv-03010-APM*, 5 August 2024, storage.courtlistener. com/recap/gov.uscourts.dcd.223205/gov.uscourts.dcd.223205.1033.0_2.pdf (archived at https://perma.cc/SBS2-FQ9W)

9   IKEA. 'IKEA Place Data Privacy Policy', 1 April 2023, ikea.com/global/en/ privacy/apps/ikea-place/data-privacy-policy/#:~:text=1.,you%20have%20 questions%20or%20requests (archived at https://perma.cc/NN7Q-V682)

10   Grand View Research. 'Smart Contracts Market to Reach $73,773.0 Million by 2030', May 2023, grandviewresearch.com/press-release/global-smart-contracts-market (archived at https://perma.cc/ERC3-L6VT)

11   McDowell, Maghan. 'Four Things Brands Should Consider When Developing AI Protocols', *Vogue Business*, 14 October 2024, voguebusiness.com/story/ technology/four-things-brands-should-consider-when-developing-ai-protocols (archived at https://perma.cc/DS2L-7VKS)

12   Bithell, Laura. 'Supporting the CISO: Building an Organisation of Cybersecurity Champions', *Raconteur*, 29 July 2024, raconteur.net/cybersecurity/building-an-organisation-of-cybersecurity-champions (archived at https://perma.cc/ LQH7-RWFW)

13   Cognizant. 'Data Ethics, What is Data Ethics?', cognizant.com/us/en/glossary/ data-ethics#:~:text=Data%20ethics%20is%20a%20branch,Data%20 privacy%20compliance (archived at https://perma.cc/X2WD-AADP)

14   Amnesty International. 'UK: Big Tech Platforms Play an Active Role in Fuelling Racist Violence', 6 August 2024, amnesty.org/en/latest/news/2024/08/uk-big-tech-platforms-play-an-active-role-in-fuelling-racist-violence (archived at https://perma.cc/4M8G-LG8P)

15   Regehr, Kaitlyn, et al. *Safer Scrolling: How Algorithms Popularise and Gamify Online Hate and Misogyny for Young People*, UCL / University of Kent, January 2024, ascl.org.uk/ASCL/media/ASCL/Help%20and%20advice/ Inclusion/Safer-scrolling.pdf (archived at https://perma.cc/H2QT-JHRQ)

16   Weale, Sally. 'Social Media Algorithms "Amplifying Misogynistic Content"', *The Guardian*, 6 February 2024, theguardian.com/media/2024/feb/06/ social-media-algorithms-amplifying-misogynistic-content (archived at https:// perma.cc/3WMZ-7DYD)

17 Instagram. 'Introducing Instagram Teen Accounts: Built-In Protections for Teens, Peace of Mind for Parents', Instagram Blog, 17 September 2024, about.fb.com/news/2024/09/instagram-teen-accounts/ (archived at https://perma.cc/22F7-TZYK)

18 Business of Fashion. 'TikTok to Block Teenagers from Beauty Filters Over Mental Health Concerns', *The Business of Fashion*, 27 November 2024, businessoffashion.com/articles/technology/tiktok-to-block-teenagers-from-beauty-filters-over-mental-health-concerns (archived at https://perma.cc/3NVE-JVJH)

19 Boseley, Matilda. 'Is That Really Me? The Ugly Truth about Beauty Filters', *The Guardian*, 1 January 2022, theguardian.com/lifeandstyle/2022/jan/02/is-that-really-me-the-ugly-truth-about-beauty-filters (archived at https://perma.cc/P9H6-5D3P)

20 Chalk, Andy. 'Roblox Adds New Rules for Players Under 13 Following Scathing Child Safety Report', *PC Gamer*, 18 November 2024, pcgamer.com/software/platforms/roblox-adds-new-rules-for-players-under-13-following-scathing-child-safety-report (archived at https://perma.cc/9SRG-N5WZ)

21 Ritchie, Hannah. 'Australia Approves Social Media Ban on Under-16s', BBC News, 28 November 2024, bbc.co.uk/news/articles/c89vjj0lxx9o (archived at https://perma.cc/8VC3-NPLZ)

22 Carroll, Mickey. 'Students Adapt Meta's Smart Glasses to Dox Strangers in Real Time', Sky News, 3 October 2024, news.sky.com/story/students-adapt-metas-smart-glasses-to-dox-strangers-in-real-time-13227034 (archived at https://perma.cc/ZG2B-QS6H)

23 Richardson, Kalia. 'One Year After the Actors' Strike, AI Remains a Persistent Threat', *Rolling Stone*, 14 July 2024, rollingstone.com/tv-movies/tv-movie-features/actors-strike-sag-aftra-ai-one-year-later-1235059882 (archived at https://perma.cc/MWA4-43UA)

24 Fazlioglu, Müge. *Privacy and Consumer Trust*, IAAP, 2023, iapp.org/media/pdf/resource_center/privacy_and_consumer_trust_report_summary.pdf (archived at https://perma.cc/3HTL-LKGT)

25 McClain, Colleen, et al. 'How Americans View Data Privacy', Pew Research Center, 18 October 2023, pewresearch.org/internet/2023/10/18/how-americans-view-data-privacy (archived at https://perma.cc/G8EW-39CZ)

26 Arbanas, Jana, et al. 'Data Privacy and Security Worries Are on the Rise, While Trust Is Down', *Deloitte Insights*, 6 November 2023, deloitte.com/us/en/insights/industry/telecommunications/connectivity-mobile-trends-survey/2023/data-privacy-and-security.html (archived at https://perma.cc/J7UM-YZ99)

27 Amnesty International. 'Briefing: Gender and Human Rights in the Digital Age', 10 July 2024, amnesty.org/en/documents/pol40/8170/2024/en (archived at https://perma.cc/2S8Q-HRRG)

28 Shields, Ronan, and Seb Joseph. 'Assessing the Fallout of Google's Ad Tech
    Antitrust Trial', *Digiday*, 2 December 2024, digiday.com/media/assessing-
    the-fallout-of-googles-ad-tech-antitrust-trial/?utm_medium=email&utm_
    campaign=digidaydis&utm_source=daily&utm_content=241202 (archived at
    https://perma.cc/CD2C-7K6U)

29 Committee of Energy & Commerce. 'Committee Chairs Rodgers, Cantwell
    Unveil Historic Draft Comprehensive Data Privacy Legislation', 7 April 2024,
    energycommerce.house.gov/posts/committee-chairs-rodgers-cantwell-unveil-
    historic-draft-comprehensive-data-privacy-legislation (archived at https://
    perma.cc/LAJ5-2XSD)

11

Anticipating crisis

Proactive measures for brand resilience

My mum has always said that the only guarantee in life is change. I am always ready with a Plan B, C and D. I have always practised the skill to rapidly flex and adapt when unexpected things happen or my circumstances change. This early-learning system has been foundational in the way I live my life and the decisions I make.

Brands need to build resilience to inevitable but unpredictable and unprecedented change in this transformational era, where the only certainty is uncertainty. Take a moment to consider some of the real-world drivers and cultural shifts, and how your audience's behaviours have been impacted by them, in just a few years: world changing geopolitical tensions – about to be ramped up over the next few years – awareness of toxic algorithms and the regulations coming in thick and fast, the rise of privacy when it comes to data, the impact of social justice issues as the Global South's inequalities and injustices continue to be live-streamed driving a new generation of global activism, the beyond-urgent climate emergency, the rise of dis- and misinformation and conspiracy theories, and AI. Simultaneously, we are gaining a better and deeper understanding of how businesses affect and are affected by these, which are becoming more and more widely protested against or justified by brand audiences.

Today, brand resilience not only anticipates, but withstands, responds to and, importantly, bounces back and recovers from difficulties. It adapts with the challenges and, ultimately, creates new opportunities and innovations to be relevant and thrive in a variety of never-before-seen overlapping and intersecting scenarios. A resilient brand does this again and again. Resilience as a practice is not static because the world and people are not static.

MICHELLE LAVIPOUR

In terms of crisis management, there's a lot of steps people can take, and there's a lot of preparation you can do. So, people shouldn't feel unempowered in a fast-moving, issue-rich environment. I think the obvious place to start is mapping all the potential issues or scenarios that could impact your business and brand. There are always going to be things that happen that you can't predict, but there will be others you might be able to plan for. Your team will probably be able to brainstorm what the majority of them are, but then I think it's about going out to people in the business who work in all sorts of different roles and ask them, 'What keeps you up at night? What are you worried about? What are you hearing from customers and from consumers that we should be thinking about and working to get good visibility of? What are those areas?' Simulations and practising scenarios are a crucial part of preparedness.

In the Introduction to this book, I outlined my belief that brands are judged through their response to the impacts of all these cultural issues and challenges on our full culture stacks. In Chapters 8 and 9, I presented my thoughts on the importance of DEI and the climate crisis on business impact. Chapter 5 covered how I would approach consumer insights and Chapter 7 focused on the power of cultural voices. This mix of relevant cultural intelligence can ensure your brand, products, services and organization are fit for purpose today and tomorrow by addressing your most pressing business and brand critical challenges, in the face of these generational shifts. Tapping into AI models can help unlock insights that you may have missed, surface unexplored breakthrough-thinking and inspire new, un-thought-of ideas and innovation, enabling new, enhanced or evolved offers fit for purpose today and tomorrow. The right intelligence not only informs your cultural positioning, it continually feeds it.

Done right, cultural relevance will foster curiosity of what is happening in the world and the credible role that brand has to play in it, encourage creative new ways of working and driving innovative ideas and updating processes and systems to be fit for purpose in the 21st century. And it happens because your cultural positioning acts as the filter to ensure your messaging is consistent and recognizable, rooted in the brand even if your product looks unexpected, if you are a global brand dealing with a market crisis and/or have content shared across multiple channels in multiple formats. This can help build resilience against decision paralysis and concerns around call-out culture and achieve resonance by credibly engaging with existing, latent and employee communities and consumers.

Reputation as the business backbone

Consumers and employees are sceptical after what seems like a deprioritization of brand promises and pledges since 2020, and there is an understandable fear of backlash in the face of corporate allyship. In 2023, *Raconteur* interviewed global business leaders about how to respond in today's polarized landscapes.[1] No one had an exact answer. There were views on ensuring that personal opinions should not impact business decisions, but, of course, these do, especially where unconscious bias and stereotypes come into play. Some suggested that a way to ensure those cultural mishaps don't occur in the first place is to be transparent about how the business is transforming, with corporate communications and narrative going beyond investors and shareholders, and championing diversity and inclusivity overall. Other views included making decisions only rooted in your area of expertise and credibility: your brand values. It was noted too that sometimes there are bigger issues that businesses should not stay silent about, where there is a societal red line and a responsibility for businesses to speak up, for example hate crimes or the climate emergency.

ETE DAVIES

I don't know if anyone truly trusts brands. That's why you've got to engage with community and culture. Brands have to start from a point of values and authenticity. So, what do their values say about how they want to exist in the world and how they want to service their customers and to be absolutely true to that? And if the truth of that is about the environment, or equality, then they have to stand by those things, and take positions that might make them unpopular with a potential market segment or customer profile. But, this means that they're building and growing customers more aligned with their values, who are ultimately more likely to be loyal, more likely to be advocates, and ultimately provide them with better long-term growth.

Back in the day, if there was an issue that could damage a brand's reputation, the corporate comms department would spring into action. This was at a time when damage limitation was the objective and it was easier to control the narrative and influence through traditional gatekeepers like the media and politics, as I talk about in Chapter 1. We only knew what the brand wanted us to know. In other words, we were receivers of 'brand out' information, whether we were consumers or employees. It was easier for a brand to maintain and build its reputation by simply reacting to the issue. It worked because we felt reassured by the familiar or at least those we 'trusted'. This enabled big brands and businesses to thrive, no matter the crisis.

Fast forward to today and this monopolistic power and way of working seems to have parallels with the recent anti-trust cases in Big Tech – this time connected to people's data and the related implications. This back-and-forth debate by anti-trust critics and advocates rumbles on, affecting all of us. The digital and technological advances of the early 1990s opened brands up to closer scrutiny by us and, importantly, their consumers, shifting some power from the company to consumers. It was uncharted territory before the climate emergency and Covid pandemic exposed brands' and businesses' inner workings (and lack of ability to flex and adapt to this 'new normal'). This inflection point supercharged and redefined how a brand needs to build resilience. It is no longer only the impact on consumers that organizations need to be concerned about. Employees also expect their companies to take a stand on global issues and decisive action on environmental or social issues. So, the power has evolved to include employees and wider society as key audiences for a brand, directly linked to culture stacks. Today, that reputation can no longer be controlled from a brand-out perspective – it has to be earned by and through all your audiences.

In a world where reputation and trust are inextricably linked, transparency, over the traditional brand-out, risk-management, damage-control narrative, is crucial. This is a key pillar in both withstanding and responding to expected and unexpected crises. In Chapter 5, I dug into my version of cultural intelligence – real time, real world and ongoing. I explained why 21st-century brands need to go beyond the traditional demographics to understand audience behaviour and their needs, to make the brand, its activities and product or services relevant to them and society at large. This intel, filtered through your cultural positioning, is key to informing and feeding internal knowledge and can help in making decisions in service of earning that all-important reputation. After all, this is the translation of your brand DNA and values relevant for all your audiences today (and tomorrow), reflecting the shift from 'brand out' and 'consumer in' to 'culture led'.

Live the brand values

As purpose-driven millennials reach senior leadership, Gen Z enter the workforce and Gen Alpha/Beta become incoming consumers, these tech-enabled generations expect their organizations to align with their values and push things forward. Both millennials and Gen Z are vocal about this, using their collective power across channels and platforms. They prioritize well-being, ESG, transparency and inclusivity over pure profit, while AI-fluent and unfiltered Gen Z, already entrepreneurial in thinking, have an innate knowledge of how to navigate uncertainty and ongoing change. That means attracting and retaining talent are as important as each other, with employee engagement key to nurturing resilience and HR shifting from an executional function to a strategic one.

In a 2025 outlook on HR, Gartner found that only 15 per cent of organizations currently practise strategic workforce planning,[2] highlighting inconsistent and non-scalable processes that limit HR's capacity to plan for and respond to changing circumstances (competitor moves, M&A, recession, pandemics and so on) and its ability to align with business-critical initiatives. To be a resilient brand or business, an inclusive and resilient workforce – whether in office, remote or hybrid – is your greatest asset. In times of crisis, your colleagues are the creative trouble-shooters, adaptable and agile as they pivot, and, in the longer term, if they can manage stress better and be more productive, they drive innovation. Business transformation is driving an evolution of hiring practices, as I showed in Chapter 6, with change management itself driven by the people within the business. I showed how inclusivity is underpinned by the long-overdue diversification of the C-suite in Chapter 3 and the cultural agility discussed in Chapter 2.

JAMIE GILL

If you want to make a commitment to be more inclusive, to be more diverse, you will reap the benefits as an organization both in reputation terms and in bringing your workforce together on the journey with you and attracting new talent. To set an agenda, to have a strategy and to be clear about it, is only going to be seen as positive. The reality is that the only risk the brand might perceive is whether they truly want to commit to this and are they prepared to put in the necessary work and investment. If it's not done properly, that's where the reputational risk is. An inauthentic strategy, without the commitment from leadership, won't deliver the results, and, if we're saying it publicly, we have to deliver updates. There's no downside of having a public, committed, clear strategy to benefit from a more diverse, inclusive team, to make your business more commercially viable. There is no harm, it will only enhance, and it will only give cultural gravitas. Kudos to new people wanting to work for the organization that stands for those brand values. And you will only benefit from all the positive business case studies that we've been discussing for years.

SARAH WATSON

My whole work is getting in touch with your deeper self, with who you are, because, once you're coming from that place, you can have any conversation. When you're out of yourself, you're a headless chicken. You can't do it. Humans are built for change, we're built for complexity, but we have to access that deep, stable part of ourselves. And if we're dysregulated and off-kilter, we can't do it. So, a lot of my work with leaders is getting to taste yourself, getting to taste who you really are, which is completely different from anyone else. If you can get into that mode, then you can lead from that place and it's really powerful.

To be a truly inclusive organization, employee wellbeing is directly linked to resilience, and vice versa. And that goes beyond the employee wellness traditionally connected to physical health and manifests in benefits like health insurance and subsidized gym membership. Gallup defines wellbeing as the broader holistic dimensions of a well-lived life,[3] finding five elements that employers need to take into account: career wellbeing or liking what you do every day; social wellbeing or having meaningful friendships in your life; financial wellbeing, meaning you manage your money well; physical wellbeing, meaning you have energy to get things done; and community wellbeing, meaning you like where you live. In another report, Gallup finds that the impact of wellbeing extends far beyond how people feel.[4] For businesses, it affects the number of sick days employees take, their job performance, burnout and the likelihood of leaving your organization.

Today, customized wellbeing policies feel even more relevant – after all the needs of someone going through the menopause are different from someone becoming a parent. Importantly, we should also talk about reactive wellbeing. This means seeing the workforce as humans first, impacted by their culture stacks as momentous – and perhaps traumatizing – personal and global events occur in real time. A trauma can manifest in a number of different ways, and companies, leaders and HR practitioners, who themselves may be impacted, need to approach employees and be approached with care. Personal trauma can include the death of a loved one, injury, divorce and financial worries associated with an event like a natural disaster. Company-wide trauma could include a cyber-attack. Global events, especially when polarizing and when connected to your inherited culture, can impact people profoundly, including with heightened anxiety and burnout. While these may all be opportunities to build resilience, how this is done in the workplace needs empathetic consideration – this in itself drives resilience as it establishes the brand and business in the 21st century.

Embrace change

As we establish ourselves in Industry 4.0, becoming more efficient and productive through the use of technology and connectivity; and evolve into Industry 5.0, focused on human–machine collaboration, new ways of working, a new and different skillset will be needed, and novel decisions will have to be made. What is sure is that brand resilience stems from leadership decision-making.

KEITH CHENG

There are two ideas that act together. First of all is to build up a 'change is inevitable' attitude to the employees, to ensure no setbacks whenever the team faces challenges from the market situation. And to push further, we also teach the employees to 'welcome changes', and to 'look for changes', because using the old way cannot solve the new problems. Change is the only way to improve the brand and the employee. However, we are also very mindful that changes should happen following the overall brand positioning, and can happen if it serves well for the core consumer groups.

Resilient leadership is rooted in proactive persistence, a never-give-up optimistic attitude and the will to move things forward, especially in the face of adversity. Could this be a new type of role in leadership teams built from a mix of legal, comms (corporate and consumer), operations and HR functions? Or, should every leader (and every department) have resilience capability training? For me, both would be ideal. This mindset accepts change as inevitable and is comfortable with uncertainty. This type of leadership harnesses these as potential and opportunity to drive positive growth – personally and professionally. Importantly, this type of leadership fosters adaptability, empathy and curiosity and bakes resilience in through the whole business by prioritizing cultural agility, inclusivity and new approaches to transformation.

Cyber resilience at the forefront

Like brand resilience, cyber resilience is also affected by interconnected impacts of global movements – driven by social, political, environmental and technological changes. Initially, a bit like past-era corporate comms, cyber security felt more reactive; today a business needs to be cyber resilient as a basic need for survival. In Chapter 10, I mentioned that all it would take is just one privacy breach for consumer trust to be lost. There is a clear link to brand reputation from brand resilience.

MICHELLE LAVIPOUR

The reality of managing an issue or crisis is that it's a high-pressure time. There's lots of demands on the team, and you need to go into these periods with a team who feel confident to manage whatever is thrown at them. And that requires practice and giving people a safe environment to try things out, test, learn and fail before a real situation arises. And I think one thing that's really important about preparing and practising is it can't just be the comms team that does it. You have to involve cross-functional teams, and you have to involve people at all levels of the business, because you'll require the mobilization of lots of different people and lots of different functions when you're in a real issue or crisis situation.

Sometimes these issues are not malicious. That doesn't mean the impact on trust is less.

Remember the 2024 Microsoft outage. Tough as it was, the response by Crowdstrike, the company responsible, was heartfelt and empathetic, but, as mentioned earlier, it's the post-crisis work that matters. As new technologies accelerate, so do newer security vulnerabilities – both inside business and outwardly to the supply chain and consumers. The connectedness of today's organizations means that, like privacy, brand resilience must take a proactive, over preventative, approach, moving beyond only the IT department to converge with any and all operational technology (OT).

Brands that get privacy right are the ones that will win.

The route is clear: when a brand earns trust, it creates a relationship where consumers willingly share their data. That is a privilege, not a right. When done ethically, it's also an opportunity. Ethical data practices allow you to monetize that trust in a way that feels authentic and fair. But it all starts with earning that trust. Without it, you can't collect the data you need to break out of your category and drive relevance. In a world where competitive advantage is increasingly tied to advantaged data, those who approach it responsibly and transparently will come out on top. Trust isn't just a nice-to-have; it's the new currency of growth.

Respond, don't react to a crisis

In the past, where known financial risk felt like the main focus of corporate crises, today a variety of challenges and difficulties can occur globally within minutes. A crisis can be created by an internal situation – something the organization has done, like a non-compliant product, an angry consumer or an employee that shares online, or it could stem from an external situation, like a natural disaster. The worst is where these overlap, as described at the beginning of this chapter.

How a business responds is the key, not least because your audiences are watching.

MICHELLE LAVIPOUR

My view is that the starting point for communications leaders is reflecting on what role the business or brand plays in the lives of consumers and asking whether the brand or business has the right and credibility to show up in a space, and what value the brand or business can add. But I think that, of course, there are going to be scenarios where brands have a legitimate perspective to add, but brands need to really scrutinize whether they have a right to step into a discussion. It's important to ask some big questions: Are we adding value here? Is this just something we're saying, or is it something we're doing? Are we comfortable with our record in this space? If not, what are we going to do about it? If we are, but there's some stuff we're worried about, are we being sufficiently transparent?

Audiences remember how crises are handled and view the brand accordingly. The traditional strategies of the corporate comms department calling a press conference or issuing a press release outlining legal compliance no longer works. Today, it's also important to balance the speed of response – too fast or too slow could make the perception worse. Additionally, for me, I feel like it is no longer possible for one department, like corporate comms, to be responsible for brand crisis management. Capabilities must be embedded through the business, with response strategies built into cross-functional collaborative teams as we aim to move beyond the silos and towards an AI-powered future. When that crisis hits, ensure you move fast to get the facts, verifying and assessing them from the perspective of *all* your audiences – employees and suppliers, consumers and customers, stakeholders and investors and society at large, proceeding to make a plan of prioritized communication to and with these audiences. Simultaneously, make sure to issue some type of initial public acknowledgement, all the while using real-time monitoring online and across social media. This may even help in surfacing what must be addressed in the final response. Once you understand what has happened, own your role in it, take accountability, apologize if necessary and also have clear solutions and next steps.

Transparency is both the input and output.

Importantly, the post-crisis work is to take learnings, identify bubbling and future weak spots through real-time intelligence and try to reduce the future risk by creating end-to-end processes ready to respond to the next inevitable shock. This is also where AI can help through real-time tracking of social media and rising news stories, alerting the team about potentially incoming situations to tackle or plan for.

MICHELLE LAVIPOUR

When it comes to social listening, being equipped to interpret the huge amount of data you get back is just as important as having lots of information. It's important to identify what's worth listening to and taking into account, and what is just noise. I often like to think about social media being like a football match. If you're watching the game and someone 10 rows behind you starts shouting at you, you're probably not going to turn around and answer them. But, if someone next to you taps you on the shoulder and says, 'What about this?', you'll probably have a conversation about whatever it is. When it comes to identifying who you should really listen to, often the best are the people at the front line of your business and brands who are closest to your consumers. So, whether that's your customer service team, if you're a retail business, the people on the shop front of your store, people in your supply chain, I think those are the people that you need to have really honest conversations with about how we are being seen, what feedback we are getting from consumers or stakeholders, and have a culture which allows real openness. I think that's probably your strongest line of defence for detecting any issues.

Plan for multiple futures

In an uncertain world, businesses have to place their bets in places and spaces that involve significant risk, with no certainty of the ideal outcome. So, managing that risk and future-proofing a brand in the traditional ways has never been more difficult. The outcome of this is that businesses are super-focused on short-term wins, nervous of predicting too far in the future. And who can blame them?

The concept of the Futures Cone first emerged publicly in 1988, introduced by Charles Taylor in *Alternative World Scenarios for Strategic Planning*.[5] Taylor used the concept to map out geopolitical scenarios, providing a framework for strategic foresight. Since then, futurists like Trevor Hancock, Clement Bezold and Joseph Voros have adapted and modernized the cone,[6] creating simplified versions of alternative futures that continue to shape how industry thinks about future possibilities and planning. This, as with any future planning, has its limitations, but is the most used framework for brands and businesses to have some type of structure to explore what's possible – as far and wild as your imagination can go. It explores what's plausible; in other words, what could realistically happen based on current knowledge, what's probable or likely to happen if we follow a linear path from where we are today, and what's preferred, which is what you or your team actually want to happen. The latter is subjective and may, unfortunately, be based on trend reports and industry buzzwords, and it may not align with what the business actually needs. I do have to caveat too that, in this day and age, it would be impossible to predict anything with 100 per cent confidence, whether plausible or probable, because, today, that linear projection is not guaranteed at all. 2020 really showed us that, and since then, we have continued to see that brands and businesses can be blown off-course beyond even the wildcard or preposterous parts of the futures cone. But, the main point of weakness with the cone is in the assumption of a singular starting point, along with an obvious question around whose perspective that is through. This lack of nuance can lead to specific outcomes based on flawed or incomplete input and one-off future scanning.

A culture-led brand is proactive in exploring multiple scenarios for an unknown future. The difference is that it takes into account how we get to that point in time: by leaning into the past and present to explore overlapping future challenges and opportunities from the perspective of all your audiences. This is where ongoing, real-world and real-time cultural intelligence, potentially enhanced by AI, can really add value, both through sorting through past data, but also as an early warning sign as data from the present is inputted. It's this relativity, interconnectedness and intersectionality of the full culture stacks that can be the most important areas to unpack when attempting to map out the right or new potential scenarios for the brand.

Once this multitude of interrelated starting points, incorporating sub- and emerging cultures based on both the past and the present, is selected, the job needs to happen of identifying your specific brand and business-critical uncertainties (internal and external) in the future. This is also done by projecting the path of those also-interconnected impacts of global movements – driven by social, political, environmental and technological – on audiences' culture stacks so you can consider your audience's behaviours tomorrow. This needs to be established as ongoing. This approach tries to both mitigate risk and showcase realistic opportunities for the business, brand and product as it moves forward. Filtered through your cultural positioning, these relevant indicators and drivers can help you identify and ultimately decide on the big bets for the business.

The final part of this work is then mapping out a variety of entry pathways for product design, marketing and communications to achieve that future state, stress-testing these out across multiple scenarios. This should by no means be a one-off piece of work. For this work to be meaningful, each pathway needs clear criteria and related actions against each potential activity, with built-in processes to both protect any connected systems and flex and adapt depending on how the projected and non-controllable futures play out in reality.

This 21st-century business strategy is where cultural intelligence meets cultural strategy and where your cultural positioning can help identify the big bets for your brand and business.

Be consistent and dynamic

Whether it's your futures planning as just outlined, your product offer or product innovation, ways of reaching all your audiences, and particularly those with now-expected personalization demands, embracing both agility and adaptability is an unlocker for resilience, short and long term. The reality is that the traditional 18-month planning can become outdated too quickly. Tech brands, with their ongoing software updates, and brands like those in fast fashion, with adaptable supply chains creating new products in response to consumer needs, do this well. It is understandably harder for big brands, especially if the internal operational processes are rigid. Agility and adaptability need to be cascaded through the business, and, once again, it starts from leadership. Agility and adaptability by no means equate to lack of consistency in your brand.

This ability to flex, while leaning into the role that is unique to you is especially important. It enables the creation of a variety of brand activity upon which multiple connected projects can be attached in the language, spaces and places of your audiences, reaching and engaging core, new and/or target audiences and delivering exciting and breakthrough culture-led creative work that resonates, while staying rooted in your brand. I look back at some of my personal work – brand side at adidas or Diageo and even with my clients at Spin and Platform13: the codes, slogans and KBAs of a brand are hugely valuable. In Chapter 4, I covered how they can be played with, and, importantly, how you can break a brand and category formula or even potentially go into new categories, but still be totally recognizable. For me, this is where the magic happens. This creates relevance and brand heat, enabling new distribution and growth opportunities… and it builds resilience.

Whether it's TikTok or the next comms channel or new tech innovations, if identified as relevant for your brand, you need to test and learn at pace, creating proof points as fast as possible. Now, more than ever, infusing a constant stream of fresh and relevant culture-led perspectives into the creative process is imperative. One of my favourite examples has to be the Orange advert, created by Marcel Paris, for the 2023 football Women's World Cup,[7] showcasing the French national team. First, the brand has been a partner of the French Football Federation since 2018, so has some equity in the sport. It wanted to challenge an outdated gender skills bias in the game by flipping the script with 'La Compil des Bleues', a video compilation that seems to feature the French men's team (nicknamed Les Bleus). However, it cleverly transitions to highlight the technical prowess of the women's team. Through sophisticated visual effects, it initially disguised the gender of the players to convey a powerful message: supporting Les Bleus is the same as supporting Les Bleues. Using archive imagery from the Federation, the ad involved meticulously matching the women's technical moves with similar actions from the men's team and then seamlessly integrating these using visual effects. I loved it.

AYESHA MARTIN

Relevance is resonance, and, at the heart of cultural relevancy is sparking an emotional connection that speaks to a community. So, in order for a brand to achieve cultural relevance, it firstly has to acknowledge the responsibility that comes with informing or shaping culture with the narratives it crafts and the artefacts (directly impacting generations) it creates. Any brand that understands the intersectionality of story, community and impact, overlaid with the nuance of timing or trends, could be set up to be culturally relevant. And then the people decide.

A raft of new creative production platforms such as Blender and Unreal Engine, mixed with new business models created out of Web3 behaviours that are intuitive for the incoming Gen A consumer segment, is about to upend the industry again. Beyond traditional outputs, the threat and promise of AI – from internal productivity tools and external facing creativity – gives much-needed opportunity for legacy brands to create their own AI assistants, using their own datasets, leaning hard into their unique expertise to drive relevance. If brands are set up with cultural relevance as a growth driver, these real-world insights and emerging behaviours would be flagged, understood and implemented, avoiding a too-late knee-jerk reaction or competition FOMO. No one has all the answers, however, so embracing uncertainty here is important too.

Add value to your communities

I have spent quite a lot of time on this already, but wanted to add a quick reminder about how this embeds resilience. In Chapter 4, I introduced the cultural pipeline. Interestingly, these early socio-cultural signals can also be enhanced by keeping an eye on subcultures and/or niches. After all, these usually crop up in response to the mainstream.

Scenario-mapping for multiple futures is becoming a normal tool for brand foresight and, ultimately, brand activity. This then means engaging in those big bets identified in scenario planning at their emerging stage of the cultural pipeline. It's too late by the time these scenarios hit the mainstream because that's when your brand looks like it's trying to jump on the band-wagon. This is where audiences might come for you and where there has historically been inaction and a fear of backlash.

I have defined a culturally relevant brand as one that is also advocated for and defended by consumers, whether target or not. In the face of adversity, especially if a brand has negatively impacted a community or culture, having cultural voices who will advocate for and defend you is priceless. They will do this if you have added value to their lives, communities and cultures.

Bring the outside in

Resilience is deeply connected to brands and businesses being open to new perspectives that help them to adapt and transform as inevitable changes occur, and one way to achieve this is a diverse and inclusive workforce.

The traditional big-brand–big-agency relationship is breaking down, as brand budgets tighten and layers of agency overheads and heavy teams with large fees and drawn-out schedules become more challenging. AI is also start-ing to play a role, especially where clients may see cost efficiencies. Today, agility, adaptability and innovative ideas and ways of working are needed. In an interview with *The Drum* in December 2023, I discussed the shift from traditional client–agency models to one closer to Platform13, highlighting the need for innovation and adaptability in today's dynamic industry landscape.[8] I emphasized the importance of integrating cultural relevance into business and brand strategies, noting that understanding global contexts and their impact on target audiences is crucial. We chatted about my new ecosystem for working with brands and organizations in two ways: through P13InsideTrack, focused on support *inside* the business to answer business-critical challenges, through consultancy, advisory and intelligence services for all levels in marketing, product, creative and insights teams; and P13TheDepot, our dedicated creative studio for culture-led brand storytelling to resonate with existing communities and fans and reach new ones.

The benefits of opening the gates and bringing new perspectives into play are clear. Supporting in-house teams by bringing the outside in, positively impacting team and departmental learning and development, or embedding cultural intelligence into your work as fan culture drives business and new consumers demand innovation, or delivering work that is ahead of the curve, in the cultural pipeline – these could all be helpful. Having worked on the brand side, this was one of the key reasons why I pioneered an innovative business model of curating diverse project teams according to category, culture and community and those experimenting with new creative formats. It means our clients have credible access to an agile and fast-moving brand partner, an extension of their usually tightly resourced in-house teams. Importantly, the brand also has access to those who shape and represent cultural territories, whether inherited, interest or stacked, and to new creative skillsets and audience spaces. Where we are different is in the ability to speak and translate the languages of corporate to culture and vice versa, creating a positive exchange for both sides.

Working with new types of partners and people needs brand-side clients who understand the value of this type of work, who themselves have done this type of work, and those who are open to new ways of working. This includes sharing your *challenge* – not a traditional brief – allowing us to understand how this work will impact the challenge and the rest of the business. While this may have become more normal now, when I was brand side and when I launched Platform13 in 2017, it definitely wasn't. What is even more crucial is to have a plan to cascade the project through the business and build learnings and resilience.

As I mentioned right at the beginning of the book, a modern brand, like culture, needs to be living and breathing, changing and evolving all the time.

There is no single way to build resilience in business today, but there is a crucial need for brands to expect changes so they are proactive in trying to identify the impacts and variables before or as they happen, and credibly flex around these changes to pivot brand and business plans accordingly.

Making cultural relevance a business growth driver could be a solution for survival because it enables your brand, product or service to make sense in the world, at any time, and receive positive advocacy – this is where brands can win or lose hearts and minds. It also builds resilience, internally reducing decision paralysis. Both play a key role in driving meaningful and sustained growth for the business.

Notes

1   Forsdick, Sam. '"We Can't Be Silent": How Does Business Know When to Get Political?' *Raconteur*, 19 January 2023, raconteur.net/leadership/business-leaders-speak-out-political-issues (archived at https://perma.cc/3232-FDB4)

2   Gartner. 'Top 5 Priorities for HR Leaders in 2025: Actionable Insights to Navigate Challenges and Drive Business Impact', 2024, gartner.com/en/human-resources/trends/top-priorities-for-hr-leaders (archived at https://perma.cc/4E65-A7JE)

3   Pendell, Ryan. 'Wellness vs. Wellbeing: What's the Difference?' Gallup, 22 March 2021, gallup.com/workplace/340202/wellness-wellbeing-difference.aspx (archived at https://perma.cc/MXX6-F57Z)

4   Gallup. 'Employee Wellbeing is Key for Workplace Productivity', 2024, gallup.com/workplace/215924/well-being.aspx (archived at https://perma.cc/EMS2-VSXG)

5   Taylor, Charles, W. *Alternative World Studies for Strategic Planning: Futures Report*, 1988, Strategic Studies Institute, U.S. Army War College, apps.dtic.mil/sti/tr/pdf/ADA201065.pdf (archived at https://perma.cc/A89C-4TKL)

6   Voros, Joseph. 'The Futures Cone, Use and History', The Voroscope, 24 February 2017, thevoroscope.com/2017/02/24/the-futures-cone-use-and-history (archived at https://perma.cc/K453-SNSB)

7   Nichols, Conor. 'Orange France Ad Takes a Powerful Shot at Tackling Long-Held Issues in Football', *Creative Salon*, 20 July 2023, creative.salon/articles/features/orange-france-marcel-publicis-fifa-women-s-world-cup-2023 (archived at https://perma.cc/BY4P-VXDK)

8   Bradley, Sam. 'Network Shops Aren't the Only Agencies Exploring a Product-Led Service Model', *The Drum*, 21 December 2023, thedrum.com/insight/2023/12/21/network-shops-aren-t-the-only-agencies-exploring-product-led-service-model (archived at https://perma.cc/CUC3-6327)

12

The culture-led business growth strategy

What it means for changes in your organization

In the 21st century, brands are complex, needing to navigate ever-changing consumer expectations and societal shifts in the face of increasing distrust in both capitalism and brands by all audiences. The big unlearning started in earnest a few years ago, with 2020 sparking the long-needed rise against racial injustice, rekindling movements that reverberated around the world, increasing the global urgency around the climate, especially in the Global South, changing things forever. Today, we're navigating an era marked by uncertainty and complexity, where traditional business planning of immediate profitability in the fiscal short term and strategic planning of three to five years ahead are easily impacted. Alongside the advent of spatial computing driving mixed-reality media such as VR and AR, technological forces are dismantling the traditional boundaries of brand experience, retail, commerce, marketing and media, giving established brands a once-in-a-generation opportunity and licence to reinvent their business from product-led to culture-led.

KATIE DREKE

We're at the beginning of a fascinating time, where companies are going to be feeling serious pressures, enough pain and tension, that true business model innovation will become transformational across multiple categories. I'm expecting things to start getting really exciting, really soon. Brands will become more competitive and ambitious in a race to show the world that you *can* make

> choices different from the current playbook, and you *will* still win. It will actively demonstrate that the old game is over, and we're playing a new game now. Most large enterprises are massive machines designed for a different age. This is where small to mid-sized brands have the advantage. They can change the rules, and pull the rug out from under the incumbents. And just like that – they're irrelevant and extinct. Whoever wants to be a part of the future is going to have to play by these new rules.

Even before 2020, global cultural shifts, such as the climate emergency, technological advancements and political influences, started changing audience behaviours and mindsets and called for big brands to ensure they have a credible role in people's lives. Done right, those culturally relevant brands transcended their category leadership by adding real value to that community or culture and became culturally relevant.

The four Ps must evolve

For many brands, what feels like right up until the pandemic, category leadership to sell more product was, and for some still is, the key objective. The Cambridge Dictionary defines category leadership as 'a company that sells more of a particular type of product than another company'. Category leadership style brands have always felt 'brand out', based around the four Ps of product, price, place and promotion – an academic framework made famous by E. John McCarthy in the 1960s.

Things have changed since then.

Product/service

It still all starts here. Overconsumption and planned obsolescence – the process of becoming obsolete or outdated and no longer used – in the 20th and early 21st century has led to product and production overload. Because of the need for convenience, personalization, inclusivity and awareness of the climate emergency, a business needs to honestly decide if its core product answers the needs of both the contemporary consumer and the world. Deciding what to keep, what to reformat, what to innovate around and what to get rid of can be an exciting brand exercise in an oversaturated market. What is clear is that there is an urgent role for brands to support, educate and help their audiences navigate their way forward, and to create a concerted industry-led effort to reduce and innovate their products or services with robust ESG at the heart.

ESG is a set of standards measuring a business's impact on society, the environment, and how transparent and accountable it is. It demands both broad and detailed adjustments, driving innovation and embedding inclusivity and sustainability into every facet of operations, meaningfully and sustainably. From a human perspective, I understand that living sustainably and/or waste free is a wealth privilege. I am also fully aware that flexing the newest car, sneakers and bag is a form of status and expression, especially if you are from humble beginnings. But brands from FMCG to lifestyle and luxury have the weight, responsibility and obligation to make positive change for people and the planet.

Price

This is directly related to the value that the consumer attaches to your product or service. This, of course, is linked to cost of production and the perception of that product or service. Additionally, cost of production directly impacts the real cost of production. When it comes to perception, I will use the example of Supreme. It began as a community-focused skate shop on Lafayette Street in downtown Manhattan and transformed into a global powerhouse,[1] drawing long lines of fans outside its stores in select city locales and achieving rapid sell-outs there and online. A masterclass of storytelling, scarcity and hype, this brand made the humble T-shirt into a collectible. In 2024, it released *30 Years: T-Shirts 1994–2024*,[2] a three-volume book set that looks back on its T-shirt archives. I can't think of another established brand that can tell its entire history through T-shirts. Whether we agree with the elevated prices or not, this brand commanded a premium based on brand perception, a key driver of growth. What lesson can we take here about fast fashion? Could we look at how we drive brand value through products that we want to keep, instead of simply disposing of at a whim? How do brands credibly tap into fandom as it grows through new types of fragmented, marketing-savvy communities – both online and offline – to ensure they value your product enough to buy it? And how do we approach price transparency and price value, as consumers can easily find out the true cost of a product or service, instead of the price of what the business sets?

Place

The traditional 'place' used to be directly related to where to buy your products in real-life locations: your retail and wholesale footprint. The change has been marked by the usually bustling and busy shopping centres of Hong Kong now quiet and shuttered.[3] Today, the point of purchase needs to be easy for consumers to find and buy your products or services, in the formats and places where they are. Platform innovations like TikTok Shop have opened the door to social commerce, and purchase behaviour involving algorithmic recommendations has become the norm. Real-time supply and demand through live commerce dominates, and immersive commerce is incoming fast. With the TikTok Shop marketplace model, users go directly from viewing a post showing the products to purchasing the product within the app or via a key online retailer.

eMarketer forecasts that ad spend in retail media – retailers that act like media channels – will increase by more than $75 billion over the next four years, representing nearly $1 of every $4 spent on media by 2028.[4] And when a consumer's AI starts autonomously buying for them, things will shift again.

Connected commerce through payment innovation and solutions upending transitional transactions deeply impact purchasing behaviours, especially relevant for new immersive worlds on platforms like Roblox – a server-based platform where players can access millions of games created by each other. Different from social UGC, Roblox users identify through their UGC – items created by players that can be used to customize their characters in the game, like avatars and skins created themselves or bought through a digital currency called Robux. Roblox Avatar Shops is a new space for digital fashion, where users can create UCG and try, buy and share their items and look with their friends using Robux – community meets commerce. This is being explored with activity such as the 2024 'Walmart Discovered on Roblox' innovation, allowing users to purchase IRL goods and receive free digital twins directly on the platform, driving both revenue and new forms of loyalty activity.[5] There is, of course, still an important role for 'place', and it is still an important part of an omnichannel approach.

Promotion

So, onto the last P: promotion. The 20th century focused on driving one-way messaging through mass media channels, and now, even through established social media channels, this sits squarely in that 'awareness' part of the traditional funnel. This way of promoting was about product benefit and functionality, even if it was and still is wrapped in groundbreaking 'emotional' creative advertising or featuring the biggest influencer or celebrity of the time. The arrival of the internet heralded a new method of communication, liberated through social media, the removal of brand gatekeepers and the beginning of the fall of that structured marketing funnel. Yes, there are brands that did heed the signals of the early internet pioneers and online marketers extolling the virtues of two-way conversations with consumers. They quickly incorporated 'data' into their business operations, but, ultimately, that was all still in service of understanding how their consumers bought their product so that they could target them in even more efficient ways, still to travel through the traditional marketing funnel, with brands becoming media channels. The thought was still that with better 'consumer insights' brands now had the ability to communicate their product benefits or functionality even faster. Performance marketing, newsletters, anyone? WARC reported in 20203 that performance marketing effects have declined by 62 per cent over the previous two years in the face of subdued consumer demand.[6] It notes that creativity is being severely underutilized in the performance marketing space and highlights that this is a big opportunity for advertisers aiming to stop the decline in response effectiveness.

And... the funnel is obsolete

As social platforms become new commerce channels, gaming becomes the new social, new forms of commerce emerge, mixed reality and phygital strategies become normalized and search becomes conversational, this generation's behaviours and expectations are changing drastically in real time.

You might call awareness top of funnel, consideration as middle, and conversion as lower funnel. Even if you add the 'social' elements of more recent years into the funnel and add engagement and loyalty to the bottom, the original sales funnel was conceived of in 1898 to work in a unified way, top down, from one stage to the next. It was simple, its demographic-focused media planning through measurable mechanics was a dream... for a different era. Even though it's been updated since then, the funnel just doesn't cut it any more for truly reaching and engaging with consumers. It's outdated because the way consumers find out about brands is no longer linear and not all consumers can be segmented by traditional demographics.

Google's Messy Middle from 2020 came closer to the reality of how people shop in the digital age.[7] Its report noted that people were constantly seeking out information about products and brands, diving deep into their options. The authors illustrated that this journey involves two distinct mental modes that make up the 'messy middle': exploration, where people expand their scope, and evaluation, where they narrow their choices down. Whether a consumer is browsing search engines, social media, aggregators or review websites, their activities fit into one of these categories. They cycle between exploring and evaluating, looping through these processes repeatedly until they reach a decision to purchase from that brand site. This upended the linear form of the funnel and rightly reflected how complex and iterative the decision-making process is. Companies were not wrong if traditional (and paid) search was front and centre, but, of course, organic search is based on SEO optimization or the keywords that people may search for on the journey to ensure your website appears.

There is no doubt that competition for audience attention is the fiercest it's ever been. With a media and commerce landscape with a wide variety of options and opportunities, both digital and virtual, and AI going mainstream, the traditional funnel is no longer fit for purpose. Instead, a spectrum of mindset and behaviour, based on the culture stacks, makes consumers close to purchase at many touchpoints. Today, social commerce reigns, live commerce is exploding and immersive commerce is brewing (I talk more about that in the next chapter). As the AI wars hot up, reminiscent of the browser wars back in the day, traditional search is additionally shifting to new platforms such as ChatGPT, TikTok and YouTube, so discoverability may eventually become a prompt-oriented conversational format for us all. Soon, additional to SEO will be AI/LLM optimization because your brand will have to be in the query or response to even be considered. Brands need to understand how their brands are presented for relevant prompts and described accurately in conversation, not only keywords.

Ultimately, big brands and companies have a huge challenge on their hands: how to grow while being credibly part of this ever-changing world, and how to build meaningful relationships with all their audiences – in other words, how to be and stay relevant.

This means a culture-led strategy is needed.

Cultural-led brands

Resonance, resilience and the right growth

Throughout this book, I have shared my observations and thoughts on what a culturally relevant brand is… and what it is not. I have shared my experiences and suggestions on what that means in terms of inputs and outputs to deliver audience resonance and brand resilience, driving business differentiation, growth and longevity if done right. I explained why and how brands need to read and analyse relevant cultural shifts, signals and conversations that impact the world and their audiences through their culture stacks, and flex and adapt in ways that are right for the business and the brand.

A cultural positioning ensures you find a unique role for your brand – the thing that only your brand can do, outside your traditional product offer. Externally, that means attracting consumers and potential employees to you, while internally fostering innovation and curiosity. Creating and then continually feeding your organization with the right cultural intelligence to identify insights and signals relevant to your brand and category enables innovation across your marketing, product and business, making it relevant for today and tomorrow.

The combination of these new behaviours and mindsets caused by these monumental shifts has changed how we live and work forever, catalysing a new era for brands marked by radical inclusivity and pioneering product and systems innovations. Culture-led lenses of your audiences impact their path and their decision to purchase even more than any category wins, so feeding your cultural positioning with ongoing and relevant cultural intelligence (related to your positioning) can keep your brand or business relevant and growing in a positive way for all (summarized in Figure 12.1).

What this means for change in the organization

Brands, businesses and industries are under pressure, and there is no option but to transform in some way, impacting how the business is set up and organized by what you sell and the best way to sell it. To be and stay relevant, brands must become culture-led. Cultural relevance must be brought upstream in brand and business strategy. It's not just simply about understanding

FIGURE 12.1 A culture-led business strategy

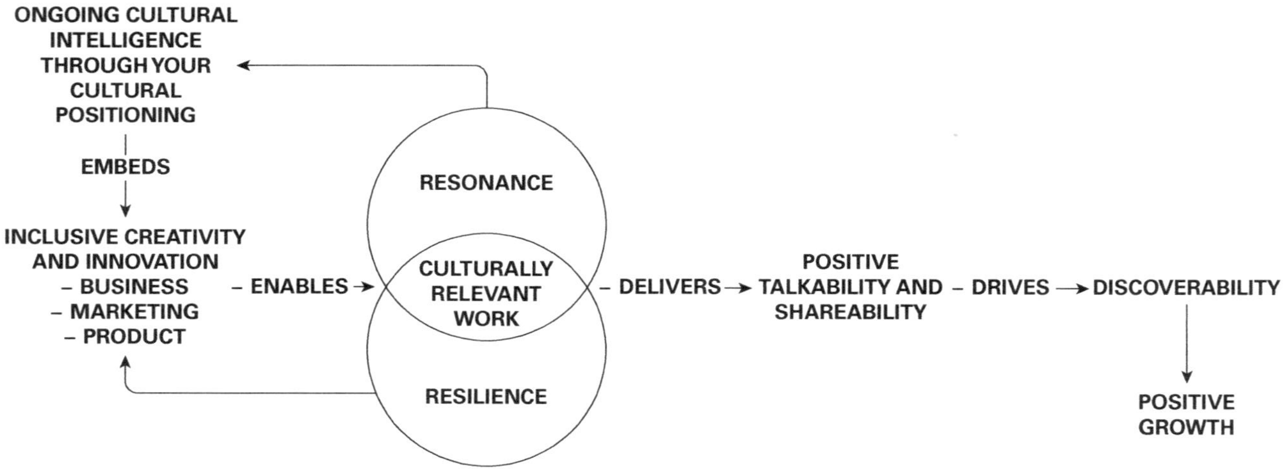

ONGOING CULTURAL INTELLIGENCE THROUGH YOUR CULTURAL POSITIONING

EMBEDS →

INCLUSIVE CREATIVITY AND INNOVATION
– BUSINESS
– MARKETING
– PRODUCT

– ENABLES →

RESONANCE

CULTURALLY RELEVANT WORK

RESILIENCE

– DELIVERS → POSITIVE TALKABILITY AND SHAREABILITY – DRIVES → DISCOVERABILITY →

POSITIVE GROWTH

cultural nuances, it's about skilfully incorporating these through the business, embedding it into both long- and short-term brand plans.

ETE DAVIES

From my personal experience, as someone who comes from an ops background, process and operations exist only to serve an outcome. Environments change, and as those things change, the same process is not going to deliver the same outcome. So, there always has to be an expectation that there will be adaptation or evolution in processes. And any process only needs to remain as long as it's delivering the desired outcome. It's always about continual improvement, adaptability and keeping up with the pace of things. I'm the result of the school of thought that you should be continually evaluating your processes, particularly when it comes to decision-making. Going back to whether you are scientific – having your trusted sources that are informing your point of view, but also making sure that you have sources which are counterintuitive to your experience, biases and assumptions. So, there is that critical evaluation in the decision-making process.

In each section here, the people interviewed and I share some proactive steps to drive resonance and build resilience to future-proof the brand and business. In addition, the following includes a non-exhaustive list of overarching areas that I think need to be addressed.

A HUMAN-FIRST VISION

As established brands and traditional agency talent pools diversify and include new-generation ways of thinking, this shift from category to culture leadership means a new type of company North Star needs to be created. This is to ensure that the whole business moves in one direction. In a world of change, an optimistic and imaginative culture is needed. One that is always critically challenging and rapidly reimagining everything from marketing to product to business models, in service of possibility and progression. This vision needs to build something new and fresh or even pull disparate parts of a brand together so that it makes credible sense for all its audiences. This can only happen if the input – the value you can add to all your communities from employees, consumers (whether current or target), partners, suppliers and so on is as valued as the output, which seems to be how success is currently measured through traditional KPIs. This means reframing what success and growth look like.

ETE DAVIES

So, the big global agencies and the big global holding companies, I'm not sure the current model survives another 20 years. I think that era is over. I think back to a quote which references that corporations and companies don't rise and fall like the Roman Empire, but more like the Venetian Empire, whereby at some point the trade and business just moves elsewhere. I think, in the next five years, we'll see even more of that change. I think it will be very good for creativity. I hope it will also be very good for employee wellbeing and representation, because we're in a world where people understand that legacy structures don't work. They understand that there are better ways to get to good work that are more enjoyable and rewarding.

KWAME TAYLOR-HAYFORD

The bigger shift is going from a shareholder mindset to a stakeholder mindset. It's moving from profit at all costs to this idea that if we do the right thing with our employees, with our suppliers, with our community, it's going to float all boats. And that comes down from shareholders, the board, and what they task the CEO to do, and how the CEO, that leadership team, all the employees, embrace the directive. It's a big shift.

MICHELLE LAVIPOUR

Being really clear on your enduring values as a business or brand and what you stand for is really important. And, just to be clear, that doesn't mean they necessarily have to be worthy things. It can be innovation, it can be creativity, etc. But being clear on your brand and the role you play for consumers or your customers is foundational.

JAMIE GILL

There are two things to unpick here. We're talking about aligning DEI initiatives with core values of a business and integrating them into the business strategy. The first step is clarity on brand values. Is the business clear and certain about what these are? Does everyone know what they are and do they show up in the everyday work culture, being led from the top? This requires an exercise involving leadership and the wider business, ensuring core values are integrated into overarching business strategy and everyone is aligned on the vision and plans for executing the strategy. It's crucial to be clear on what the business stands for. From there, you can move forward with aligning your DEI strategy with these core values.

I've learned over the years that the concept of authenticity is severely overused, but it remains crucial. If you don't really believe in what you are saying it won't land with your team or your customer. You can no longer fabricate this. Even if your primary belief is that the goal is to generate substantial profit, being authentic about that focus will attract a team that is aligned and wants it too. Therefore, it's quite straightforward to connect these goals to the people and the culture, and to ensure that those who embody them are aligned with the vision. That's what the DEI link is for me.

In this exercise of introspection, you might discover that your culture is conflicted. Your people are conflicted. Both of which will lead to a culture of confusion and misalignment which is never going to lead to positive business. Getting your people on board with your business values means clarity for everyone and you can build on this to create a stronger sense of purpose and belonging. This has been proven time and again to deliver productivity and results.

AYESHA MARTIN

Historically, marketeers have taken a very binary, linear approach to marketing and driving growth. Our reality is more fluid. Cultural relevance and being inherently more human are what now drives business growth and it reflects this shift by approaching growth through acknowledgement that we exist within an ecosystem powered by trust, authenticity and community. Purpose must be superseded with intention, business acumen needs to be reframed as human-centred design thinking and there is a need for courage, curiosity and co-creation – a kind of intrapreneurship.

OPTIMIZED OPERATIONS

Flexing outside the traditional brand playbook brings much-needed innovation and shifts product, design, distribution and/or marketing. Additionally, AI adoption means, for many brands, that this requires a fundamental shift in how they do business and what products and services they are offering, requiring new, adaptable systems fit for today. Important are how they are set up internally and who they work with externally. With a unique cultural positioning, driving meaning with all a brand's audiences can create differentiation and sustainable, positive growth. Imagine the power to foster curiosity and innovative ideas, update systems to build resilience, transform internal playbooks to achieve resonance by credibly engaging with existing, latent and employee communities, fans and consumers.

ETE DAVIES

There are two things that I've done across my career. One – I guess people call them shadow boards now, but we did them a long time ago. Basically, you get a community of people within the business that have different skillsets and experience, culturally connected in different ways, and they're operating as a mirror to the leadership and the executive team with free remit to input into, evaluate and stress-test the leadership team's plans and ideas.

The other thing is actively driving the business to radically collaborate. One of the big challenges agencies have is with collaboration, both internal and external. We build agencies to be ideas factories where we expect perfect ideas to always come from within. But we don't look externally often enough to find inspiration, and what we can learn from the specialisms that people have externally.

In big brand creative agencies, we're generalists. We think we're specialists, but we're not. And the only way you get to interesting things is diversity in imagination and collaboration. And that means you have to pull in other people who are specialists alongside your generalist thinking to help you constantly learn, innovate and evaluate your ideas and get to new places in creativity.

The business consultant I interviewed highlights an undeniable and urgent need for robust business architecture, data and technology architecture and engineering within businesses – not just now, but as we move into the future.

He says he has yet to see a single company fully address this challenge. His warning is stark: in five years, 50–90 per cent of the jobs in most companies simply won't exist as they do today. This raises fundamental questions about responsibility. What is a company's role versus society's role in helping its workforce adapt to this seismic shift? How do we prepare people for roles that don't yet exist while still delivering on today's demands? And, perhaps even more critical, how do businesses attract and retain the incredibly scarce talent needed to build this future? For him, these aren't just HR or strategy questions – they're existential challenges. He believes that companies that rise to meet them will define their place in the world for decades to come. Those that don't will be left behind. He is convinced that the time to reimagine the future of work isn't tomorrow – it's now.

MORDECAI

If I could imagine this in any way, I would say it's a reimagining of the COO. A COO should lead the operations and organization to success, which includes optimizing all resources, in turn overseeing human resources.

I was having this conversation because I was reading some work where this person had talked about adversarial attacks in the C-suite. And one of the statements this person was making was, 'I'm speaking about things that HR does get involved in.' And I said, 'I don't know of a single C-suite executive that's calling HR for anything. HR is for middle managers. Then they get burned and realize when you're in the C-suite, you are looking at HR as another department that you're probably sceptical of.' And she said, 'Well, what about sexual harassment? That is for HR.' I replied, 'That's for lawyers. If you called me up and said, I have a problem, there's no way I'm ever going to say, did you talk to your HR person?'

My point is, we have a broken HR. So, you're at a crux where this could be a thing because HR is broken. They are not your DEI leader. And unfortunately, they are bucketed as it. And we all know what happened to the chief diversity and inclusion officers. So, to me, it is the COO's role to make sure that the organization is operating at its highest efficiency. They need to upskill into it. They would write the job description that says, my COO needs to lead this. It's too intense for a CEO to lead.

ANA ANDJELIC

So, it's an operational question, organizational question and business modelling question. Basically, when you think about it, retail companies, apparel, fashion, they are still operating the way they were set up for mass people, for mass media, for mass markets. And really, when you think about it now, you have niche markets, niche media, niche retail. There is nothing 'mass' any more. There is no monoculture any more. And so, in that sense, they need to be able to quickly respond to a portfolio approach to put a lot of different ideas that live in the real world. The emphasis is from this gigantic strategic planning to actual execution and creative production. And in terms of creative production, that means that you can't have those silos any more. That linear way of doing things is more of a Hollywood model when you bring different talent in a creative production of a campaign of our ongoing cultural output and so on.

CONTEXTUAL COLLABORATION

Your cultural positioning belongs upstream, impacting the whole business, breaking the silos to drive collaboration that integrates both across the business and with new types of external partners.

KWAME TAYLOR-HAYFORD

I think maybe one of the biggest things is shifting the mindset a bit from campaigns to initiatives. It's starting with the community, taking action, creating results, then a message to inspire more action from more people. It's a cycle that starts to drive meaningful progress. We work with several teams, at the brand, because we're developing these initiatives to work across the entire organization. People have to really embrace them in order for them to happen. And then when it happens, it makes the marketing piece much easier to talk about.

ETE DAVIES

It sounds like an obvious thing, but it's so anti-agency for operating models to collaborate with each other. It's like everything is zero-sum competition, I've got to eat my enemy. But, if we have the right partnerships with the right people, we can continue to evolve creativity, continue to be inspired, continue to stay culturally relevant, and also give something back to those partners. So, I think it can be a mutually beneficial ecosystem, but getting that in place in the business requires lots of operational and cultural change within the industry because it's not designed to be mutually beneficial. And partnerships can be simple things, or really hard. And then there's also a behavioural and cultural change within our employees to know that actually collaborating with an external party who has experience, especially an understanding of a sector, isn't compromising your ownership of the idea or the integrity. It's actually the opportunity to amplify it. Those are the two big things: internally, more equitable evaluation, and then also driving collaboration, particularly external collaboration and partnership.

AYESHA MARTIN

My personal journey that reflects making progress in this space is fostering a centre of purpose driven innovation – where we learn by creating, doing and connecting. This dynamic approach has pivoted traditional frameworks and created the fluidity needed to drive brand confidence within a captive audience of historically disenfranchised (with our brand) audiences. This approach has now been adopted across the business and beyond. Starting with community and leading with culture, it creates buy-in and sustained advocacy. The greatest joy of the work we do is reflected back by the community we serve. We've shifted perception and sparked an emotive connection to the brand that had faded.

KATIE DREKE

There's been a strange resurgence of vanity metrics on the back of growth marketing optimization: likes, shares, views, downloads, etc. We all know you can simply buy those results. They are not durable and resilient data points. What brand marketing is really about are the intangibles you can't buy. It's about that rent-free time in the hearts and minds and spirits of people. It's about emotional resonance that lasts *beyond* and *inbetween* transactions.

My business is called DRKE, or Deep Record Knowledge Exchange. Deep Record is a pillar focused on leveraging learnings from the past to leave intentional and meaningful impacts upon the future. It's about thinking long and short at the same time – about business, about brand, about product; where we've been, and where we're going. Knowledge Exchange is about bringing fresh energy, fresh voices, fresh faces into the centre of the work constantly, not just every once in a while when you're reminded that it's the right thing to do; a constant refreshing of people, experiences, skills, methodologies and ideas – a rich knowledge exchange that then sends those qualities back out into the world again to do the same thing somewhere else. The whole central tenet of my business is to think deep and long, and to share with radical generosity.

PEOPLE POWER

The creator economy, born out of side-hustles and early experimentation on social media, enhanced by full creative studios on your phone, have upended traditional work pathways. Now, even product creation is in the hands of audiences and consumers, meaning that Gen Z and Gen A are as likely to become entrepreneurs as they are to work for a brand. If they do work for your brand, they expect flexible, remote and/or hybrid working, inclusivity as standard and wellbeing built in. They expect empathetic management and on-the-job upskilling.

JAMIE GILL

We're in a permacrisis, a volatile global market that has never been so uncertain. There are wars, divisions of power, cost-of-living crises, and businesses are trying to navigate through challenging cultural nuances. Mistakes are made when there isn't enough diversity in the room, people empowered to speak up with ideas on how to navigate these challenges. By incorporating greater representation from diverse cultures and groups around the table, you can better mitigate risks associated with limited perspectives. If decision-making lacks LGBTQIA+ representation, or any other under-represented groups, you miss out on valuable insights and risk overlooking critical viewpoints. You can't capture that insight from a third party or analysis alone. It must be present and live in the room because it comes from the lived experience of someone who has been through it.

KWAME TAYLOR-HAYFORD

D&AD has always represented the pinnacle of creative craft. The organization has done such a great job of keeping the bar extremely high when it comes to the very best of the disciplines that feed what we do. I'm excited to continue that legacy, but to also ensure that we are modernizing it for the time that we're heading into. We need to build a creative industry that is still focused on excellence, but we have to redefine what excellence means, and how we can have many more people and disciplines as part of the conversation. How can we have many more conversations about mid-career talent? How can they grow into leadership with support from the right mentors? How can we build the right culture that will inspire and stimulate and educate the next generation of creative thinkers and makers? All exciting challenges that I'm eager to take on.

SARAH WATSON

Post-Covid, the workplace is unrecognizable. In America in general, people haven't returned to work at all in the same way as they've done in London. Leaders have to show up for constant change. The sheer complexity of running brands now, many of which are customer service machines, means that it can take years not months to fully onboard people. There is a whole cohort of leaders that's been lost; a generation that wasn't physically in the workplace during those years and didn't have the opportunity to truly step up. You need to be forged in the fire to be taking responsibilities for really tough, deeply interpersonal things. The contract of work has broken down. It is hard to care when you buy a house any more. So why should I show up and take your bull****? Many leaders find it really hard to hire hungry people who want to be in person. The need to be flexible, the ability to really listen, to hear and to change. I would say, capital-C conversation, the ability to speak and to hear someone and to be in dialogue, in constant dialogue and to be very accepting of what is emerging.

ECOSYSTEM MANAGEMENT

In marketing and communications, as new metrics and measurements evolve, relevance must blend both hard and soft metrics. Soft metrics include positive and unprompted brand advocacy. Sometimes those are not in the places that can traditionally be measured, so, when audiences (from employees to consumers and non-consumers) feel compelled to work for your brand, talk positively about your brand, share your activities and advocate for and/or defend it, outside the traditional marketing calendar, you know you are relevant. This is important as both discoverability and promptability become key drivers of commerce.

ANA ANDJELIC

You have to be nimble and flexible in the approach to problem-solving. So, if you say, 'I want to do this capsule really quickly,' it's all about having the organizational motivation and your organizational approach to doing things. Like Banana Republic – the procurement, the production, the supply, they really quickly sourced vintage items and set them up. So, it's just having the right motivation. We are now doing these things. We have never done them before, but let us figure it out. CMOs are usually operators, engagement planners, media planners, asking how do I use my media budget and so on. I'm creative in a sense that it's about reordering this because this is your vision. Let's see how we can get there. Let's see what people we need. It's more breaking things to put them together again. The creative, how the operations need to look, and that you really need to inspire and motivate people – those are the most important things. I just think that good ideas come from everywhere. And that's why, again, going back to this middle, I think that we put too much emphasis on cultural creativity. It's important and maybe Netflix is going to do that. Maybe Apple has been doing that, back in the day, and so on, but even if that doesn't happen, great ideas still happen. Your idea is still an amazing idea.

MORDECAI

The consumer side to me is you're saying the funnel is out the window, but, as a consumer, I'm still going to use the term and what I call it, but it's a different thing. I don't need you to buy any more. I need to figure out who you are in the ecosystem once you're in the ecosystem. But, you know, it's Web3. I don't need you to buy any more, I need you to be in there.

PETER SEMPLE

I'm going to coin an acronym – maybe this already exists – but it's thinking about 'AI SEO'. So: how are you going to optimize for not just the content of your website but also the things people are saying about you in the world. And how do you think about optimizing that for an AI-discovery first world? That's fascinating.

The evolution of digital in marketing made everyone then addicted to digital tracking and digital visibility and digital footprint – and that eroded some focus on brand and cultural intention. Then you have these grand shifts like privacy, effectively removing all of the consistency of digital visibility, and then everyone begins to lean back into brand.

In an AI world, that will probably mean people have to think a lot more about what the people are saying about you versus what you're putting through a marketing channel.

SITUATIONAL COMMERCE

We are in a generation of financially empowered consumers, creating new forms of revenue and using new payment tech, who highly value their privacy and the integrity of their data, rewriting the rules of commerce and redefining what growth for brands means today. AI is already reshaping the shopping journey beyond e-commerce search and convenience. This will mean new, increasingly connected personalized phygital – where physical and digital merge – business models and therefore new objectives and metrics for success. From competing in marketplace models like Amazon, Alibaba and eBay, to ensuring your brand is alive and kicking on TikTok (both from a discovery and sales point of view), and the emerging customer-to-manufacturer model with flexible supply chains that reacts to consumer demands, compounded by the Web3 behaviours of decentralization, person-alization and co-creation – this new era is already here.

KWAME TAYLOR-HAYFORD

The very idea of a global business needs to be reconsidered. In the past, there was this value of business being the same everywhere... recognizable and consistent. But I don't think that's it any more. If you're a global company, you may sell the same or similar product, but how that product shows up in every market needs to take into account a lot more cultural nuance and context. In the age of AI, people have come to expect a level of customization and personalization that's responsive to their needs. I don't think that's going to go away.

KATIE DREKE

Hermès is 187 years old. How does a brand remain contextual through 187 years? One example in its case is the Hermès scarf: a truly iconic piece. Imagine this icon travelling the passage of time, going through the 1950s, 60s, 70s, 80s, 90s, etc.

The 70s, for instance, was a counterculture time that rejected many things from the previous generation. Symbols of 'the establishment', like government and military, formal education, even home ownership and automobiles – all of these took a hit in the 70s. Culturally, there was a recognizable persona driving these counterculture ideas – hippies – people who were more about living simply, challenging the status quo and the establishment, and not at all about this 'keeping up with the Joneses' consumerism thing. How does a luxury brand survive that? One thing Hermès did in the 70s was develop an ad campaign where it photographed the scarves, tied around a backpack, tied around an upper arm, fashioned into a kerchief and worn on the head of a young woman wearing denim jeans. Placing the icon directly into the context of the day.

To be clear – fashion is not luxury, particularly to Hermès's upper-echelon customer. Fashion is frivolous, fast, trendy. Fashion at this moment was all about denim and ripped jeans and long hair and cat eyes and all these new trendy, fresh things that were a bold departure from the 50s and 60s. Denim was right in the centre of it all. But denim had absolutely no place in the Hermès world. So, it decided to take a bold step and to recontextualize an iconic product to live within the world that was actually happening. It took the risk, made the bet, and the bet worked.

Similarly, I completed an audit report a year ago of luxury and fashion brands using humour. In the process of that project, I discovered a television ad from 2010 that Hermès created which was quite unexpected. The ad features their classic exquisite luxury items, like a leather wallet, a beautiful handbag, hats and watches, its memorable orange boxes, and the iconic Hermes scarf – but this time Hermès had hired a skateboarder who used his hands to 'ride' a fingerboard, a miniature version of a skateboard, ridden with the fingers instead of the feet.[8] This film is humorous and whimsical, which is completely on brand for Hermès, but skateboarding was totally unexpected. And that's kind of the Hermès jam: to quite successfully recontextualize time and time again.

It is an art and a science to be able to recontextualize a brand for resilience and longevity. And you can often tell when a brand is not thinking at all about time, when they have become hyper-focused on their marketing in a closed-in way, immediate, narrow, commercial. They become a brand that is stealing from their own future. Shortening their own lifespan. Narrowing their own options.

PRODUCT INNOVATION

A study by PWC showed that 45 per cent of total economic gains by 2030 will come from product enhancements, stimulating consumer demand.[9] It believes AI will drive greater product variety, with increased personalization, attractiveness and affordability over time.

These breakthrough products could redefine boundaries, creating new playing fields and potentially much larger pay-offs, but with that potential comes greater risk. For a brand like Nike, that risk is part of the 'Just Do It' brand story. For example, in 2024 it announced its Athlete Imagined Revolution (AIR) – a new co-creation process between teams of Nike designers and innovators and 13 of the brand's elite athletes, from Wembanyama to Sha'Carri Richardson to Kylian Mbappé, experimenting with the most cutting-edge technologies, amplified by AI, to co-create the future of the 50-year-old Nike Air.[10] A key way of working was outlined by Roger Chen, Nike VP of NXT digital product creation. He explains that a truly inspiring aspect of the project was bringing together such a diverse group of creatives, each layering their unique techniques and technologies. He notes that they were in a constant state of learning from one another, building on the Nike ethos of merging varied disciplines to forge something groundbreaking. It is a great way to augment human capabilities rather than replace them. The AIR project is part of Nike's bigger internal AI LLM model, which leverages its rich pool of athlete performance datasets, gathered from its cutting-edge laboratories and authentic training sessions. This exclusive 'private garden' of data gives Nike a distinct competitive advantage. It enriches this with selected insights from the 'public garden', ensuring all this information remains within the confines of what it uses to train its models. This strategic blend of private and public data underpins Nike's innovative product approach.

Mixing the product range could be a smart way to embed ESG practices along the journey. The best way to do that could be that a cross-functional team across the business and borders creates and manages products, breaking down those traditional silos, with a human–AI team to support it. For my interviewee business consultant, this is positive, highlighting the opportunity for sustainability technologies to accelerate things like energy management, decarbonizing heavy industry, and breakthroughs faster than we have seen before.

MORDECAI

When I say inclusive innovation spaces, I'm talking about linking someone that's new to the company with someone tenured at the company, someone that's creative with someone technical, someone that learns in a different way with someone that learns like a book way, people with a high school education, someone who's an MBA. There's a ton of internal support and years-old research which continues to be updated, that dictates if we are inclusive in our early processes, nearly 2x in-business growth is delivered through increased productivity and change-readiness. This is what comes out of it. Without inclusive space, you become more susceptible to unforeseen experience errors as much as being cancelled by the culture.

PETER SEMPLE

The cultural relevance and business growth question, obviously, to some degree, depends on what the business is and the context in which it's operating. I'm a believer that, if a business can find ways to make itself interesting to people and find ways to give them artefacts to talk about and to reflect on, it'll deliver more value and have more of an impact. Maybe one of the learnings is that, just because you take a shot at it doesn't mean it will necessarily land the same as every other activity. You can do a PLA campaign and it may not be effective, but attempting to meaningfully contribute to culture is a valid thing for businesses to try. And just, if you can't read the results, or, in fact, for whatever reason the intention didn't land the first time, don't then give up on it. Then think about other ways you can more meaningfully contribute.

Culture-led brands blend short-term and long-term brand plans in an agile way, identifying what parts of the brand are fixed, and what parts can and must flex and respond to cultural shifts, both through people's culture stacks and advanced technological shifts. A culture-led brand blossoms and shines when all these combine respectfully and credibly.

Brands and businesses need to reimagine outdated business processes and create fit-for-purpose systems to both transform your brand and push our industry forward. Holding a mirror up to yourself truthfully and addressing both the product offer and the operational gaps to become a culturally relevant brand can move the brand from being really good or acting as expected as a category lead to being really great, by blazing a trail and making a positive impact for all your audiences as a cultural leader.

Notes

1   Sullivan, Robert. 'Charting the Rise of Supreme, from Cult Skate Shop to Fashion Superpower', *Vogue*, 10 August 2017, vogue.com/article/history-of-supreme-skate-clothing-brand (archived at https://perma.cc/X2RK-LTPH)

2   Supreme. '*Supreme 30 Years: T-Shirts 1994–2024* Book', Supreme News, 19 December 2024, supreme.com/news/958 (archived at https://perma.cc/ME5E-S8XG)

3   Bloomberg. 'Hong Kong Luxury Shops Sit Empty as Chinese Spending Plunges', *The Business of Fashion*, 3 September 2024, businessoffashion.com/news/global-markets/hong-kong-luxury-shops-sit-empty-as-chinese-spending-plunges (archived at https://perma.cc/A8AJ-494Q)

4   Lebow, Sara. 'Retail Media Will Make Up One-Fifth of Worldwide Digital Ad Spend This Year', eMarketer, 26 February 2024, emarketer.com/content/retail-media-accounts-one-fifth-of-worldwide-digital-ad-spend (archived at https://perma.cc/PH4S-XXTJ)

5   Roblox. '[Free UGC] Walmart Discovered', roblox.com/games/13398230007/2X-XP-Walmart-Discovered (archived at https://perma.cc/PUM6-3679)

6   WARC. 'Performance Marketing Effectiveness Needs to get Better', 26 May 2023, warc.com/content/feed/performance-marketing-effectiveness-needs-to-get-better/en-GB/8234 (archived at https://perma.cc/2WGF-3JTC)

7   Rennie, Alistair, and Jonny Protheroe. 'How People Decide What to Buy Lies in the "Messy Middle" of the Purchase Journey', Think With Google, July 2020, thinkwithgoogle.com/intl/en-emea/consumer-insights/consumer-journey/navigating-purchase-behavior-and-decision-making (archived at https://perma.cc/RHC6-FX8D)

8 Highsnobiety. 'Hermès Fingerboard Skate Viral', youtube.com/watch?v=I0JbqXM_HFM (archived at https://perma.cc/JV66-DLMH)

9 PwC. *Sizing the Prize What's the Real Value of AI for Your Business and How Can You Capitalise?*, 2017, pwc.com/gx/en/issues/analytics/assets/pwc-ai-analysis-sizing-the-prize-report.pdf (archived at https://perma.cc/ACM6-TTCD)

10 Nike. 'Creating the Unreal: How Nike Made Its Wildest Air Footwear Yet', 11 April 2024, about.nike.com/en/stories/nike-design-athlete-imagined-revolution (archived at https://perma.cc/K5MT-XZ2A)

13

Conclusion

The win-win of cultural relevance in business growth

Today, the world is at a historical turning point focused around three major and interconnected cultural factors: geopolitical tensions and social justice, the climate emergency and the acceleration of AI – shifting global and collective attitudes and mindsets and behaviours, the narratives around them driven by the mainstream news and new media. Clearly, our traditional global establishments and rules are breaking down, demanding a re-evaluation and reconstruction of existing systems. A new type of mindset is at the forefront of this change, not merely experiencing it, but actively spearheading a transformative movement as agents of change, navigating and shaping the future.

Since 2023, the number of significant global conflicts has put Western democracy, global security and international law on trial. The Global South, 'developing' countries, are increasingly influential players in global politics, asserting their presence and stake in shaping international agendas and finally dismantling the view of the world that many of us have grown up with. These regions of the world, which lie outside the West or the Global North, are younger and growing more rapidly than their Western counterparts, yet they are also more susceptible to the impacts of climate change and generational injustices, compounded by global cost-of-living crises and inflation surges. I believe the learnings, inquiring mindsets and collective empathetic behaviours kicked off in the early 2020s are still being practised, further expanded by critical thinking skills and the search for truth.

This time, we are seeing such changes play out in real time, on demand and livestreamed.

It was telling and hopeful that Cannes Lions 2024 honoured Maria Ressa, co-founder and CEO of Rappler, the top digital-only news site leading the fight for press freedom in the Philippines, as its 2024 Lionheart winner.[1] This is a special accolade given to a person who has harnessed their position to make a significant and positive difference to the world. The impact of contemporary truth-tellers has driven deeper public understanding of the forces that influence and impact all our realities, fostering much-needed curiosity and delving into what we have historically been fed and how we get our information. It starts with the truth.

The great relearning

Today, brands and businesses simply cannot grow at any cost. The climate crisis remains a critical, unavoidable issue, with 45 per cent of global youth reporting that climate anxiety impacts their daily lives, according to UNICEF.[2] As awareness of the interconnectedness of climate change and the negative impact on people to supply the demand of overconsumption, a report by Tim Jackson for the Sustainable Development Commission outlines why prosperity lies in our ability to thrive as humans while respecting the ecological boundaries of our finite planet.[3] He says the real challenge for our society is to create the right conditions for this to happen. This means that companies, industries and governments must work together to dismantle systemic issues to drive, at scale, decarbonization – reducing CO_2 emissions resulting from human activity, with the eventual goal of eliminating them – and waste management.

In a longer article in 2022, with *Nature*, Tim explains that the global economy currently revolves around the notion of growth – the expectation that companies, industries and countries must increase production each year, whether it's necessary or not.[4] This relentless drive is a key factor behind climate change and ecological breakdown. He identifies high-income economies, dominated by powerful corporations and wealthy elites, as primarily responsible, consuming energy and materials at unsustainable rates. Yet, many industrialized countries are now finding it challenging to sustain economic growth due to disruptions from the Covid pandemic, resource shortages and stagnant productivity. Tim admits that governments are in a tough spot as their efforts to stimulate growth often clash with the need to enhance human wellbeing and reduce environmental harm. He and other ecological economists advocate for a shift in focus: wealthy economies should abandon GDP growth as a primary objective. Instead, they should reduce harmful and unnecessary production, cut down on energy and resource use, and prioritize economic activities that enhance human wellbeing and meet essential needs.

As verified truths are being revealed, people are seeing and understanding how traditional economic systems and global organizations have been set up to benefit only the few, at the expense of 'others' and the environment. This knowledge will not be forgotten and means that we all will need to think critically about everything we thought we knew – racism, liberation, religion, stereotypes and much, much more. Hate movements have also expanded this awareness, bringing the word 'woke' into the mainstream and into the language of the masses, now being (mis)used as a catch-all for demonizing left-leaning or progressive attitudes interested in social justice. This contributes to further division, polarization and hatred towards minorities and marginalized people being used as a shortcut to outrage, connected to cancel culture and perceived political correctness.

For us all, understanding context and nuance is essential for critical thinking.

This word and attitude to 'stay woke' is a deep part of Black American history. To be woke in the Black community means that someone is informed, educated and conscious of social injustice and racial inequality. Deeply entwined with the Black Lives Matter movement, it has also come to encompass a broader awareness of other social inequalities such as sexism and LGBTQia+ rights.

The past few years have seen us all navigating intense periods of social, political and economic instability, worldwide polarization and deepening divisions continuing to drive a sharp decline in public trust towards governments, institutions and corporations. This is important, because all our (and future generations) culture stacks are impacted by our governments' politics and policies, which are highly motivated by economic growth. The truth is that systems and policies in industrialized countries have been created to fuel economic growth. This is essential because wealth and subsequently international power is measured, wielded and valued by the GDP of that country. This makes staying at the top of the leaderboard very important and, yes, of course, there are major benefits if a person lives in a 'wealthier' country. This focus on financial wealth for a few, however, is counter-intuitive to serving the poorer or more marginalized people of that country or territory. Since the Covid pandemic, this gap is ever widening. So, depending on which side of the wealth fence you were lucky to be born on, both multi- and inter-generational inequalities are so deeply rooted that it's hard to get out of… and the cycle continues. Trust me, I know.

Set against this backdrop, today's pace of technological advances in AI, Web3, mixed reality media and spatial computing is accelerating marketing, product and commerce innovation, upending traditional brand management like never before. We must ensure that the profound changes of recent years are remembered and addressed. It's our duty to shape a future that serves both humanity and the planet authentically, steering clear of superficial commitments like greenwashing, pinkwashing and, especially, culture-washing. All this is creating some of the biggest and most radical shifts in global dynamics in history.

The great reset

Recent years have seen a very long list of global events that have driven a powerful moral and political reckoning that will deeply affect us and future generations. The rebalance of power will take years of unrest and uncertainty, pushed by people deeply affected – students, consumers and workers – to provoke long and much-needed accountability and transparency from businesses. Today, there is no denying that brands are under the microscope and that their behaviour during this time won't be forgotten. We want brands that match our shared values and we want them to take positive action when those values are threatened or challenged. So, how a brand responds to the impacts on people's culture stacks – the core essence of us all – is the first barrier or influence if we see, engage with, work for, defend and advocate for or buy the brand (see Figure 13.1).

The role of brands and business in the 21st century and beyond is clear and culture-led. Big businesses can positively influence and impact at scale. They have the ear of the political powers that can change things and the ear of the masses through their brands, giving them a unique opportunity to help solve global issues and push society forward. For example, they have the ability to break stereotypes, build bridges, change traditional narratives, challenge the status quo on product creation processes, and create new, inclusive systems that empower communities. Brands can transform their brand, category, industry and wider society to shape all our futures.

So, I outline here some 'what ifs' if we approached this with an 'and', not an 'instead of' mindset – an idealistic set of questions.

> **What if** *we start with rethinking the countries in the Global South as overexploited not underdeveloped? What would that mean for your operational and supply chain practices when it comes to people and planet?*

For brands, the response to this needs to go beyond 'purpose marketing' or siloed CSR to a cultural positioning – the foundational and fundamental

FIGURE 13.1 The culture-led brand

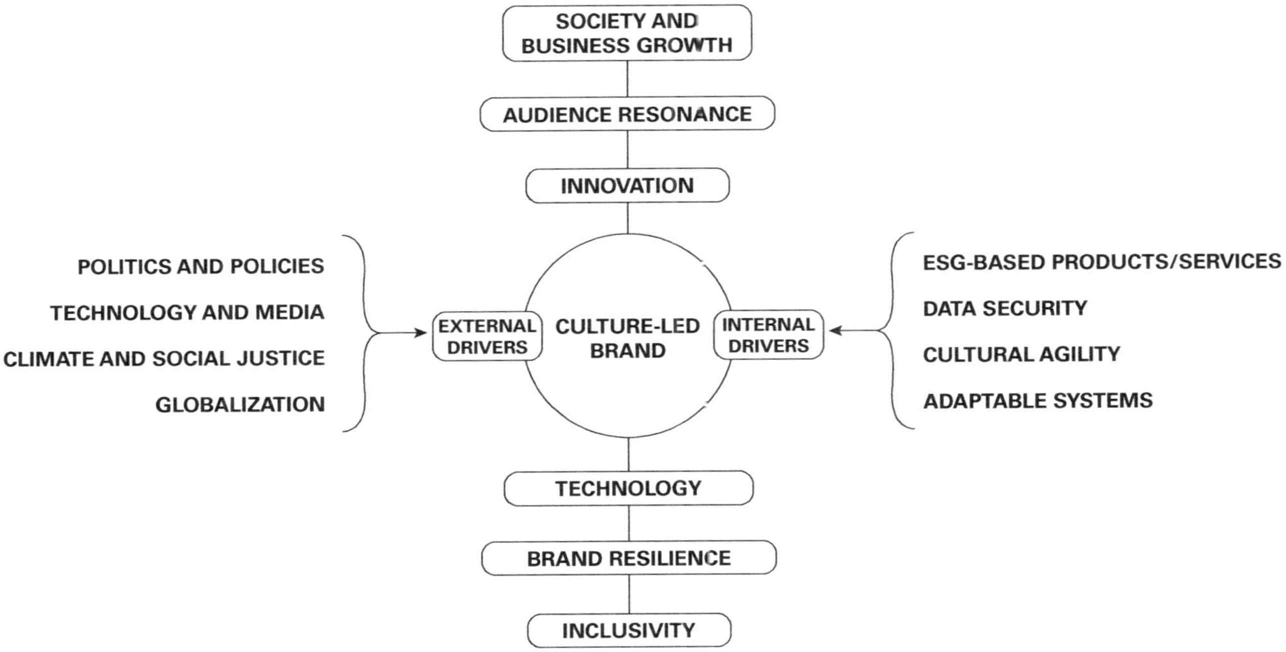

values of 21st-century business, embedding cultural-led strategies horizontally through the whole business, integrating and cascading through traditionally vertical corporate departments and policies like inclusivity, ESG, ethics, marketing, product and the like, to stay relevant. Culture-led brands that read and analyse changes relevant to their intersectional audiences, add value to their lives, and make a positive impact on the world will continue to stay culturally relevant. The business consultant agrees that in five to ten years from now, the cohesion of society itself will become a critical challenge. We agree on the need to keep communities united in an increasingly fragmented world. He thinks that it's unlikely to be by product brands, and ponders if it's the brands of nations or brands of cultures and communities.

But Africa cannot and is not waiting for the West. Ghana is one of the continent's leading receivers and importers of used clothing, clogging up their beaches and cities.[5] So, amazing projects like the Or Foundation are doing something about it.[6] Its mission is clear. In Accra, it is at the forefront of catalysing a justice-led circular economy in solidarity with Kantamanto, the largest second-hand clothing market in the world. Ghana's Obroni Wawu – translated from Akan to 'dead white man's clothes' – is a festival of thrift, beach clean-ups, live DJs and upcycling fashion attended by fashion designers, artists, models, photographers and thrift vendors from around the world. A model for the fashion industry, perhaps.

> **What if** *we centred humanity within new systems of digital, data and AI literacy, with critical thinking, resilience, adaptability, entrepreneurship, collaboration, empathy, curiosity and creativity as essential?*

UNESCO has declared future literacy an essential competency for the 21st century, which 'empowers the imagination, [and] enhances our ability to prepare, recover and invent as changes occur'.[7] In Chapter 1, I talked about being human as a competitive advantage. I often think about the need for radical optimism, hope and possibility, especially in the transformational and polarizing era we are living through.

Brands play a significant role in shaping societal norms and our attitudes, while our varied access to and adoption of technology is crucial to our behaviours. We are truly in a time of radical transformation, and integrity and humanity need to lead as acts of modern form of resistance and change. By embracing these cultural shifts and changes with optimism, brands and companies foster new mindsets and behaviours internally. This results in personal (human) growth and empathy, pushing ourselves and each other to innovate, adapt, learn and develop resilience. It encourages a new growth mindset, enabling us to see challenges as opportunities for development rather than obstacles, to find ways to collaborate, not compete at any or all costs. This growth can positively impact all of intersectional audiences and communities to build a better future.

JAMIE GILL

The biggest cost for any business is human capital – your people. When you look at big corporations, this is evident. Without the right people, nothing else matters. Your manufacturing supply chain can be rebuilt, but without the right people in the right roles, it isn't going to work. I find that here in the UK, we are conflicted on being transparent and confident around our commerciality. The intent is there, but it means we're juggling between these values. We know we want to drive successful commercial businesses, but we don't want to talk about it. Instead, we anchor our business claims on other values, which means the people are striving for unknown goals. I think the beauty is in bringing the purpose and commerciality together. It's a magic formula that is possible, but generally businesses aren't doing it.

AYESHA MARTIN

I think having a clear corporate compass defined is imperative. That's not informed only by growth in sales, but rather creates accountability across other areas of impact as a global corporate citizen. And this in turn will inform a sound approach to product creation, elevation and storytelling. Blind spots because of empathy and culture gaps are no longer tolerated, which is why leadership and the concept of agility needs to expand in matrixed centuries-old brands. Acknowledging the generational shift in senior management happening right now that favours a democratized version of creation (marketing) perhaps marks an imminent transformation that will change the future of brands.

KATIE DREKE

It's incredibly disappointing to watch such a low bar currently being applied to AI. We're playing small-ball, and it's not going to serve anyone well. We need to demand better. *We don't need* more algorithmically optimized content, faster. In fact, we can see that it's slowly driving us to depression, anxiety and a sort of collective madness. Luckily, there are some incredibly smart folks that recognize the real applications for AI are still to come – very serious, big, hairy, audacious issues that the human brain struggles to wrestle with. The human mind can only handle so much; it struggles to wrangle big concepts of exponentiality; it struggles to wrap around multi-generational time beyond our own lifespans. These machines and algorithms can do this work quickly for us, and can help us understand ourselves in our changing world better. Imagine things like studying ancient, dead languages, mapping interplanetary travel, solving cancer, optimizing recycling machines and agriculture, understanding the massive complexity of our global interconnected ecosystem. In the end, it's quite possible that the impending pressures from the climate crisis will be the driving force that focuses the use of AI where we really need it, so that we don't exterminate ourselves. Let's hope we get there fast enough.

What if *we embed inclusive strategies through the business, leveraging the power of the diverse communities that define the world? What could it be to make business decisions with deliberate intent of integrity, fairness, purpose, courage and empathy?*

This approach not only enhances the work but also amplifies brand reputation, recognition and fame, building loyalty and driving the right business growth, all while making meaningful social and financial impact on communities and cultural voices that may have historically had limited access to brands and business career paths. This means prioritizing the expansion of diverse talent pools and exploration of new hiring and procurement methods, both internally and with external teams and partners. Including for your employees, business ethics should become part of the day to day, with deep consideration of people's culture stacks. True inclusivity enables how your internal culture, organizational set-up and business policies impact humanity and society. For example, creating an accessible website goes beyond simply broadening your audience reach or ticking a box; it's fundamentally about inclusivity and ensuring everyone has equal access.

This commitment to accessibility is not just strategic; it's ethical. It allows us to forge deeper connections, cultivate loyalty and build an internal culture and external consumer base that reflects the diverse world we live in.

KATIE DREKE

What I would like to encourage brands to do more of is to ask themselves: 'Are we on the right side of history here? Are we participating in the right things? And are we doing what we can where it makes sense to recognize inequities and historical flaws in society and in capitalism specifically?' Identifying them, making a choice not to participate in them, and inviting others to do the same. It doesn't need to be a radical act, but brands do need to act with self-awareness. And every brand ought to be building towards a legacy they can be proud of.

JAMES KIRKHAM

If you were doing a workshop now, everyone would mention Patagonia. The thing with Patagonia, we know what Patagonia's political stance is. We know what Ben and Jerry's is. But you don't have to know about Patagonia's political stance to know that everything it does is just an action. It's pure action generally braced around a self-sustaining, global climate, positive and green. Everything about it is for the good. It's unequivocally for good. That shouldn't need to be political. From a brand perspective, I think if they just demo its actions, as we know, Gen Z and certainly with Gen Alpha, it's going to be important. It is everything, it is so vital. They will find it comical and absurd that they could perhaps go to a brand that doesn't have those values, they'll simply move on, filter them out.

JAMIE GILL

Talent needs to be empowered to bring their intelligence, to bring that bloodline of knowledge and heritage into a professional capacity, because they have the skill and authentic knowledge. It's not just on the shop floor, it's not just in retail or in the back office, lower admin support functions. It's in leading roles at decision-making levels. They should be empowered to share that insight to support the whole business to deliver. Why are we relying on outside analysis from trend reports believing that gives us the knowledge we need to know how best to serve a market? It's so flawed. And the business is setting itself up for massive risk and missing the biggest opportunity in developing a workforce that is representative of the customer base. It's an easy route to a big win.

What if *the value added was to society? If business success was shifted from only financial performance to prosperity for all and positive profit for businesses; where businesses were both values and results driven, and coupled economic with social progress?*

ETE DAVIES

I think the whole thing is going to start to get turned on its head. Not to get too philosophical, but many of our legacy institutions and systems, whether they are macroeconomic or corporate, are being evaluated, by everyone, because the world has moved to a place where there is more democratization of information, even if some of that is, unfortunately, misinformation. Lots of communities and groups who were historically marginalized and oppressed have found their voices and found their courage and found ways to connect with each other and are refusing to be marginalized and oppressed. Even economic value is shifting because, before, your wealth was your house; now it's also wellbeing, personal freedom, mobility, etc. You see it being reflected in corporate culture. The pandemic happened and, globally, industries still can't figure out what they want to do in terms of return to the office – because the paradigm has shifted. People talk about an era of disruption. I think what we've experienced the last 20 years, and more, is an era of acceleration. So, everything, whether it's disruption or innovation or whatever else, is going faster than it has before.

KWAME TAYLOR-HAYFORD

My perspective is that creativity is the most powerful and transformative force in the world. When harnessed by brands with significant resources and scale, there's an ability for us to move the world forward in a way that is incredible. And we can do that while we're making tons of money.

What if *brands took the lead in redefining underconsumption to suitable consumption, and making that desirable? What would it mean for product innovation by design that encourages circularity? What if we mix indigenous wisdom and innovation? How could brands educate consumers on the value of products, instead of only driving volume, so that what we are buying we care more for and we take better care of?*

KATIE DREKE

You buy a piece of Hermès for the rest of your life. Ten years later, 50 years later, if it needs repairing, it'll get repaired. It's an extreme example because it is an extremely luxury brand. But repair and longevity are finally becoming a viable revenue stream again.

Let's look at what the sportswear category is doing, for example the On Cyclon running proposition.[8] A customer can subscribe to its running shoes and apparel, and never actually own them. The On products will come to your house, and you run in them. When you run them down, run them out, you send them back. A new product comes again, brand new, and you keep going. What happens to the used product that you return? The company deconstructs it, recycles it and creates new products again – circularity in practice. The customer doesn't have the burden of recycling, of reselling, of giving away, of rebuying. Pretty soon, the burden of ownership is going to get real. I'm very enthusiastic about all the brands starting to experiment and innovate in this space, such as Arc'teryx with its ReBird programme, for example, and Houdini Sportswear with its Circle Hubs where you can buy new, buy used, get your gear repaired, or subscribe temporarily to products you don't need permanently.

PETER SEMPLE

Circularity, behavioural change, positive momentum on those things – they're ultimately great for the world. Depop is a circular fashion marketplace. The thing we are fundamentally trying to drive is behavioural change – helping people understand there is a different way to interact with and consume fashion versus buying new, buying seasonal, buying more than you need, buying all the time.

Fashion itself is sort of this grand entertainment module that we're all somewhat addicted to. The role we're trying to play as a business is driving behavioural change at mass scale. And we're obviously not the only business trying to do that across spaces or in fact in this particular space. But we see the job that Depop is capable of doing: we have to find a way of effectively competing with the entertainment and the engagement that fashion offers and has offered throughout the entirety of our lives. Second-hand fashion and access to good products in second-hand fashion – that's not a new idea. We grew up in this country with second-hand shops and charity shops. And in the US, they have thrift and they have Goodwill. All of that stuff exists because great clothing was built to last in the first place. But access isn't enough. You actually have to think about this kind of equation of access and desirability. Fashion is desirable, new sneakers are desirable.

If we want people to really think about changing their consumption behaviour, we need them to be excited to do the second-hand thing rather than buying new. There isn't a silver-bullet way to make people excited about it, but that's the brand world we're building. You can get things that are no longer available or things that are different from what's available in the first-hand market – uniqueness and individualism are things the second-hand market can provide – as well as low prices. And underpinning all of that is the sustainability impact. We look at sustainability and that kind of moralistic, underlying purpose bit as really important to people, but it isn't necessarily what's actually going to motivate them in the first place. It's more of a validator. So, we have to be at least as exciting as new fashion, and then underpin that with the fact that you're making a good choice. You can tell people to feel proud that they've made this decision to shop here or to sell or buy another thing here versus contributing just to the mass piling up of new stuff.

What if *brands helped us all navigate our way in a digital and complex world, instead of trying to commoditize our data? How could brands help us find meaningful ways for us to both lean into our individuality and connect with each other, online and in real life?*

KATIE DREKE

What is the next era? I'm looking at mid-size brands that are coming up and I'm advising them to slow their roll and to be very intentional as they grow; to not get caught up in speed and scale, but to fall madly in love with building something that will last, building a durable business that's beyond any single quarter or FY, something that truly understands and obsesses their core audience. We're actually reverting, I believe, back to some familiar behaviours from maybe the early 19th century. More small, more local companies that make exceptionally beautiful and thoughtful products and services for a specific and particular audience. And then the company stops right there – they don't try to expand across the globe, they don't try to create more SKUs, they don't try to 'scale' – they find their ideal calibration for profit, quality and satisfaction, and they stay wonderful right where they are.

Cultural relevance isn't something you achieve overnight. I've learned it's something you earn, through consistency, ongoing positive contributions to your communities and respectful relationships with consumers. This doesn't emerge from crafting new mission statements or launching stand-alone social initiatives; rather, it develops through a continuous stream of strategic, creative and operational choices that respond to the evolving global dynamics impacting your audiences.

This does not have to be boring. Doing this in exciting, innovative and creative ways shouldn't discourage brands and their partners to take risks for fear of strict compliance or call-out culture. I have always used 'guidelines' as a catalyst for culture-led creativity, championing diverse perspectives and creating breakthrough ideas.

Final word

To be truly culturally relevant, you must realign your brand, to discover your brand's special role and place in the world for your audience and community – a role only your brand can fulfil, addressing or navigating the global shifts affecting the target audience and positively impacting that much-desired brand differentiation score.

With *cultural relevance* as both the business objective and the outcome, this new role for brands can drive much-needed innovation in product, commerce and marketing, incorporating ethics, ESG and inclusivity at the heart of the organization, building new metrics of effectiveness and, ultimately, responsible business growth and success beyond mere profit. Brand and business strategies fed by real-world cultural intelligence ensure a company fit for an uncertain and ever-changing world.

This is not easy. It takes leadership, courage, empathy and commitment to positively challenge the status quo. This is not a situation that can be fixed overnight, but it is a journey all brands should be on. This work is necessary and must be continuous, underpinned by tangible actions and a fundamental shift on ways of working fit for the 21st century. If executed correctly, this can put companies on the path to sustainable, equitable and meaningful business success.

This is a culture-led brand.

Notes

1   Cannes Lions. 'Cannes Lions Honours Maria Ressa as Its 2024 Cannes Lionheart', Cannes Lions International Festival of Creativity 2024, 9 May 2024, canneslions.com/news/cannes-lions-honours-maria-ressa-as-its-2024-cannes-lionheart (archived at https://perma.cc/CH4L-C8ZF)

2   UNICEF. 'The Climate Crisis Is a Child Rights Crisis: Introducing the Children's Climate Risk Index', August 2021, unicef.org/reports/climate-crisis-child-rights-crisis (archived at https://perma.cc/KF7F-WJ9X)

3   Jackson, Tim. *Prosperity without Growth? The Transition to a Sustainable Economy*, Sustainable Development Commission, March 2009, sd-commission. org.uk/data/files/publications/prosperity_without_growth_report.pdf (archived at https://perma.cc/3SEM-HCXV)

4   Hickel, Jason, et al. 'Degrowth Can Work – Here's How Science Can Help', *Nature*, 12 December 2022, nature.com/articles/d41586-022-04412-x (archived at https://perma.cc/Y45N-VB5B)

5   Odonkor, Stephen, et al. 'An Evaluation of the Socio-Economic and Environmental Impact of the Second-Hand Clothes Trade in Ghana', Ghana Used Clothing Dealers Association, 2024, humanaitalia.org/wp-content/uploads/2024/10/240514-Ghana-Evaluation-of-the-Socio-Economic-and-Environmental-Impact-of-the-Second-Hand-Clothes-Trade.pdf (archived at https://perma.cc/YER8-LH5L)

6   The Or Foundation. *Human Beings Are Not Commodities*, theor.org (archived at https://perma.cc/TVX7-2ETV)

7   UNESCO. 'Futures Literacy & Foresight: Being Futures-Literate Empowers the Imagination. It Enhances Our Ability to Prepare, Recover and Invent in the Face of Change', unesco.org/en/futures-literacy (archived at https://perma.cc/YZP7-UPZG)

8   On. 'Cyclon: Your Gear. (But Not Forever.)', on.com/en-us/collection/cyclon (archived at https://perma.cc/DQK8-N9PZ)

INDEX

Note: Page numbers in *italics* refer to figures.

Looking for another book?

Explore our award-winning
books from global business
experts in Marketing and Sales

Scan the code to browse

www.koganpage.com/marketing

EU Representative (GPSR)

Authorised Rep Compliance Ltd, Ground Floor, 71 Lower Baggot Street, Dublin, D02 P593, Ireland

www.arccompliance.com